Perhaps no classical writer has be[...]
Famous in his own lifetime as a cl[...]
to whom he dedicated several o[...]
BCE) has never really been out of [...]
elled his letters on Horace's innovative *Epistles* while also borrowing from
his Roman forebear in composing his own Italian sonnets. The echo of
Horace's voice can be found in almost every genre of medieval literature;
in later periods, this influence and popularity if anything increased. Yet,
as Paul Allen Miller shows, while Horace may justifiably be called the
'poet for all seasons', he is also in the end an enigma. His elusive, ironic
contrariness is perhaps the true secret of his success. A cultured man of
letters, he fought on the losing side of the Battle of Philippi (42 BCE).
A staunch Republican, he ended up eagerly (some said too eagerly)
promoting the cause of Julio-Claudian imperialism. Viewed as the acme
of Roman literary civilization, he was shaped by his Athens education
at Plato's famous Academy. This new introduction reveals Horace in all
his paradoxical genius and complexity.

PAUL ALLEN MILLER is Carolina Distinguished Professor of Classics
and Comparative Literature at the University of South Carolina. His
books include *Lyric Texts and Lyric Consciousness: The Birth of a Genre
from Archaic Greece to Augustan Rome* (1994), *Latin Erotic Elegy: An
Anthology and Critical Reader* (2002), *Subjecting Verses: Latin Love Elegy
and the Emergence of the Real* (2004), *Latin Verse Satire: An Anthology
and Critical Reader* (2005) and *Plato's Apology of Socrates: A Commentary*
(with Charles Platter, 2010).

'The well-known Latinist Paul Allen Miller here presents a lively and stimulating introduction to Horace, one of the great short-form poets in world literature, in all his richness and complexity.'

– Stephen Harrison, Professor of Latin Literature, University of Oxford, UK

UNDERSTANDING CLASSICS

EDITOR: RICHARD STONEMAN (UNIVERSITY OF EXETER)

When the great Roman poets of the Augustan Age – Ovid, Virgil and Horace – composed their odes, love poetry and lyrical verse, could they have imagined that their works would one day form a cornerstone of Western civilization, or serve as the basis of study for generations of schoolchildren learning Latin? Could Aeschylus or Euripides have envisaged the remarkable popularity of contemporary stagings of their tragedies? The legacy and continuing resonance of Homer's *Iliad* and *Odyssey* – Greek poetical epics written many millennia ago – again testify to the capacity of the classics to cross the divide of thousands of years and speak powerfully and relevantly to audiences quite different from those to which they were originally addressed.

Understanding Classics is a specially commissioned series which aims to introduce the outstanding authors and thinkers of antiquity to a wide audience of appreciative modern readers, whether undergraduate students of classics, literature, philosophy and ancient history or generalists interested in the classical world. Each volume – written by leading figures internationally – will examine the historical significance of the writer or writers in question; their social, political and cultural contexts; their use of language, literature and mythology; extracts from their major works; and their reception in later European literature, art, music and culture. *Understanding Classics* will build a library of readable, authoritative introductions offering fresh and elegant surveys of the greatest literatures, philosophies and poetries of the ancient world.

UNDERSTANDING CLASSICS

HORACE

Paul Allen Miller

UNDERSTANDING CLASSICS SERIES EDITOR:
RICHARD STONEMAN

I.B. TAURIS
LONDON • NEW YORK • OXFORD • NEW DELHI • SYDNEY

Published in 2019 by
I.B.Tauris & Co. Ltd
London · New York
www.ibtauris.com

A catalogue record for this book is available from the British Library.

Library of Congress Cataloging-in-Publication Data
Names: Miller, Paul Allen, 1959- author.
Title: Horace / Paul Allen Miller.
Description: London ; New York : I.B.Tauris & Co. Ltd, 2019. | Series:
    Understanding classics | Includes bibliographical references and index.
Identifiers: LCCN 2018048038 (print) | LCCN 2018048391 (ebook) | ISBN
    9781786735386 (ePDF) | ISBN 9781786725387 (ePub) | ISBN 9781784533304
    (pbk.) | ISBN 9781784533298 (hardback)
Subjects: LCSH: Horace--Criticism and interpretation.
Classification: LCC PA6411 (ebook) | LCC PA6411 .M47 2019 (print) | DDC
    874/.01--dc23
LC record available at https://lccn.loc.gov/2018048038

ISBN: HB: 978 1 78453 329 8
       PB: 978 1 78453 330 4
       ePDF: 978 1 78673 538 6
       eBook: 978 1 78672 538 7

Text designed and typeset by Tetragon, London
Printed and bound in Great Britain

CONTENTS

Caris amicis mihi ubicumque sint

Acknowledgements

I WANT TO THANK Charles Stocking, who read and gave me valuable feedback on a number of my early chapters for this book. Thanks are also owed to Francesca Martelli and the Classics Department at UCLA, who invited me to present a very early version of my *Epodes* chapter. I benefited greatly from those discussions. An altered version of that chapter will also appear in *'Pataphilology: An Irreader*, eds Sean Gurd and Vincent W. J. van Gerven Oei (Brooklyn: Punctum Books). Thanks are owed to Casey Moore, whose dissertation 'Invective Drag: Talking Dirty in Catullus, Cicero, Horace, and Ovid' inspired me to think more deeply about Canidia. Additional thanks are owed to Nick Lowe and Phiroze Vasunia, at whose invitation I gave a version of my *Satires* chapter to a seminar on ancient literature at the University of London's Institute of Classical Studies. No acknowledgements would be complete without thanking Carl Rubino, whose infectious love of Horace's *Odes* inspires me to this day.

WHY HORACE,
WHY NOW?

QUINTUS HORATIUS FLACCUS, or Horace as he is known in English, is the supreme ironist. Like Socrates, we can never be sure exactly where he stands, and like Socrates he constantly forces us to question where we stand in relation to him, to our community and to ourselves. Horace is in that sense a profoundly ethical writer: not because he propounds a strict moral code, nor because he provides unambiguous embodiments of exemplary virtues, often just the opposite. Rather, Horace is an ethical writer owing to the way he forces our attention on the habits of daily life, on our petty foibles and vanities, on our momentary lusts and desires. A trip to the market, a fire in winter, the games and wounds of love: all are occasions for both reflection and deft self-deflation that avoids the ponderous. He focuses our attention on these small moments of lyric intensity and satiric observation even as he reframes them in the context of the momentous political events that led to the collapse of the Republic, the observations of the great philosophical schools – Stoic, Epicurean and Academic – and the previous 800 years of literary tradition. A glass of wine with a friend in Horace is never just a glass of wine, even as that glass is also never simply subsumed into an allegory of the 'larger' issues that surround it.

Horace is a challenging writer because he is at once an acknowledged classic and yet dazzlingly difficult to define in terms of style and genre. He is the satirist and iambist who became a lyric poet. He is the ally of Brutus who fought at Philippi and the intimate of Maecenas and Augustus who travelled in the highest circles of imperial power. He is both the follower of the savage poetry of Archilochus and Hipponax and the exemplar of Callimachean polish in the *Epodes*. In the *Satires*, which he termed *Sermones* or 'Conversations', Horace is the self-proclaimed heir to Lucilius and his pointed critic. In the *Odes*, he claims to be the first to bring the songs of Sappho and Alcaeus alive in Latin, yet his lyre never actually sounds; and this poetry, while no doubt recited, is profoundly bookish, with each poem in its place and every word positioned for maximum effect. Horace's is a poetry of reading and rereading more than it is a song of the symposium or choral performance. The *Carmen Saeculare*, a late commissioned poem for Augustus' *ludi saeculares*, is the exception that proves the rule. Lastly, in the *Epistles*, he returns to the more prosaic style of the *Satires*, withdrawing from the ambitions exemplified in the *Odes'* monumental structure and their direct engagement with public themes. Yet these seemingly minor, intimate pieces are sometimes addressed to the pre-eminent personalities of the principate (Maecenas, Tiberius and, indirectly, Augustus). They discuss philosophical themes and often return to the gentle satire of the *sermones*, while demonstrating a craftsmanship that no prose translation can capture.

In poem after poem and work after work, Horace consistently challenges our ideas about who he is, what his work means and how he should be received. At the same time, throughout his work he is engaged in a fundamental re-engineering of the Roman ideological universe during the period of the transition from the end of the Republic to the beginning of empire. He seeks to redefine such basic terms in Roman life as *libertas* (freedom), *nobilitas* (nobility), *urbanitas* (sophistication), *amicitia* (friendship) and, ultimately, *civis* (citizen) for a new era in which the verities of the Republican past are no longer operative but in which the world of the empire has yet to be created. This ideological work is neither crude nor inconsequential but generally represents a profound interiorization of what were formerly public and political values, transforming them into complex personal interrogations and creating new modes of reflection and new technologies of existence for a changing, often dangerous world. This ideological refashioning is, in turn, overdetermined by the refined poetic structures in which it is framed, structures that allow for nuances and forms of meaning that prose would not admit.

Understanding Horace is no easy task. It requires careful attention to textual detail since, as an ironist, he never means exactly what he says and normally much more. Understanding Horace also requires a comprehension of the generic conventions within which he wrote – iambic, satire, lyric, epistle – and the complex histories of those conventions, which he self-consciously exploits. Understanding Horace requires attention to the subtle ways in which established forms not only reinforce particular meanings but also undermine and overdetermine others. It requires knowledge of not only the basic values of Roman life and how they were reshaped by the era in which Horace lived but also a tolerance for ambiguity and a recognition of the multifaceted dialogue Horace's poetry maintains with its larger historical context. These are the features this book will offer to the educated reader, the avid student and the expert looking for new perspectives. It offers at once a distillation of recent scholarship and a fresh reading of these texts, which have been formative not only of the Western poetic tradition but also of our tradition of moral reflection.

Before turning to Horace's published work, we should recap a few basic facts. What we know about Horace the person can be easily summarized, and while it would be a grave mistake to reduce his poems to autobiographical reflections, it is also the case that all meaning is contextual. Moreover, almost every Horatian poem, with a few notable exceptions, is addressed to or concerns specific, historically identifiable individuals (Johnson 1982: 4; Barchiesi 2007: 149). Thus, the more complex ironic structures of meaning which Horatian poetry produces only become visible within the frame of the specific references that make them possible. In much the same way, all the characters of the Platonic dialogues, with the possible exception of Diotima, are actual historical individuals, yet few today would confuse the dialogues with the records of actual events, let alone try and reduce the meaning of those dialogues to those events. Horatian poetry, like the Platonic dialogues, exists in the dialectical space between the events and personalities it references, the universality of its themes – love, death, community, friendship – and the specific overdeterminations, ambivalences and ironies of verbal art (Nisbet 2009). The nature of Horatian poetry, therefore, makes specific references indispensable, but also always renders them double-voiced and overdetermined.

Horace was not born of aristocratic stock. As he says in *Satires* 1.6, his father was a freedman. In what sense his father had been an actual slave is the subject of some debate; indeed, he insists on his humble origins to such a degree in this poem that scholars have wondered whether this is a statement of fact or merely an artistic device (Armstrong 2010: 11–12). Bion the Borysthenite, one of Horace's inspirations for the *Satires*, also claimed to be the son of a former slave in his diatribes. While it seems unlikely that Horace is merely acknowledging a valued predecessor in this poem, the echo nonetheless transforms what seems a statement of fact into a generic citation that, of necessity, problematizes the boundary between the referential and the literary. This much, however, seems certain: if Horace's father had been a slave, he was no field hand. Horace, the elder, was better off both financially and culturally than the average *libertinus*: he was, Horace tells us in *Satires* 1.4, able to move to Rome when Horace was a boy, and there acquired for his son the finest education available, before sending him to what counted for university in the ancient world, philosophical training in Athens (Freudenburg 1993: 205; Williams 2009).

Nonetheless, even if Horace exaggerated his youthful poverty, we can be sure that he was of relatively humble origins when compared to Lucilius, the founder of Roman satire and a very wealthy equestrian, and to the senators and magnates of the late Republic and early principate with whom he rubbed elbows. The last days of the Republic were a period of social instability and offered opportunities for ambitious young men, the sons of wealthy and talented freedmen, to advance quickly, even if the mark of their humble beginnings could never be completely erased and even if a certain amount of whispering and innuendo had to be endured (Armstrong 1989: 13; Stampacchia 1982: 210–11). Horace was among the *arrivistes* who populated the second tier of the principate's new aristocracy, although he always disclaimed any pretensions to power and prestige.

Horace was born on 8 December in the Apulian town of Venusia in 65 BCE. Little more is known of his early life, and while his father is praised in *Satires* 1.4 and 1.6, he never talks about his mother. Indeed, Horace mentions almost no women in his poetry unless they are courtesans, slaves or objects of disgust. He never married and had no legitimate children. Thus, while many of Horace's greatest modern readers have been women – Margaret Hubbard, Emily Gowers, Michèle Lowrie, Lowell Bowditch and Ellen Oliensis, to name only the most prominent – there is little in Horace's poetry, from a thematic point of view, for a feminist to love. Indeed, it is one of the paradoxes of Horatian poetry that, as Robin Nisbet observed, while Horace's 'tolerant humanity had a long-term influence on the European enlightenment [...] he is one of the most brutally sexist of the Augustan poets' (2007: 21; cf. Oliensis 2007: 221–2). Nonetheless, one suspects that this situation is less anomalous than it first appears, since ancient misogyny is commonplace. The writers of the ancient world do not as a rule share our assumptions about human rights, gender equality, slavery, torture or capital punishment, and yet our most basic conceptions of beauty, justice and goodness trace their genealogy to these same writers. The recognition of this fact should serve as a cautionary tale in two specific senses: first, we are perhaps a good deal less free, tolerant and enlightened than we imagine; and second, the positive legacy for Western culture may have less to do with a presumed inheritance of universal themes or values, and more to do with a certain quality of attention, a certain critical relation of the self to itself and a certain ethic of care that makes possible the creation of complex systems of reflection that are both resistant to dogmatic reduction and capable of producing moments of genuine utopian imagination. It is for these reasons, I would assert, that understanding Horace remains an urgently contemporary task.

As noted above, when Horace finished his rhetorical instruction at Rome he went to Athens to study philosophy, the customary capstone of an upper-class Roman education. There he met Brutus, the assassin of Julius Caesar. He apparently impressed him, for when Horace joined the army of the conspirators he received a commission as a military tribune, a rank that required him to have already attained or to be promoted to the status of an equestrian, no mean feat for the son of a freed slave. After the defeat of the Republican cause at Philippi in 42 BCE, Horace returned to Rome, where he obtained the position of *scriba quaestorius* (treasury clerk). Such positions were relatively prestigious, so Horace's claim that he took up poetry out of poverty (*Epistles* 2.2.50–2) must be taken with a grain of salt. Nonetheless, while Lucilius and Catullus take their elite status for granted, Horace, especially in his earliest poetry, reveals a self-consciousness concerning his social standing unseen among both his immediate predecessors and his Augustan contemporaries, all of whom are comfortable equestrians (McNeill 2001: 65). In the early thirties, Horace made the acquaintance of Virgil and Varius, who approved of his poetry and in 38 BCE introduced him to Maecenas.

Maecenas played a key role in Horace's life and poetry. *Satires* 1.1, 1.5, 1.6, 1.9, 1.10, 2.3, 2.6, 2.7 and 2.8 are all either addressed to, or make prominent mention of, Horace's relation to his patron. Maecenas is also the dedicatee of the *Odes*, the *Epodes* and the *Epistles*. No one in the history of previous Latin poetry had been 'as lavishly and consistently advertised by any poet' (White 2007: 197). Yet Maecenas is not the sole object of Horace's attention. His poetry constitutes a virtual prosopography of the Roman cultural and political elite of the early principate, a fact which testifies both to Horace's own upward mobility and to the cultural capital his poetry possessed and was able to bestow on others. Poetry in Rome was not only a way by which the notable were acknowledged, but also a way by which the great deeds of some and the foibles of others became immortalized. As we shall see, then, throughout this book, Horace's relation to Maecenas, Augustus and the other addressees is one of the primary means of access to his poetry, even though Horace's relationship to these figures is complex and changes over time (Citroni 2009; Bowditch 2010: 65).

Maecenas in some ways defines the first half of the Augustan era. An equestrian from an old Etruscan family, he never sought elective office. He was one of Octavian's earliest supporters and fought with him at Philippi. He became his trusted friend and agent, assuming political control of the city when the *princeps* was away. He also functioned as the chief poetic patron of the new regime. Maecenas recruited Virgil, Varius, Horace and Propertius to endorse, or at least acknowledge, the emerging Augustan settlement. He appears to have been neither overbearing nor inattentive as a patron. If one accepts what the poets say at face value – a dangerous thing to do – he encouraged the production of poetry that would reflect well on the emerging principate, yet it is clear that he gave those under his protection a great deal of leeway. He neither attempted to micromanage their productions nor to censor work that could be considered critical of the regime, such as Propertius 2.7. As a result, some of the finest poetry in the history of the West was produced during the Augustan era. This was no mere act of disinterested aesthetic patronage, but a shrewd investment in image management. It is largely as a result of this poetry that the principate enjoys an image of peace, moderation and prosperity to this day (Galinsky 1998). That would certainly not have been the case if the only picture we had of Octavian was that of the young *triumvir*, who allowed Marc Antony to slaughter Cicero in the proscriptions, or of the bloody victor at Perusia (Gold 1986; White 1993).

In the period between 35 BCE, after the publication of the first book of *Satires*, and the Battle of Actium (31 BCE), in which Octavian defeated Antony and Cleopatra, Horace received the Sabine farm from Maecenas, a gift that gave the poet the personal and financial independence celebrated in *Satires* 2.6 and which is continually referenced in the *Epistles*. The second book of *Satires* was published circa 30 BCE at about the same time as the *Epodes*, which appear to have been composed intermittently over the previous 12 years. At this point, Horace's personal and poetic life takes a decisive turn, making him more than ever a member of Octavian's inner circle. At the same time, he undertakes an important shift in genre, abandoning the satiric and iambic vein that had characterized his previous poetic activity in favour of lyric in the manner of the canonical Greek lyrists of the archaic and classical era, in the *Odes*. This is a genre that in the strict formal sense, aside from a few brief experiments by Catullus, had largely been untouched by previous Roman poets, and one which would not be taken up again by any subsequent Roman poet (Lowrie 1997: 39; Tarrant 2007: 71). The *Odes*, in fact, are a singular monument to poetic ambition and genius that cannot be separated from Augustus' own extraordinary recomposition of Roman political and social life (Nisbet 2007; Bowditch 2010: 57).

Exegi monumentum, 'I have built a monument', begins the last poem of the three books of the *Odes.* In some ways this phrase signals the end of Horace's early career of generic experimentation in the *Satires* and the *Epodes* and the crowning success that was the three books of the *Odes.* The final portion of Horace's career is marked by both a return to the achievements of the past and an increasingly explicit pose of philosophical reflection. The period after the publication of the *Odes* circa 23 BCE sees the poet both revisiting the conversational hexameter poetry of the *Satires* in the *Epistles,* and producing two codas on his lyric achievement: Book 4 of the *Odes,* which while retaining the formal perfection of the first three books is more explicitly devoted to praise of the imperial family than anything we have seen before (11 BCE), and the *Carmen Saeculare,* a commissioned choral lyric to celebrate the Secular Games revived by Augustus in 17 BCE. While the last two works are certainly worth study, and several spirited defences of them have been launched in recent years (Putnam 1996; Johnson 2007), nonetheless few would argue that they equal the accomplishment of the *Odes.*

Among Horace's late works, it is the *Epistles,* however, that will draw most of our attention. These came out in two books. *Epistles* 1 (21 BCE) contains a variety of short- to medium-length poems addressed to the poet's various friends and acquaintances, including Maecenas. While the tone is often bantering and mildly satiric, gone is the pose of the speaker of diatribe found in *Satires* 1 and the social self-consciousness of the freedman's son entering the highest reaches of late Republican society. These modest masterpieces position themselves as notes to friends about the daily cares of life, the proper attitude to death and the obligations one owes one's benefactors. While we have collections of letters that predate Horace's – Plato's, Epicurus', Cicero's – this is the first self-conscious collection of poetic epistles and constitutes the last of Horace's major generic innovations. Their tone of tolerant good humour and ironic reflection not only prepares the way for Boileau and Pope in the seventeenth and eighteenth centuries but also creates an artistic discourse of intimacy, one that sculpts an image of the poet in maturity and establishes a zone of personal autonomy that, nonetheless, recognizes the ineluctably social nature of the self. The second book of *Epistles* contains two long poems, one addressed to Augustus, both of which are primarily concerned with theoretical reflections on the nature and role of poetry. The *Ars Poetica*, whose exact date is much debated, is also often included in this collection, dated shortly before the poet's death in 8 BCE (Rudd 1989: 19).

The *Ars*, while one of Horace's most influential works, is also one of his most puzzling. Scholars in the Early Modern period, hungry for the secrets of classical achievement, latched onto this rambling, disjointed letter and tried to extract rules from it, in the same manner as they did from Aristotle's *Poetics* (Laird 2007: 132, 138). Moreover, while there is no debate that Aristotle's work is intended to be a serious study of classical Athenian theatre, in the case of the *Ars* the tone is more difficult to discern, and at least one scholar has argued that the entire letter should be read as a parody (Frischer 1991). At a minimum, it is quixotic that most of the poem is given over to a discussion of tragedy, comedy and satyr plays, three genres Horace never practised, while precious little insight is to be gathered about how he actually conceived the *Odes*, *Epodes*, *Satires* or *Epistles*. Indeed, one of the greatest ironies, as Denis Feeney has observed, is that it is quite likely Horace had actually been banned from attending the theatre at this time as a result of the social legislation Augustus passed to encourage marriage and the production of children. Horace, as a lifelong bachelor, would after 22 BCE no longer have been allowed to sit with Maecenas in the rows reserved for the married members of the equestrian order (Feeney 2002: 184).

One of the classic debates about the *Ars* is how much it owes to a lost Hellenistic work by a certain Neoptolemus. Porphyrion, the ancient commentator, makes it appear in one brief comment that the entire text is derived from this source (Havthal 1966b: 649), a claim that, as we shall see in the coming chapters, should be viewed with a certain amount of scepticism. Horace is a writer who is very aware of his predecessors and always seeks to situate his work within the tradition, but he is anything but a slavish imitator, and lampoons those who are in *Epistles* 1.19. What we know of Neoptolemus is largely preserved in the fragments of Philodemus, an Epicurean philosopher and friend of Virgil. But all attempts to make the *Ars* cohere in any simple fashion with Neoptolemus have failed to yield general assent. Indeed, it seems likely that if there is a substantial presence of Neoptolemus in Horace it is as much in the form of parody as model (Laird 2007: 133–5).

The *Ars* presents itself as a list of dos and don'ts for the Pisones, a father and son who were literary critics and patrons and who had poetic aspirations of their own (Rudd 1989: 19–21). In part, the *Ars* serves as a gentle reminder that just because you are of noble birth, it does not mean you possess poetic genius (Oliensis 1998: 206–11). But the tone is still more complex. This is a poem that appears to have a source text but does not follow it. It gives advice on the theatre, a form Horace never practised and likely no longer saw. If the Pisones or their early modern avatars thought they could simply pick up the *Ars*, follow its dictates, and, *voilà*, poetic art would appear, they were sadly mistaken. The fun is only increased when we recall that our major source for Neoptolemus is Philodemus. Philodemus was a client of the Pisones, and the reason he preserved a fair amount of Neoptolemus was so he could attack him; one suspects that the recognition of the intertext would have inspired amusement in the reader more than a desire for emulation. Indeed, as Frischer observes, Horace 'may be treading a fine line between angering and amusing Piso' (Frischer 1991: 65–6).

This is not to say we can learn nothing about poetry or about Horace from reading the *Ars*: quite the opposite. Horace's comments on style, while not earth-shattering, give a good guide to what he practised. He is, for example, a master of poetic arrangement. His poems have been compared to mosaics in which each word is a tile, whose placement produces the sought-for effect (Nietzsche 1997: 86). Early in the *Ars*, Horace makes the following recommendation:

> Ordinis haec virtus et venus, aut ego fallor,
> ut iam nunc dicat iam nunc debentia dici,
> pleraque differat et praesens in tempus omittat;
> hoc amet, hoc spernat promissi carminis auctor.
> in verbis etiam tenuis cautusque serendis
> dixeris egregie notum si callida verbum
> reddiderit iunctura novum.

> This is the virtue and the seduction of arrangement, unless I am fooled,
> that what ought to be said right now, is said, and the present moment
> in time may defer and omit many things; let the author of promised
> verse love this and avoid that. Careful and subtle in the binding of your
> words, you will be called extraordinary if you make a known word new
> through a clever juxtaposition. (42–8)

The opening line tells us this is more than a simple list of precepts. *Virtus*
certainly can mean 'virtue', but it also means 'manliness' and 'courage', even
'force'. It is derived from *vir*, 'man'. While the translation 'virtue' may be
adequate in terms of the basic denotative meaning of *virtus*, *venus* activates the
word's gendered connotations. So we do not fail to get the point, Shackleton
Bailey in his edition prints *Venus*, the name of the goddess of erotic love
(2008). Rudd's choice to translate *venus* as 'value', while lexically defensi-
ble, is clearly prudish (1979: 191). When used as a common noun, *venus*
normally means 'beauty' or 'attractiveness', if it does not directly mean 'sex'
(cf. Catullus 3.1–2, 13.12, 86.6; Adams 1982: 57, 98, 188–9). Of course, in
ancient Latin there was no firm distinction between upper- and lower-case
letters, so whether one follows Rudd in printing *v* or Bailey in printing *V* is
a matter of interpretation, which in turn dictates how you translate *venus*.
But these are decisions that did not have to be made by Horace's ancient
readers, and it is precisely the ambiguity inherent in the Latin that allows
for the play between *virtus* and *venus* in this line, which in turn underlines
the point Horace is making about *ordo*, 'arrangement'. If the words had not
immediately been juxtaposed, the play between them would have been less
active, and the humorous joining of *virtus* with *venus* could have been missed.

One of the more intriguing things about this passage is how we are to
understand line 45. As reproduced above, the text follows Wickham's 1901
Oxford Classical Texts edition and prints the whole as unbroken text, but
English punctuation makes one decide whether the line should be construed
with what comes before or what comes after. The pronouns *hoc* are suffi-
ciently vague as to allow either construction, and later commentators are
undecided. Wickham's semicolon asks the reader to assimilate this line to
the preceding comments on saying what needs to be said when it needs to be

said and deferring or omitting other things. Rudd, in his 1979 translation, interweaves it syntactically with what comes afterwards: the capacity of word choice and collocation to renew the meaning of worn-out words. But in his 1989 text, Rudd creates paragraph divisions and section headings so that line 45 is grouped with what comes before it, returning to Wickham's text and contradicting his own decision ten years previously. Bailey (2008) also creates paragraphing, but uses it to reinforce a reading in line with Rudd in 1979, rather than his 1989 text. Again, these are problems that are more a creation of modern editorial practices and the needs for translation to adhere to the demands of English syntax than they are a reflection of either confusion in Horace's text or poor writing on his part. The poet has just spoken about the importance of order and about the need to say things when they ought to be said rather than including extraneous material. He then follows with a discussion of powerful artistic effects created by exercising care in the joining of words and the value of collocation and juxtaposition. In between, he creates a line that with perfect economy illustrates these points through its ability to be taken with both what comes before and after.

The final example is to be taken from Horace's discussion of the *callida iunctura*, 'clever joining', 'juxtaposition' or 'collocation', which is able to renew a known word, giving it new point and poetic power. Again the lines illustrate the points made: *notum* and *verbum* frame *callida* in line 47, creating an artistic or 'clever' arrangement of language which English syntax is unable to reproduce. Together, these words are in a chiastic relation with *novum* in the following line. Thus the 'known [...] word' becomes 'new' through its artistic 'joining' or *iunctura* with that very word, *novum*.

The lines in this passage must be read slowly, with close attention to multiple levels of meaning on both the syntactical and the lexical levels. Clearly, when Horace says a few lines earlier that your poetic composition should be whatever you want, 'as long as it is simple and one' (23), his notion of simplicity and unity is neither simple nor univocal; but neither is it nonsensical or incoherent. What it is, however, is ironic. When Plato's Socrates in the *Apology* says he is the wisest of men because at least he knows that he knows nothing (21d), he does not mean that he is a simpleton or completely ignorant; rather, he forces us to rethink what we mean when we speak of knowledge and wisdom. He is both jesting (he recognizes the paradox) and completely in earnest. Likewise, when he says in the same work that he is the teacher of no man (33a), he does not mean that no one ever learned anything from him – least of all Plato, who is writing the dialogue – but he forces us to question on a fundamental level what it means to teach and what it means to learn (Miller and Platter 2010: 177–8). As I shall argue throughout this book, Horace's sense of irony is similarly acute and challenges the reader to think again, to reread, to question fundamental terms and to come to new conclusions, or at least refresh the old. We will see numerous examples of this in the pages to come, and often the Socratic precedent or Platonic intertext will be clear, but within the *Ars* there is one passage in particular to which we should pay attention in this regard. There are few places where he is more direct:

> To be wise is the first principle and source of writing correctly: the Socratic books will be able to show the matter to you, and the words will follow with ease once the matter is envisioned.   (309–11)

This is not a call for the poet to include simplistic moral lessons: the Socratic books offer few, if any. What they *do* teach is a style of thinking and communicating that is profoundly self-conscious, and deeply seductive – Socrates is after all accused of corrupting the youth. The *Ars Poetica* is indeed no simple recipe book for creating poetry but an exemplification of Horace's complex ironic style, a send-up of the pretensions of academic criticism and a text that doubles back on itself in ways that often seem to undermine its own precepts.

This last point is perhaps nowhere better exemplified than in the *Ars'* famously self-deflating finale. A poem that had begun with a plea for simplicity and unity, while demonstrating complexity, and which had insisted on wisdom as the key to proper writing, ends with an image of the poet as mad, diseased and avoided by the wise:

> Those who are wise flee and fear to touch the insane poet as they do someone who is afflicted with the foul scab or royal jaundice, or the

wandering fanatic and moonstruck lunatic. Only children and the reckless harass and pursue them.

One poet, as he wandered aimlessly, belching forth heavenly verses, fell head first into a well or pit, just as a fowler intent on catching blackbirds, and although he for a long time shouted 'help me, fellow citizens', no one took the time to pull him out. If anyone were to make the effort to bring aid and throw him a rope, I would say, 'how do you know that he didn't throw himself in intentionally and doesn't want to be saved?' and I would tell him of the death of the Sicilian poet. When Empedocles wished to be considered an immortal god, he coolly jumped into burning Mount Etna. Let this be the law, and may it be permitted to poets to perish. He who saves a man who does not wish it, does the same as killing him. The poet hasn't done this just once, and it's not the case that if you pull him out now he would become human and put aside this love for a spectacular death.

Nor is it clear why he persists in making verses, whether he pissed on his father's ashes or perversely disturbed the gloomy site of a light-ning strike.

He is certainly mad, and just like a bear, if he were able to smash the bars before his cage, this painful reciter would drive off the learned and the unlearned alike. But if he grabs someone, he will hold on to and kill him with reading, and he will not let go of his flesh except like the leech once he is filled with blood.   (453–76)

Many pages could be filled examining the diction and images of these lines, more than we can devote to them. What is clear, however, is the *Ars* does not present us with a treatise or an essay on the rules of poetry. It is a complex poem that is not simple and never quite one, yet deeply composed and always challenging. It is a poem that works on multiple levels at once, ironic, parodic, but also exemplifying its principles. In doing so, it is a profoundly Horatian poem, and the finale of what most believe to be his final poem serves as a fitting introduction to his work as a whole.

*

In the end, understanding Horace, from first to last, is to take him seriously as a poet, thinker and ironist, and ultimately to see these functions as indissociable. It is not that Horace first thinks and then decides to wrap those thoughts in poetic finery. But rather his thought, even at its most playful, ironic and self-deflating, *is* his poetry. And this is important: for, if that were not the case, then we would hardly need read the poetry at all; we could simply summarize the contents and discard their troublesome external garb. Such an exercise, however, would not simply be an aesthetic loss, it would be an impoverishment of Horatian thought. The heresy of paraphrase is not simply a critical nostrum but a recognition, at least in the case of Horace (but I would argue in the case of any poet worth his salt), that what we call the 'content' or 'meaning' of poetry is inseparable from the experience of its reading, from the momentary perplexity provoked by a peculiar turn of phrase, a daring coinage, an ironic understatement or an outlandish hyperbole. These moments of perplexity, or, to use a more technical philosophical term but one with a particularly Socratic resonance, aporia, are created by an overabundance of meaning, an inability to choose the one true meaning, and hence the ensuing need for reflection, criticism and, ultimately, self-exploration. The reduction of those moments to a simple message or meaning that the poet wishes to 'communicate', one which is separable from that experience of deeply engaged reading, is the confession that poetry is a vain bauble, a plaything that can be discarded before the serious events of life. Nothing could be further from the case for Horace, and nothing could be further from the case if we are to 'understand' Horace, to take Horace seriously. The answer to the naive undergraduate question when confronting a puzzling syntactical construction, a harsh hyperbaton, or deliberate paradox – 'Why didn't Horace just say what he meant?' – can only be, 'He did.'

I

ROMAN SOCRATES

IRONY IN THE SATIRES

IN 1963, WILLIAM ANDERSON published a remarkable essay, 'The Roman Socrates: Horace and his Satires'. It was later anthologized in his collected essays on satire, which were published in 1982. This was widely read when I was in graduate school in the 1980s and still shows up in many bibliographies on the subject. This is no small feat for a bit of scholarship now more than 50 years old, but I want to argue that this essay has *yet* to receive its due. How can I say that? It has certainly long been recognized that the satires have a strongly philosophical background: the polemics with Stoicism are obvious (1.1.120; 1.3.127–8, 139; 1.4.14–16; Brown 1993: ad loc.; Gowers 2012: ad loc.). The influences of diatribe and the popular Cynic philosophy of Bion the Borysthenite have been well documented (*Epistles* 2.2.60; Duff 1936: 28–9, 33; Rudd 1982: 17–18). Horace's own Epicureanism and the influence of thinkers like Philodemus has been observed (Rudd 1982: 24, 31–2; Freudenburg 1993: 87–8, 125; Oberhelman and Armstrong 1995), and Horace acknowledges Plato to be as much an influence on his writing of satire as Archilochus or the comic poets (*Satires* 1.4.1–5; 2.3.11–12).

Philosophy of various kinds is everywhere in the satires (Moles 2007), then, so how could Anderson's observations in 1963 have yet to be truly appreciated or, for that matter, be even controversial? Of course, with so many different kinds of philosophy in the mix, how can there be any philosophy worthy of the name? Is this not just pastiche? Are the satires not just a literary exercise? Rather than being a serious philosophical undertaking, we are often told, Horace's satires represent either some kind of popular eclecticism, a bit of picking and choosing from the common themes of the day, or they use philosophy as a literary motif, deploying it in much the same sense Virgil writes about shepherds in the *Eclogues* or Aristophanes about amphibious life in *The Frogs* (Mayer 2005: 153–5; White 2007: 201). In both cases, it would be foolish to consider Virgil an authority on shepherding or Aristophanes a naturalist. And likewise, it was argued, only the obtuse would consider Horace a philosopher, would take him seriously as a thinker (Veyne 2001a: xviii-xix). He is, after all, a poet, and while the *Satires* and *Epistles* may contain bits of philosophical verbiage, only the armchair moralist would be convinced that these constitute actual philosophical arguments.

Hence the brilliance of Anderson's choice of Socrates! For Socrates' main trait, the one for which he is recognized by everyone in the ancient world from Aristotle (*Nicomachean Ethics* 1127a–b) to Cicero (*De Oratore* 2.269–70) to Quintilian (9.2.46–7), was not for being the exponent of a set of philosophical doctrines – and certainly not for being merely the mouthpiece for Plato, as he is sometimes now understood – but for being an ironist: a shammer, a guy who walks up to you on the street and asks a few simple questions, and when he is done leaves you stunned, confused and fascinated, and ultimately desiring more. Horace is that Roman Socrates, the questioning Socrates, and this is as true in the *Satires* as it is in the *Epodes*, *Odes* and *Epistles*. Such at least is the thesis of the present book and the basis for my contention that Anderson's essay has yet to be fully appreciated.

Two passages from Plato will illustrate both sides of this Socratic equation: the aporetic and the irresistible. The first passage comes from *Meno*, in which the title character famously responds with exasperation to Socrates' incessant questioning and seemingly feigned ignorance:

> Socrates, I used to be told, before I began to meet you, that yours was just a case of being in doubt yourself and making others doubt also: and so now I find you are merely bewitching me with your spells and

incantations, which have reduced me to utter perplexity. And if I am indeed to have my jest, I consider that both in your appearance and in other respects you are extremely like the flat torpedo sea-fish; for it benumbs anyone who approaches and touches it, and something of the sort is what I find you have done to me now. For in truth, I feel my soul and my tongue quite benumbed, and I am at a loss what answer to give you. And yet on countless occasions I have made abundant speeches on virtue to various people – and very good speeches they were, so I thought – but now I cannot say one word as to what it is. You are well advised, I consider, in not voyaging or taking a trip away from home; for if you went on like this as a stranger in any other city you would very likely be taken up for a wizard.   (*Meno* 79e–80b; Lamb 1967)

This passage illustrates the famously perplexing character of Socratic discourse. Far from providing answers to questions, Socrates often only gives us more questions and questions that we cannot answer, and yet in the end, those who stay around to hear, who do not react in anger, are driven to question themselves, to seek to know themselves, even to care for themselves (*Apology* 31b; Brown 1994: 165–6; Hadot 1995: 55–7, 105; Blondell 2002: 100, 124; Hunter 2004: 86–7). And this drive for an adequate self-knowledge, for a sense of self that is at once separate from the world and yet better equipped by that separateness, and indeed by that questioning, to navigate the world, is endlessly compelling and attractive, as Alcibiades observes at the end of the *Symposium*:

Even now I am still conscious that if I consented to lend [Socrates] my ear, I could not resist him, but would have the same feeling again. For he compels me to admit that, sorely deficient as I am, I neglect myself while I attend to the affairs of Athens. So I withhold my ears perforce as from the Sirens, and make off as fast as I can, for fear I should go on sitting beside him till old age was upon me.   (216a; Lamb 1925)

Socrates, then, according to both Roman tradition and his portrayal in many Platonic texts, is a figure at once puzzling and endlessly attractive, at once impossible to define in himself and yet producing in his interlocutors an endless drive to understand and define themselves, often to the neglect of what other more conventional persons might assume is important. I will argue that when Anderson calls the Horace of the *Satires* the 'Roman Socrates', it is precisely to this set of traits that he gestures. Indeed, as I shall argue throughout the remainder of this book, this characterization of Horace is apt not only for the *Satires* but also for his *oeuvre* as a whole, although at each stage we must take account of the particular generic histories the poet is invoking and the way in which those histories condition the reader's expectations and offer different resources and limitations to the poetic ironist (cf. Davis 1991: 1; Plaza 2006: 169–70). We begin with his satires, then, not only because *Satires* 1 was Horace's first published collection, but also because the satires give us what is in many ways the most unfettered insight into Horace as ironic moralist.

Before delving into the meat of our argument, it is necessary, however, to provide the reader with a brief background to the satiric genre, which Horace inherited from its founder Lucilius and made his own; while the *Satires* may be Horace's most direct link to the Socratic tradition, they are nonetheless peculiarly Roman. Quintilian, the second century CE rhetorical theorist, says famously, 'Satire indeed is wholly ours' (10.1.93), and this has been interpreted to mean that Latin verse satire is a Roman invention. Whereas epic, tragedy, comedy and lyric all have Greek models, and their Roman imitators prided themselves on being able to produce these forms in Latin, satire, Quintilian argues, is different. He is not alone in this: not one of the canonical satirists disagrees. Horace says he is following in the path of Lucilius (1.4, 1.10 and 2.1); Persius cites the precedents of Lucilius and Horace (1); and Juvenal acknowledges Lucilius and Horace while quoting Persius (1). They often cite Greek Old Comedy as well, but while these plays were satiric in tone, no one would confuse them with Roman *satura*, which is written in dactylic hexameters, often features a single first-person speaker and is only dramatic in the same sense as Plato's dialogues.

Satura had two important qualities in the Roman imagination. First, it was a poetry of blame. This was especially true, according to Horace, in the works of Lucilius (1.4.1–10), but is also reflected in Horace's own diatribes and later in Juvenal's famous *indignatio*. Nonetheless, *satura* grew in Horace's hands into a complex, self-reflective literary form. In part, this is reflected in the fact that Horace himself never uses the name *satura* but instead refers to his poems as *sermones*, 'conversations', even 'dialogues' (Coffey 1976: 24–5; Rudd 1982: 96). The focus of Horace's criticism in these poems often becomes ambiguous and multilayered, ultimately calling into question the critical function itself, as the satiric voice becomes both the object and means of criticism (Anderson 1960: 237; Schlegel 2005: 6, 101).

Satire's second important quality for the Roman imagination was that it pursued a variety of topics (adultery, travelogues, gastronomical excess, etc.), both within individual poems and in the genre as a whole. It is not unusual for a *satura* to start off in one direction and end somewhere very different. If we ask ourselves what a form of discourse would look like whose salient points were variety and blame, we would also need to imagine the perspective of a specific individual (a voice, a persona, a character), for blame can only be assigned from a point of view. Satire, then, is a discourse of strong personalities who often in their very strength function as both subjects and objects of the discourse. While this is clearest in the satires of Book 2 in which Horace becomes the object of attacks delivered by his friends, neighbours and slaves, even in Book 1 he appears as the sexually obsessed speaker of 1.2, the obtuse travelling companion of Maecenas in 1.5, and the social-climbing poet who must himself fend off the approaches of another less couth version of himself in 1.9 (Rudd 1982: 82–3; Oliensis 1998: 17; Reckford 2009a: 70).

Within these parameters, satiric discourse will often take the form of a claim to speak the truth without regard to social niceties, known in Latin as *libertas*. This was Lucilian satire's essential quality, according to Horace (1.4). *Libertas* is a complex and contested term to which the translation 'freedom' or 'liberty' does not do justice. On one level, *libertas* is the quality that defines the Roman citizen as opposed to the slave or foreigner. On another level, *libertas* denotes a set of prerogatives that are only able to be exercised fully by the aristocratic elite (Welch 2008: 66), the most noted of which is freedom of speech. *Libertas* also signifies a fundamental notion of self-determination, commonly understood as the ability to be subject to the will of no one else and hence implying the capacity to enforce one's will upon others. *Libertas* was actualized most concretely by traditional Roman elites through their participation in competitive politics (Wirszubski 1950: 38; Syme 1960: 155), yet it was precisely their ability to continue in that role that was called into question at the end of the Republican period and the beginning of the principate (Welch 2008: 49).

These are poems, then, that no matter how light the tone and how deft the touch address issues fundamental to the Roman elite's self-understanding. What could *libertas* mean in a world where the fullest realization of the free man's potential was no longer the capacity to govern others, to assert one's own *dignitas* above the contending claims of others? What could *libertas* mean in a world where one was always, at least in principle, subject to the authority, if not the direct power, of another? And in that sense, even a great senator was unfree – perhaps even, as Tacitus avers, a slave (*Annales* 1.2). In such a world, the Stoic paradox that only the wise man is free, the topic of *Satires* 2.7, while absurd taken at face value when confronted with actual chattel slavery, appears less and less counter-intuitive.

Thus, in *Satires* 1.4, Horace begins by contrasting his own practice of satire with that of Lucilius, who censured the faults of others freely (*cum libertate*) like the Greek Comic poets. Those poets acted in the manner of a traditional Roman *censor*, he says, who would place a mark (*nota*) next to the names of leading citizens who failed to exemplify the behaviour expected of the senatorial elite. In this manner, Lucilian satire becomes a fusion of Roman norms with Greek literary precedent:

> Eupolis atque Cratinus Aristophanesque poetae,
> atque alii, quorum comoedia prisca virorum est,
> si quis erat dignus describi quod malus ac fur,
> quod moechus foret aut sicarius aut alioqui
> famosus, multa cum libertate notabant.
> hinc omnis pendet Lucilius, hosce secutus
> mutatis tantum pedibus numerisque [...]

> The poets, Eupolis, Cratinus and Aristophanes, and others of those
> men who wrote Old Comedy, they marked down with great freedom
> if anyone was worthy to be written up because he was a criminal and a
> thief, because he was an adulterer or an assassin or in some other way
> infamous. Lucilius wholly descends from here, having followed them
> with only the metre and rhythms changed.   (*Satires* 1.4.1–7)

Poem 1.4, however, also negotiates Horace's departure from his Lucilian
model, as he both explicitly embraces and distances himself from his great
forebear. This new satire will be urbane and polished; its image is the pure
stream of Callimachus' *Hymn to Apollo* (108–12), as opposed to the great
muddy river of Lucilius (1.4.9–13). It will come closer to the comedy of
manners we associate with Menander (1.4.45–56) than to the tradition of
personal attack associated with Aristophanes.

   Horace then goes on to redefine the practice of satiric censure as a private
matter of self-formation learned from his father (a *libertinus*). *Libertas* in this
sense is defined not as public control or political reproof but the cultivation ✗
of private virtue, a concept that would have been recognized by Greek phi-
losophers but not the traditional senatorial aristocracy. In Horace's hands,
satire is no longer a discourse of the competitive elite in which humour
is a political weapon; it represents instead a version of the refined speech
(*sermo merus* 1.4.48; cf. Cicero *De Officiis*, 1.132–7) and social intercourse
that underwrites an as yet undefined but ultimately very different political
vision which will become the principate and then the empire. Near the end
of this complex and multilevelled poem in which the poet simultaneously
lays claim to and distances himself from the Lucilian tradition, Horace
concludes by apologizing if he has spoken a little too freely (*liberius*, 1.4.103;
Oliensis 1998: 24–5). It would, of course, have been missed by no one in
Horace's audience that the satirist had risen to the rank of military tribune
with Brutus and the defenders of Republican *libertas* before their defeat
at Philippi (1.6.46–8; Armstrong 1989: 13; Lana 1993: 60; Roller 2001:
215; Armstrong 2010: 9). What then is freedom in this context? Is it the
right to criticize others like Lucilius, the fact of no longer being a slave like
Horace's father, the ability to shape one's life as one sees fit, a privilege that

can be abused if overused (*licentia*), a principled resistance to autocracy, or a willing submission to it? The multiple ironic levels on which Horace defines and redefines what it means to be 'free' in this poem are worthy of a Roman Socrates and force us to engage with these fundamental questions in all their complexity and ambiguity (Plaza 2006: 208; Muecke 2007: 115–20).

Horace in 1.4 and the surrounding poems defines satire for a new era. He is moving from an essentially political definition of free speech and self-determination towards a vision of private virtue and ethical freedom (Freudenburg 1993: 72–88). In the process, he is redefining what it means to be *civis Romanus* for an era in which the politics of competitive elites has become a dangerous anachronism. In 1.6, thus, where Horace recounts his introduction to Maecenas, Octavian's right-hand man in Rome and informal minister of culture, the satirist contends that even though his father had been a freedman, Horace nonetheless lives a less constrained, and hence freer, life than that of a famous senator. This statement would have been absurd in the mouth of Lucilius. Horace is free, however, precisely because he has no pretensions to public honours, because he does not seek to wield power over others, because he cultivates himself and because he is happy in his own skin (1.6.19–22; Classen 1993: 117). In short, Horatian satire redefines *libertas* as the virtual opposite of its normative meaning in Republican literature, without overturning the fundamental social distinction between free and slave (1.6.7–8; cf. Stampacchia 1982: 208). His is not the power to speak his will and to enforce it upon others, but to go where he wants on a gelded mule, an image of lower-class emasculation, a freedom which he contrasts with the *praeclarus senator*'s enslavement to the demands of public life (Freudenburg 2001: 59–60).

> nunc mihi curto
> ire licet mulo vel si libet usque Tarentum
> [...]
> hoc ego commodius quam tu, praeclare senator,
> milibus atque aliis vivo. quacumque libido est,
> incedo [...]

> I can, if I want, ride a castrated[1] mule all the way to Tarentum [...] In
> this and a thousand other ways, my life is more pleasant than yours,
> famous senator. I go wherever I want.   (*Satires* 1.6.104–12)

The senator is beset by a thousand obligations: the burden of societal expectations weighs upon him constantly. Horace, however, is free. The contrast between the grand man trapped by his retinue and humble Horace on his impotent ass is at once comical and poignant.

Horace claims to enjoy a freedom superior to that of the traditional aristocrat because his is internalized and self-determined. Similarly, in 1.4 and 1.10, he contends that his satire is better and more polished than that of Lucilius. Horatian satire is a literary form characterized not by anger, censure or blame, but by self-control. Horatian *libertas* is not the freedom to seek public office and control public affairs, but the freedom to mind his own business, write poetry and go wherever he likes (Rudd 1982: 44–50; Freudenburg 2001: 61; Freudenburg 2002: 136; Schlegel 2005: 8–9). In Socratic terms, it is the freedom to care for himself.

The first book of satires, then, is in many ways very different from the work of Lucilius. *Satires* 1.1, 1.2 and 1.3 borrow heavily from the tradition of diatribe and are generally considered the most Lucilian. The precise degree of Lucilian influence can be hard to judge; while we have more than 2,000 lines of Lucilius, very few of the surviving fragments are more than two lines long. But, as we shall see when we read *Satires* 1.1, even those satires that seem most characterized by a distinctly Other-directed form of invective are themselves thoroughly ironic and in the end both Socratic and self-reflective. Nonetheless, the common reading of poems 1.1 to 1.3 has a clear basis. After 1.3 – unlike what is found in the fragments of Lucilius – no living person of note is lampooned and, even in the opening satires, there is no real political combat; the unsettled times would not have permitted it. As Coffey observes, 'In the 30s it would have been dangerous, especially for a freedman's son, to write political lampoons' (1976: 90–1; cf. Bailey 1982: 3). What Maecenas and Octavian needed, and what Horace sought in *satura*, was a poetic form in which fundamental Roman values were redefined for a new era. Horace produces a satire that is both politically and aesthetically disciplined, shorn of the Republican excess that, in the view of Octavian, Maecenas and their circle, had led the Republic to collapse (Ruffell 2003).

To this end, Horace relies more on paradox and self-deprecating irony than the full-frontal assault of traditional invective. This new satiric programme is outlined most explicitly in the central satires of the first book, 1.4–1.6. In 1.4, as we already observed, Horace draws a direct contrast between Lucilian *libertas*, which he identifies with the work of the Greek poets of Old Comedy, and his own brand of highly restrained and polished work. Old Comedy was a poetry in which personal attack was considered *de rigueur*, and while there may be debate over how seriously the political criticism it featured should be taken, that criticism is certainly prominent. In contrast, Horace's satires follow the quieter, more character-driven tone of New Comedy (Gurd 2012: 98). Where Horace's father, like Lucilius, used to point to the examples of various kinds of behaviour exhibited by individuals as a source of moral instruction for the young Horace, the mature poet has internalized those lessons (McNeill 2001: 66–7, 127; Schlegel 2005: 42–5, 79), pursuing an inner freedom rather than the externalized speech of his generic and biological fathers:

> ex hoc ego sanus ab illis
> perniciem quaecumque ferunt, mediocribus et quis
> ignoscas vitiis teneor. fortassis et istinc
> largiter abstulerit longa aetas, liber amicus,
> consilium proprium; neque enim, cum lectulus aut me
> porticus excepit, desum mihi. 'rectius hoc est;
> hoc faciens vivam melius; sic dulcis amicis
> occurram; hoc quidam non belle: numquid ego illi
> imprudens olim faciam simile?' haec ego mecum
> conpressis agito labris; ubi quid datur oti,
> inludo chartis. hoc est mediocribus illis
> ex vitiis unum.

Thanks to him [my father], I am free from these defects and the harm they bring, and I am held only by minor ones that you should overlook.

And perhaps even from these, long life, a free-speaking friend, or my own counsel will have delivered me. For I am not absent from myself, even when my writing couch or the shelter of a colonnade has received me. 'This is more proper; doing this I will have a better life; thus I will be a welcome sight to my friends; this indeed is not well done; would I ever foolishly do something similar to that?' I turn these things over with myself with my lips tightly sealed. When I have a bit of leisure, I mark up some paper. This is one of those minor vices. (1.4.129–40)

It will repay our attentions to pause for a moment and remark on certain features of this passage. It is very much about *libertas* in both its traditional and new Horatian sense, and it is in the ambiguity between the meanings that the irony lurks.

Horace begins by noting that he is largely 'free from' (*sanus ab*) the graver moral flaws, owing to the power of the examples his father had drawn from others (Gowers 2012: ad loc.). Yet it is not 'freedom' in the classical sense of *libertas* that Horace names in line 129, but freedom as moral health. This relation between health and freedom implied by Horace's use of *sanus* is clearly metaphorical, and the attentive reader could be forgiven for observing that the use of *sanus* ('healthy, rational, sound') is hardly identical to *liber* and might therefore charge that our translation of it as 'free' is tendentious, even granted the presence of *ab* denoting 'separation from'. Yet the next sentence almost mandates this translation insofar as Horace describes the minor vices that still afflict him not as a disease, a wound or some other form of *insania*, but as something by which he is 'held' or 'bound' (*teneor*), by which his movement is restricted.

Thus the *libertas* of Horatian satire is a particular kind. On one level, it is identical with moral health. As such, it is something that can be described as a state or a condition that exists with regard to our internal constitutions. On another, it is imaged as a form of freedom of movement, as the condition of not being held or bound, which is produced by an external act of freedom in the more traditional Lucilian sense of observing the faults of others and 'noting' them or marking them down (*notare* 1.4.5; Gurd 2012: 88–9). But it is the subsequent internalization of this image that produces its power and yet also gives the satire a certain ironic undecidability. What does freedom mean if it is defined as a form of health? What does a lack of constraint mean that is also a fully internalized form of determination, of modifying one's behaviour to conform to or to avoid an externally observed exemplar? These are indeed philosophical questions, yet we hardly notice them as such. The comic frame of the moralizing father, a staple of New Comedy (cf. 1.4.48–56; Freudenburg 1993: 34–5), represents philosophy as what Aristotle terms the 'liberal jest' of Socratic irony (*Rhetoric* 3.18.7), rather than as a series of propositions or the product of a metaphysical system.

At the same time, this passage from *Satires* 1.4 presents the project of caring for the self (*Apology* 36b6), of moral perfectibility, as a possible outcome of experience as we age (*longa aetas,* 1.4.132). It comes as the result of a friend who feels free (*liber,* 132) to speak the truth to us. Or it is the internalization of that experience and of that advice so that they become our own counsel (*consilium*), even as the boundary between outward conformity and inward determination becomes difficult to discern (133). Most of all this project of caring for oneself is presented as a form of mindfulness, of self-presence. Horace is never absent from himself, never simply absorbed in business or governmental affairs (*neque* [...] *desum mihi,* 133–4). His freedom is not that of the thoughtless. It is certainly not freedom from himself, but rather it is a form of constant vigilance, an attentiveness to his own behaviour that many might find constraining. This self-surveillance takes place in the form of a silent internalization of the outward observation and criticism of others undertaken first by Lucilius and then on a more intimate scale by Horace's father (Miller 2018). Its final distillation appears in Horace's poetry, the pages he marks up so that the project of self-liberation through attentiveness becomes one with the satires themselves (140), as what began as a completely externalized act of blame and criticism becomes internalized as a form of self-care and then is finally re-expressed as the polished work of art we hold in our hands. Each of these moments of transformation is an occasion of ironic tension, but each also offers the potential for Socratic self-questioning (Classen 1993: 117; McNeill 2001: 127; Schlegel 2005: 79; Plaza 2006: 169–70).

Thus, at the end of *Satires* 1.4, we have a programmatic statement of what Horatian satire will be: a form of self-care that promotes moral health rather than a public indictment of vice, through a quiet and refined form of ironic self-reflection. In 1.5, this programme is enacted. Where Lucilius spent the whole of Book 3 of his *Satires* leisurely recounting a trip he made to Sicily to visit his estates, Horace polishes off the journey to Brundisium in 104 lines. Yet while the Callimachean polish is evident in Horace's pared-down version of Lucilius, the tone is anything but arch. Our narrator is charming, self-deprecating and largely clueless about the political events in which he is participating. In 38 BCE, Maecenas was sent to Athens to arrange a meeting between Antony and Octavian. That meeting took place in 37 BCE in Tarentum, and successfully mended fences between the two triumvirs for the next six years. The dramatic date of the satire is either 38 BCE, when Maecenas left for Athens from Brundisium, or 37, in which case Horace's party is supposed to have stopped at Brundisium while Maecenas continued on to Tarentum to meet with Octavian and Antony. The period between the assassination of Julius Caesar (44 BCE) and the Battle of Actium (31 BCE) was one of constant instability and intermittent civil war, yet in 1.5 we have not Old Comic political invective aimed against Octavian's foes but a New Comic satire of personal foibles and comedic situations. The focus is on friendship, on the minor inconveniences of the journey – bad food, country bumpkins, fickle call girls – and on the poet's recounting of his own ineptitude. This is *libertas* with a small *l*, but it is also the triumph of an aesthetic and an ethic fitted for a new political era in which there is little room for the larger-than-life personalities that dominated the end of the Republic (Welch 2008: 68–70; Gowers 2009).

In poem 1.6, we are told the story of how Horace was introduced to Maecenas, with repeated emphasis on Maecenas' aristocratic background in contrast to Horace's status as the son of a freedman:

> Maecenas, not because some element of the Lydians settled Etruscan
> land – no one is nobler than you – nor because your maternal and
> paternal grandfathers once commanded great legions, do you, as many
> are accustomed, turn up your nose at those of obscure birth, like me,
> the son of a freedman father. (1.6.1–6)

For Maecenas it is character, not genealogy, that determines an individual's worth: 'you deny that it matters from what father you are born, so long as you are noble/free/well bred' (*ingenuus*) (7–8). The ambiguity inherent in the translation of *ingenuus* demonstrates the shift between a culture in which status was largely determined by externalities such as wealth and birth to one in which, at least in Horace's ideal world as well as that of the philosophers, inner nature (*in-genium*) was determinative. It was your moral health (*sania*) that determined your status and your freedom, not accidents of birth.

Poem 1.7 offers a brief comic anecdote about a legal conflict between two lower status characters, Rex and Persius. It is filled with puns on Rex's name and much hay is made from the fact that the judge in this brief farce is Brutus, descendant of the Brutus who overthrew Tarquinius Superbus, the last of the Etruscan kings, and himself one of the leaders of Caesar's assassins. Poem 8 is another farce, this time concerning Horace's bête noire, Canidia, and a farting statue of Priapus. We shall return to Canidia when we deal with the *Epodes* in Chapter 2. In 1.9, Horace subtly pays a compliment to Maecenas for the integrity of his household, while portraying himself as the hapless victim of a social-climbing boor. And 1.10 recapitulates Horace's poetic programme as articulated in 1.4 and 1.6 and exemplified in 1.5.

In 2.1, which introduces the second book of satires published in 30 BCE, Horace presents a new, more dialogic style. In this book, he will seldom be the only speaker in the poem, and rarely its central protagonist. In 2.2 we receive a lecture from the rustic Ofellus on the virtues of simple fare. In 2.3, the longest of the satires, Damasippus breaks in on Horace in his Sabine retreat to lecture him on the Stoic paradox that all men are mad, save the sage. In 2.4, Horace runs into Catius and asks him to repeat a speech that he has just heard and is hurrying home to commit to writing. The scene is clearly reminiscent of Plato's *Phaedrus* (Muecke 1997: ad loc.), but rather than leading to a series of speeches climaxing with Socrates' sublime discourse on love, we receive a rambling and disjointed set of comic lucubrations on the finer points of Roman cookery. In 2.5, Odysseus in the underworld asks Tiresias how he can rebuild his fortune when he returns home; the prophet replies with a discourse on legacy hunting. The advice given on various strategies of short-term self-abasement for long-term gain are strongly reminiscent of those found in Priapus' speech on how to seduce boys by Tibullus (1.4), written in roughly the same period. In 2.6, he thanks Maecenas for the gift of the Sabine farm, while the rustic Cervius regales Horace's guest with the tale of the City Mouse and the Country Mouse, a fable that gently criticizes the search for luxury for which Maecenas himself was renowned (Muecke 1997: 228). In 2.7, Horace's slave Davus takes advantage of the *libertas* granted during the Saturnalia to lecture his master on the Stoic paradox that only the wise man is free. Finally, in 2.8, he contrasts Maecenas' well-tempered urbanity with the pretentious bombast of the would-be gourmet, Nasidienus, through a story recounted by the comic poet Fundanius.

Having briefly surveyed Horace's achievement in the realm of satire, his relation to Lucilius and the role played by Socratic irony in the two collections, I want to finish by taking a closer look at three satires which have not always received the attention they deserve, namely 1.1, 2.7 and 2.8. As the first poem of the first book, *Satires* 1.1 occupies a strategic position in Horace's *oeuvre*, and in most cases the opening poem of a collection serves a programmatic function, making explicit its subject matter, its genre and its relation to its poetic predecessors. However, 1.4, with its focus on Lucilius and the question of *libertas*, in many ways takes on this programmatic role in the current collection much more explicitly than does poem 1.1. Nonetheless, while 1.1 does not engage explicitly with the expectations of the satiric genre, it sets a certain tone for the reader and establishes a set of questions that will in fact be central to the first book of satires, and we would do well to be attentive to the import of those questions.

The first words of an ancient book served as its title, hence the *Aeneid* was known as *arma virumque* ('arms and the man'), Propertius Book 1 as *Cynthia prima* ('Cynthia first') and Tibullus 1 as *divitias alius* ('riches of another man'), each of which briefly and suggestively announces the themes to come. According to this convention, the title for Horace's first book of satires would be *qui fit, Maecenas* or 'How does it happen, Maecenas'? Such a title announces a book that asks questions. Indeed, it *is* a quizzical book. At the same time, it is also a book that addresses itself, at least rhetorically, to Horace's friend and patron, Maecenas, the man who ruled the city of Rome when Octavian was gone and who was one of its wealthiest men. *Satires* 1, thus, addresses itself to power and positions itself as able to address power, to interact with it on an intimate level.

Moreover, as this opening question unfurls, it becomes clear that this will not just be a book about how things happen (*De rerum natura*), but specifically about how it happens that *we* are not satisfied with our lot in life. It is a social and philosophical book. The opening question *is*, in fact, programmatic, because, as more than one scholar has pointed out, the question of satisfaction, of what is enough (*satis*) and of how much is too much, is central to the first book of the satires, whether the topic is money, sex, status or the length of poetic composition (Schlegel 2005: 9; Muecke 2007: 112; Moles 2007: 168; Gowers 2012: ad loc.). Indeed, it is Horace's ability to conflate excesses of multiple kinds – personal, political and poetic – that creates one of the primary ironic tensions that structures the book, for the indictment of each transgression spills over to envelop the others. Each is always, in some sense, excessive. It is no accident that the pesky social climber of 1.9 also claims Lucilian prowess in bulk poetic composition (25) and promises to bribe Maecenas' slaves to gain access to the great man (57). Horace throughout the book contrasts his vision of humble internal freedom – the son of the freedman riding his castrated mule wherever he desires – not only with the ambitions of the great senator and those who long to replace him, but also with the poetic excesses of Lucilius, composing 200 lines standing on one leg before dinner (1.4.9–10; 1.10.60–1), and the gaucheries of the ambitious, the unkempt, the immoderate and the corrupt. Each level of satiric intent becomes an allegory of the others without ever losing its particularity. Lucilius' method of poetic composition never becomes simply a metaphor for Republican political excess, but the contrast between Horatian discipline and the various species of poetic, personal and political transgression, imprudence and prodigality becomes central to the first book, even as the poet's own foibles are framed and gently lampooned.

The question of how it happens that we are unsatisfied with our lot not only ironically wavers between multiple discursive levels, rendering each both complementary to and yet separate from the others, it also contains a deeper, more personal irony. The poet who poses the question, the poet who is the son of a freedman, the poet who claims to be free from depraved ambition (1.6.51–2; Oliensis 1998: 25–6), poses that question to Maecenas, arguably one of the three most powerful men in Rome (the other two being Octavian and his admiral, Agrippa). From the point of view of the traditional senatorial class, Horace, this upstart from Apulia who fought on the wrong side of the civil war between Octavian, Antony and Lepidus and Caesar's assassins, is the definition of a social climber.

Throughout the opening section of the poem, the poet continues offering a brief catalogue of characters, each of whom admires the fortune of the others. Horace then observes that, while the grass *is* always greener on the other side of the street, if a god were to come down and offer to grant our wishes to trade places with one another, we would refuse. He then adds poignantly *atqui licet esse beatis* ('and yet they can be happy') (1.1.15–19), a phrase which is profoundly ironic and syntactically ambiguous.[2] Could these characters be happy by changing roles or by remaining in place? Both are possible constructions of the Latin, and yet they yield opposite senses. Moreover, in each case we know that, while the people involved 'could be happy', they almost certainly will not be, regardless of the option they choose. As a consequence, Horace says, an exasperated Jupiter will huff and puff at us, and he will not listen to our prayers so easily the next time (1.1.20–2).

The poet, then, draws himself up short and issues the first truly programmatic statement of the collection in which he reflects explicitly on his role as satirist:

> praeterea ne sic ut qui iocularia ridens
> percurram: quamquam ridentem dicere verum
> quid vetat? ut pueris olim dant crustula blandi
> doctores, elementa velint ut discere prima:
> sed tamen amoto quaeramus seria ludo.

> But I should not just run through the rest of this like someone who is laughing at jokes: although what forbids someone who is laughing from speaking the truth? Just as teachers are accustomed to give cookies to

pupils so they will wish to learn their letters: but, nonetheless, we're
after serious stuff here, when all the play is put aside.   (1.1.23–7)

This is an oft-cited passage but one that will repay our spending time with
it. Right after the image of a comic Jupiter, his cheeks puffed out in disgust
and turning his ear from our prayers, the poet says, 'Wait! This is not just a
series of gags (*iocularia*).' The juxtaposition between the two images – Jupiter
with his face distorted in anger and the poet's claim not to be joking – is
striking and warns the reader that there is more here than meets the eye:
the satirist speaks the truth while laughing.

Horace, like Socrates, is a practitioner of *spoudaiogeloion*, 'serious laugh-
ter', and the point of such laughter is not simply to hide the bitter pill of
truth-telling but, in a real sense, to make truth-telling possible (Miller 2015;
Giangrande 1972). Indeed, the truth such laughter tells, in the end, cannot
be separated from the ironic laughter it provokes. The telling is integral to
the truth, although its wit and humour may well make the message more
palatable than would an arid paraphrase, which would also be a distortion
(Salkever 1993; Roochnik 2012; Scolnicov 2012; Thesleff 2012). When
Socrates at the opening of the *Apology* notes that his accusers have warned
the audience that he is *deinos legein* ('clever', literally 'scary', 'at speaking'),
he replies that this is only true if by *deinos legein* they mean 'one who
speaks the truth'. Of course, that is not what they mean, at least not what
they think they mean. Socrates is only 'scary' at speaking if you are scared
of the truth.

Nonetheless, Socrates is in fact a clever speaker. Despite his claims to plain
speaking, by which he means a style shorn of sophistic ornament, Socrates
is no bumpkin. It is precisely his ability to use plain language to confute
and seduce his listeners, in the fashion described by Meno and Alcibiades
above, that makes him both irresistible and fearsome. This is what his accus-
ers fear when they make their accusation (Miller and Platter 2010: 20–1).
If Socrates' speech were but a fancy wrapper that made the 'truth' attractive,
then that speech could be discarded and the 'truth' would be unchanged,
but the fact is, as Plato in the *Seventh Letter* says, that a simple résumé of the
propositions he and Socrates advance should never be confused with the

actual experience of the truth. That experience comes only through the hard work and practice of dialogue, whether performed directly or, as for most of us, read later, producing the spark of recognition. Horace in this passage makes much the same claim, arguing that poetry in general, and satire in particular, is never just a medium for communicating the truth but one that speaks the truth *while* and *through* laughing (*ridentem*).

An example of what is meant by this can be found in the last two words – *seria ludo* – of the current passage. What happens here is not precisely translatable, and hence not truly paraphrasable, and that is part of the brilliance of Horace as a poet. If, for a moment, we disregard syntax, then what we have in these two words is a precise transcription of *spoudaiogeloion*, 'serious laughter/fun'. Yet while the Greek substantive is formed from two adjectives (*spoudaios* and *geloios*), which are fused and treated as a neuter noun, Horace's Latin phrase is made of two nouns that cannot be fused into a single word. *Seria* is a neuter plural substantive in the accusative that forms the direct object of the verb *quaeramus*, while *ludo* is a masculine noun that forms part of an ablative absolute construction with *amoto* earlier in the line. The plasticity of Latin word order allows Horace at once to suggest *spoudaiogeloion* and yet keep the *ludus* at least provisionally separate from the *seria*, which is exactly what *amoto* means ('removed, moved away').

But what does *ludus* mean? It is a multifaceted noun. Its first meaning is 'game' or 'amusement', but its second and quite common meaning is 'primary school', the kind of place where one hands out cookies to children to encourage them to learn their letters (Habinek 2005: 145). Does this passage mean, then, that when all the fun and games (*amoto* [...] *ludo*) are taken away we are after serious matters (*seria*), or does it mean that when we get beyond the basic schoolhouse learning of *elementa* (*amoto* [...] *ludo*), the kind of thing where people have to be enticed with cookies to memorize the basics, then we are after serious stuff (*seria*)? The first implies that the laughter here is optional, that the language and indeed the poetry, certainly the humour, is removable (*amoto*) from the truth and the truth remains unscathed. The *spoudaion* and the *geloion* may find themselves side by side but they do not become fused: they serve different functions, they have a different syntax. The second implies almost the exact opposite, that we only get down to serious things when the schoolhouse is removed, when the kind of rote learning involved in memorizing your letters is gone beyond and learning ceases to be the seamless transmission of truths from teacher to student and starts to become something much more like the collaborative process envisaged in the *Seventh Letter*: an unrepeatable set of dialogic encounters, in which the truth is spoken while or through laughing and which nonetheless (or as a result) leaves an indelible mark. *Seria* and *ludo* may not fuse into a single substantive, but if the word order is changed, if the juxtaposition is removed, just like that between the comic Jupiter and *iocularia* earlier in the passage, then the message, and indeed the truth, is not the same, because the message is found precisely in both the juxtaposition of the two terms and that juxtaposition's conjugation with the inherent ambiguity of *ludus* in the present context.

The remainder of the poem goes on to problematize the question of what is enough, how does one know, and what is the relation between the things one has and who one is (*Apology* 36c6)? The poet at lines 49–51 asks what is seemingly a straightforward question, *quid referat intra / naturae finis viventi, iugera centum an / mille aret?* ('what does it matter to one living within the bounds of nature, whether he ploughs a hundred or a thousand acres?'). The key to the line is the play on *fines*, 'boundaries, limits'. The statement assumes the primacy or priority of the bounds of nature, as if our desires were a clearly delimited field with visible markers. Yet that sense of *finis* is self-evidently metaphorical, and its figurative or even derivative sense is highlighted by its use in the context of delimiting the size of the field one ploughs. Boundaries are first and foremost a spatial concept, one founded on the practice of marking off the limits between one piece of property or territory from another: an idea that to the Roman mind would conjure up very concrete images of boundary stones, thought to be sacred in traditional Roman religion and often receiving sacrifice (Tibullus 1.1). Thus we are faced with the paradoxical situation that what is supposed to limit our desires for acquiring ever larger estates, and prevent us from not recognizing when we have enough, is itself derived from the bounding of those estates and the complex religious and social network that surrounds Roman property law. The bounds of nature are, then, a function of the limits of our property, which according to this passage are in turn, through a process of internalization, supposed to limit our desire for ever more property.

Thus the primary and the secondary, the figurative and the literal, the natural and the conventional become suspended at exactly the moment when the question of what limits are mandated by nature is posed. And it is, in turn, the poet's ironic use of the same term (*finis*) in two different senses within the same line that makes the recognition of this paradox possible and necessary. At the same time, the lines in which this complex play is enacted are themselves harshly enjambed, one finishing with a preposition and the next with a conjunction, so that each line's syntax vividly overspills the limits of its 'natural' metrical unit.

The poem reaches its logical climax a few lines later, just beyond its mathematical centre, at lines 61–2, at *bona pars hominum decepta cupidine falso. / 'nil satis est' inquit, 'quia tanti quantum habeas sis'* ('but a good part ✗ of men are deceived by false desire. "Nothing is enough," he says, "because you are worth as much as you have."'). The problem of false desires is a traditional philosophical conundrum. You think you want *x* but what you really want is *y*. You think you want a Mercedes, but what you really want is safety, dependability, or your friends to admire your success in life. More to the point for the Roman Socrates, in the *Symposium* Diotima teaches that you think you want this boy, but then you find you really want that boy. Eventually you discover what you want is what those boys have in common, which is beauty itself, a species of the Good.

Of course, early on this Platonic logic is subject to a Cynic critique. You say you want safety and dependability, but what you really want is a cool, expensive car. You say you desire beauty and ultimately the good, but what you really want is to sleep with the boy right here, right now (McGlathery 1998). Plato himself was more than aware of the reversibility of the ladder of love. It is no accident that, after Diotima's idealizing speech, the party dramatized in the *Symposium* is broken up by the entrance of Alcibiades, so drunk he can only stand with the help of a couple of flute girls.

Which then is the false desire? The immediate object that stands as ✗ evidence of a larger, transcendental category, or the transcendental category that serves as a rationalization for grasping the immediate object? Horace is aware of both options and their respective critiques. In *Satires* 1.2, with its talking penis and the poet's counsel to rape the first slave at hand rather than have an affair with a married man's wife, he demonstrates that behind all the refinements and rationalizations of love lies a brutal desire for immediate sexual satisfaction. At the same time, in *Satires* 2.6, we are invited to picture him with his neighbours and slaves gathered in a rustic *Symposium* on his Sabine farm discussing what is the highest good and how it should be pursued, and not just as a rationalization for immediate pleasure.

The problem of false desire, which everyone has experienced, is also simultaneously in an important sense impossible. You really do, on some level, want that boy or that car, even if the possession of either one would ultimately only lead to the realization that what you *truly* wanted or, more accurately, what you *then* wanted was something else. There is a non-trivial sense in which this problem can be boiled down to the objection articulated in the second line of this passage – *'nil satis est' inquit, 'quia tanti quantum habeas sis'* – which in fact recapitulates what we have already discussed concerning the 'bounds of nature'. To what extent are your desires your own and to what extent are they a product of the expectations of others? If you are only worth as much you have, then indeed there can never be enough, because you can always have more. But that 'worth' is not intrinsic to you. It is not determined by the sacred boundary stones that mark the limits of your nature, but by external and contingent considerations: who your father is, how much money you have, what kind of car you drive. Nonetheless, the 'limits' of nature, as we have already seen and as Horace makes clear, are themselves a metaphor derived from the prior and primary realm of property and possession. Hence how can there be a false desire? Where would it come from? This is the crux of the satire. *Qui fit Maecenas*?

And yet, the premise of human integrity, the premise that our choices are meaningful, the premise that ethics, justice and beauty are not mere pretexts, requires that 'false' desires exist and that a certain limit be established which marks the boundaries of our own internal nature, even as those limits themselves are recognized to be an introjection of that which lies beyond them and therefore an example of their transgression. The nature and urgency of this paradox – that internal integrity is established by the fact of its violation – is perhaps ultimately best distilled by Horace at the opening of 1.6, when he praises Maecenas both for his noble Etruscan ancestors and for his refusal to turn up his nose at those who are *ignotos*. The commentaries inform us that *ignotos* here is the equivalent of *ignobiles*: 'unknown, obscure, of humble birth'. But *ignotus* can also mean frankly 'ignoble', or even, as the past participle of *ignosco*, 'pardoned'. All of these are applicable to Horace, because the question at the opening of this poem is: how has Horace, the son of a freedman, been received by Maecenas, the descendant of Etruscan kings?

Horace is thus 'unknown' (at least relative to Maecenas, Octavian and the senatorial elite), and he is of 'humble birth', but he is not 'ignoble' in the moral sense (or so he tells us), and it is precisely the possibility of this disjunction between the meanings of *ignotus* and other value terms around which this poem is built.[3] At the same time, it is also the fact of this disjunction that makes possible the concept of false desires, that institutes a distinction between one's internal worth and one's external possessions and accidental attributes. To say I think I desire *x* but I really desire *y* is to make a distinction between the way my experience appears to me and to others, and its underlying reality or intrinsic nature.

Thus Horace, at the beginning of 1.6, says Maecenas denies that it matters *quali sit quisque parente natus, dum ingenuus* ('from what sort of parent you are born, so long as you are *free/native/honourable/possessed of an inborn nature*'). The word *ingenuus* really says it all. On one level, the prefix *in-* essentially signifies 'here', that is, *in-gigno*: 'to be born within the bounds of our territory' and hence a 'native', and therefore not a slave, and therefore possessed of a nature that was not slavish but characteristic of a 'free person', of someone possessing *libertas* (Stampacchia 1982: 208). The *in-* refers to location rather than interiority. But once we get to the characteristics of a free and hence of an honourable person, we shift from meaning *born in* to *in-born*. We shift levels, with the hinge point between them being the ambiguous concept of freedom (*libertas*): as a social status, an inherent quality and an achieved state. Horace, then, is the humble but not 'ignoble' son of a freedman, who in spite of fighting against Octavian and Antony at Philippi was 'pardoned' and thus retained his liberty. As 1.6 tells us, he has his own in-born nature (*ingenium*) recognized by the nobly born Maecenas and he is made part of the inner circle of the ruling elite – although he disclaims knowing anything about all but the most superficial topics of their discussions (2.6.40–6). This is the Horace who proudly proclaims that he, unlike the senator who needs his entourage, is free to ride wherever he wishes. That is real freedom. The wish to rise above one's station is a false desire. We must live within the bounds of nature, says Horace with a Socratic smile, even as he forces us to ask what that could mean.

The questions of who is wise, who is free and what is the proper scope of our desires continue to be posed in Book 2, as does the meaning of such highly charged terms as *libertas*, *servitium*, *nobilitas*, *ingenuitas* and *ingenium*. In 2.7, Horace's slave Davus takes the opportunity afforded by the Saturnalia to issue a diatribe against the poet based on the Stoic paradox that only the wise man is free (Beard 2014: 62–5; Miller 2013b). The ironic switching of places that the Saturnalia allows, and which is enacted by putting Horace on the receiving end of Davus' satiric indictment, is carried to its logical, if unsustainable, conclusion that Davus is freer than his master himself. At the same time, *Satires* 2.7 is replete with references to physical punishments and torture that offer a firm if brutal retort to Davus' claim to a superior level of *libertas*. Horace may be a slave to his own folly, but Davus remains Horace's slave. And yet the ironic relation between the content of Davus' speech and the reality of his situation cannot help but make us question the justice of that situation and what freedom might really mean (Muecke 1997: 212–13; Vecchi 2013: 374–5). That irony is only heightened when Davus acknowledges that he had received the Stoic content of the speech not from his own reflection, a study of philosophical texts or listening to lectures, but from the *ianitor*, a low-ranking slave often chained to the door of his master, of Crispinus, a Stoic moralist and favourite target from Book 1 (2.7.45; cf. 1.1.20, 1.3.139, 1.4.14). Thus Davus' free expression is, in fact, slavish.

Satires 2.7, then, is a poem that is central to our preoccupations. The first passage to read is 2.7.83–8. It comes after a recapitulation of *Satires* 1.2's indictment of adultery when sex from slaves and courtesans is easily available. The tables here are turned on the satirist, with Horace now cast as the one who lusts for another man's *coniunx* (2.7.46–77) and Davus portraying himself as the advocate of practical virtue. Whether we accept Davus' reversal of roles from *Satires* 1.2, see his charge as evidence of the slave's unreliable nature or believe that he is simply repeating what he heard from Crispinus' *ianitor* is undecidable. There is a fundamental ambiguity in this passage that is unresolvable and whose irony is only further amplified the more its resolution is pursued. Each new interpretation adds itself to the others without being able to provide a definitive context from which a decisive judgment can be rendered (Rolfe 1962: 324–5; Coffey 1976: 89; Muecke 1997: 220; Vecchi 2013: 373–4). The fact that Davus turns the tables on Horace, both in terms of the Saturnalia and the discourse of *Satires* 1.2, is undeniable. The fact that Davus is a slave (and thus from a Roman perspective of doubtful veracity) and that he is able to exploit his momentary freedom is self-evident. Finally, the fact that Davus does not claim to be the origin of this discourse but only has it third-hand is clearly stated. Each of these contexts undermines the implicit claims of the others, but all of them coexist both within the structure of 2.7 and of the *Satires* as a whole, ironizing and amplifying the claims of the others. As Paul de Man argued, while irony can recognize inauthenticity, it cannot overcome it (1983: 222). We can never move directly from the recognition of irony to a conclusion about an actual state of affairs or a prescribed set of actions.

Nonetheless, Davus' basic thesis that Horace is every bit as in thrall to base desire as Davus himself and that in both cases it is only the threat of punishment and humiliation that keeps them from acting on those desires (2.7.70–4) is essentially uncontested and, as many readers might acknowledge, for most of us uncontestable. Indeed, on a certain level, Horace is all the more the slave. For, although he is the master, he is every bit as subject to determinations that are not, in any meaningful sense, his own. Yet unlike Davus, Horace can never look forward to the possibility of manumission. His slavery is that of the human condition, and only wisdom can make him free. Davus may be his under slave (*vicarius*, 79) or fellow slave (*conservus*, 80), but in the end Horace is a plaything of people and forces greater than himself, a puppet on a string (*nervis alienis mobile lignum*, 82; Vecchi 2013: 377). And so it is that the central question of the satires comes to be posed by a slave, and not a particularly wise one, while (slavishly) repeating what he heard from another slave: 'who therefore is free?'

How are we supposed to receive this question? Is it serious or do the very circumstances of its utterance render it invalid or ironic? The expansion on it that follows is far from prima facie ridiculous. Uttered in another context, these lines could be received as a straightforward statement of ethical truth:

> The wise man is he who is in command of himself, whom neither poverty, nor death, nor shackles terrify. A strong man, he is able to withstand desires and to shun honours, wholly contained within himself, polished and spherical, lest anything external be able to distract him, even slightly, against whom fortune always rushes crippled. (83–8)

This is a conventional portrait of the Stoic sage (Muecke 1997: 223; Vecchi 2013: 378). There is nothing in it, if read outside the present context, that would indicate it is anything but completely serious. The wise man alone is free because he is his own master. Rather than obeying externalities, he controls himself. He does not yield to false desires, because the boundaries of his self are firmly fixed. He is like a god or planet in the *Timaeus* (33b), a hard and perfect sphere, against whom the waves of fortune may dash but always recede. The rhetoric may be exalted, but place it in the mouth of Scipio at the end of Cicero's *De re publica* and few commentators would laugh.

And yet Davus is no Scipio; it is precisely the context, and not the content, that is the point. Indeed, this is the most radical and ultimately the most ironic (in a profoundly Socratic sense) element in the satire. For people, real people rather than gods, are not perfectly rounded self-contained spheres completely undetermined by their environment. Nor can we imagine how they could be, without ceasing to be human, without ceasing to make meaningful choices, without truly, in any operational sense, ceasing to be free. At the same time, the language in which this vision of the Stoic sage is expressed, even though it is not in itself ironic or parodic, cannot establish boundaries that separate its meaning from the context of its utterance, any more than Diotima's grand speech in the *Symposium* can be separated from Alcibiades' grotesque entrance or from the frame narrative in which

Apollodorus recounts what Aristodemus told him that Socrates said concerning Diotima. There is no pure language that is uncontaminated by the context in which it is uttered. Crispinus' doorman is only a modestly less reliable source than Apollodorus.

Indeed, the epistemological fact that is dramatized by the frame narrative of the *Symposium* or of the *Theaetetus* as well as by Davus' speech in *Satires* 2.7 is that the truth itself, at least any truth that can expressed in the form of a proposition, can never be spoken except within a frame, within a situation, and that means that there is no such thing as an acontextual true statement, one that is not in some sense already ironized. Like the Socratic ironist, the satirist is not he who denies the truth, but he who, because he is *deinos legein*, recognizes that the truth can only be sought in the space between a statement and its frame, in the moment of their revelatory difference (Miller 2015). Our autonomy is always compromised. The boundaries that mark the limits of our nature have always been secondarily derived. We are always free only within contexts that limit our freedom, and the Stoic paradox that acknowledges this condition can only do so on the condition of being self-subverting. Yet none of this makes that paradox any less true, and its truth is most powerfully realized in its paradoxical nature: only the wise man is free, and the wise man does not exist. Nonetheless, Davus insists, the paradox leads both to comic subversion and self-recognition:

> Don't you recognize anything of your own in this picture? A woman
> demands five talents from you, she harasses you, douses you with cold
> water and drives you from her doors. Then she calls you back again.
> Rip your neck from this foul yoke and say 'Free! I am free!' (88–92)

We are a long way from the music of the spheres. The immediate juxtaposition of the sublime vision of the Stoic sage with Horace as *servus amoris* ('slave of love') is a powerful example of saying the truth while and through laughing, but these are no cookies the poet offers his tender charges for learning their lessons: they are thoroughly ironized reflections. Is this what freedom really means: not wisdom, but easy sex and no more cold showers? Maybe. 'Hey, don't knock it till you've tried it.' And yet the sublimity of the image of perfect self-determination is not so easily annihilated. It too speaks to our desire, and the irony consists not in its replacement by a more mundane image of comfort and satisfaction, but in their simultaneity, their juxtaposition (de Man 1983: 225–6). Which of these desires is truly false?

In the end, the difference between master and slave becomes less and less clear, and yet as the distinction seems ever more arbitrary, it becomes all the more real, all the more poignant. It comes down to who has power over whom, who holds the monopoly of violence:

> I am worthless, if I go chasing after a steaming cake: but does your great virtue and spirit refuse rich dinners? Why is my subservience to my belly more noxious than yours? Simple, my back is striped. (102–5)

Horace does not even attempt to deny the fact. Instead, the poem closes with him threatening Davus with violence and banishing him to the fields (116–18), rather than having the privileged status of a house slave. The Saturnalia is over. Get back to work. Even this threat has an ironic twist, though. There were far worse fates awaiting slaves than being banished to Horace's Sabine farm (Armstrong 1989: 53), whose humble virtues had just been celebrated in the proceeding poem.

The *Satires* finish with a convivial scene, a *Symposium* gone awry. Horace runs into the comic writer, Fundanius, and asks him to recount how dinner was yesterday at the home of wealthy (*beatus*) Nasidienus: for Horace had gone looking for Fundanius to be his own dinner companion and was told that his friend had been drinking *chez* Nasidienus since the middle of the day. Fundanius replies, with what, as we read on, is clearly caustic irony, that he has never had better in his life. He then proceeds to recount an over-the-top meal, in which the host relates the details of each and every dish, making sure that everyone appreciates the knowledge, the expense and the refinement that has gone into each course. In the process, the pleasure of the diners is ruined and the host appears increasingly like a buffoon who lacks all sense of self-awareness (Rudd 1982: 218; Braund 1992: 24–5). At the same time, no one is really spared. Fundanius and his companions, who include Maecenas, are shown to be an arch and uncharitable lot, who have no problem consuming their host's expensive food and wine while mocking him to his face, even if he is too obtuse to recognize it (Baker 1988: 214). The fact that Horace stands to one side of the whole scene, rather than being a direct participant, is not insignificant, as both mocker and mocked are included within the satire's distancing frame. The choice to end Horace's satiric career in this fashion offers a final ironic recontextualization of the entire project, as we are invited to laugh at both the absurdity of Nasidienus' behaviour and to question whether the comic writer who indicts others escapes his own censure (Baker 1988: 226–7; Oliensis 1998: 61; McNeill 2001: 19–21).

Lines 64–74 are emblematic of the poem's tone and recall closely the technique already observed in 2.7.83–8, wherein a statement that in one context could seem perfectly reasonable is rendered ridiculous by its frame. Nasidienus has just finished describing in detail a grotesque dish in which a pregnant lamprey is laid out on a platter in a complex sauce, surrounded by arugula, bitter elecampane and sea urchins. The fish dish would normally be the climax to any elaborate meal (Benedetto 1981: 48–9; O'Connor 1990: 27; Miller 1998). At this moment, disaster strikes. Tapestries suspended overhead collapse, destroying the dish and creating a cloud of black dust. Nasidienus begins to weep as if he had lost a young son. His hanger-on, Nomentanus, begins to lament the cruel blows of fortune. Fundanius and friends can barely contain themselves, sniggering into their cups, when Balatro, whose name literally means 'jester', weighs in. Balatro serves in the role of Maecenas' *scurra*, a lower-class dinner companion meant to provide comic relief, a role that many would have assumed that Horace, the son of a freedman and a writer of satire, played in Maecenas' retinue and one he was quick to eschew (cf. 1.4.86–91; Muecke 1997: 227). Balatro offers a consolatory discourse to Nasidienus, which both exposes him to further ridicule and rallies his flagging spirits:

> Balatro, sneering at everything, said, 'This is the human condition and
> therefore fame will never give an equal recompense to your labour. How
> wracked you are, bound by every care, so that I may be received freshly
> bathed, so that the bread not be scorched, a poorly made sauce not be

put on the table, so that all the slaves may serve us properly dressed and combed! Add to that, if, as just now, the tapestries fall; or if a lackey slips and breaks a platter. But as adverse circumstances are accustomed to reveal the inborn talent of the dinner-party host, just like the general, so favourable ones hide it.'

Balatro's irony here is emblematic of the tone that characterizes Book 2. It is wholly dependent upon the circumstances of the utterance. In alternative circumstances, we might well accept the individual observations within the speech as serious (even if we ultimately judged its content to be rather silly). Indeed, it is remarkable that Horace feels the need to signal the reader the mocking tone of the discourse (*Balatro suspendens omnia naso*), as if it were possible that we might otherwise misconstrue it. For if we were to ask what individual element in the statement is not literally true, is not capable of being taken as a sincere response to the situation as presented, there is in fact nothing, aside from the poet's explicit signal and that the comic Fundanius had already recounted that Balatro and his companion Vibidius had responded to Nasidienus' previous extravagances by demanding ever larger drinking vessels, 'we will die unavenged unless we drink till we ruin him!' (33).

While within the context of a dinner party such a speech may be over the top, it is a perfectly common platitude to lament that one seldom gets credit for one's efforts. Indeed, this *is* the condition of life. Likewise, anyone who has ever hosted a high-stakes dinner party for their boss, a client or in-laws – and one can imagine few dinners with higher stakes than inviting one of the most powerful people in Rome and their retinue – will acknowledge that, while torture on the rack might be an exaggeration, it is not far off the mark. Who would not be solicitous that the bread served to one of the most powerful men in the world not be burned, nor the sauce ruined, nor the caterers show up unkempt and wearing greasy aprons? People routinely torment themselves over much less. Likewise, difficult as the situation may be, it is only made all the more so if the powerful person has brought along a snide young dandy, like Balatro, as he humorously recognizes. The passage's final simile of the host and the general again may be exaggerated, but it is certainly true in both cases that while adverse circumstances will reveal the native-born talents of the person in charge, success will often conceal them (*viz.* Custer). And Nasidienus from beginning to end is not concerned at all with trying to hide his native-born talent, his *ingenium*, and so by this same logic he will always fail or at least always be sailing into the wind.

A good part of the humour stems from the fact that Nasidienus does not recognize the irony of Balatro's speech. Indeed, he takes it all quite literally and warms to the task of setting all to rights. 'Nasidienus says in reply, "may the gods grant you whatever pleasant things you have prayed for! You are indeed a good man and an obliging table companion"' (75–6). On one level, Nasidienus' reaction is ridiculous and underlines the fact of his being a hopeless rube. On another, however, his misunderstanding is absolutely necessary. Irony only functions to the extent that two separate meanings can be understood from the same statement. If Nasidienus' understanding of the plain meaning of the words uttered were not possible the irony of the scene would be totally lost. As Richard Rorty, the American philosopher, argued, irony is nothing more than a process of recontextualization (1989). On the most elementary level, we read Balatro's statement one way because we have the benefit of Fundanius' narratorial intervention to tell us that Balatro is 'sneering at everything' when he speaks, whereas the increasingly pathetic Nasidienus is not included within the charmed circle of those in the know, like us and Horace. Yet in a different context, these same words could mean something very different, and indeed might mean what Nasidienus understands.

Indeed, one of Rorty's points is that the process of recontextualization has no logically necessary end. We may draw lines of inclusion and exclusion, like Horace himself waiting to be introduced to Maecenas, but these lines never inhere in the propositions themselves, they are never predicated on a truth separate from those propositions. Thus, while we may read Balatro's statement as an ironic indictment of Nasidienus, his pedantry and his pretentiousness – and this is certainly a legitimate and common interpretation of this passage – at the same time if we disallow Nasidienus' construction of the statement, then indeed we must also logically conclude that the gods should not grant Balatro's wishes and that he is probably not 'a good man and obliging table companion'. Indeed, if we reframe Balatro within the terms of his own discourse, then he is the hanger-on of a rich man, who has been welcomed into the home of another and served a lavish meal, one for which his host has gone to considerable time and expense, only to drink in excess and begin insulting his host. Within this frame of reference we must ask how different Balatro is from the picture Horace draws of the overly aggressive satirist and drunken *scurra* in 1.4, from whom Horace is at pains to distance himself, even as he seeks to redefine and recontextualize satire outside a Lucilian frame:

> 'His horns are wrapped in straw. Run far away. So long as he can raise a laugh, he does not spare any friend, not even himself.' [...]
>
> Often you may see a fourth person crowded onto the three couches each built for three,[4] and one of them loves to spray the rest with abuse any way he can, except for the host. Although he goes after him too once he has started drinking, when truthful Bacchus [*Liber*] opens the secrets of the heart. This man seems obliging to you and witty and free [*liber*].   (1.4.34–5 and 86–90)

Balatro, as the drunken *scurra* who will say anything to get a laugh and does not spare his host, especially after drinking to excess, fits Horace's image of the bad satirist from whom he wishes to separate himself almost to a tee. But if we recognize the parallel, then we should refuse the invitation to identify with Balatro's position. Indeed, it seems more and more significant that Horace himself was not at the party, and rather than being framed by the discourse he constitutes its frame (Muecke 1997: 228–9). Nasidienus may be a buffoon, but Balatro is at best a problematic model of what it means to be 'obliging, urbane and free'.

Yet if that is the case, why do we stop with Balatro? Fundanius is the one who recounts the story, and insofar as we identify Fundanius' position with that of the satirist, since he is both a writer of comedies and the narrator of our poem, then we must ask to what extent we are to identify with his position in the poem and how we are to separate ourselves from it. For if we can ask the question of whether Balatro is truly a good man, or whether the space between his sneering mockery and Nasidienus' pretentious buffoonery offers the possibility of a more meaningful and a more humane discourse, one which in fact ironizes both the ironist and his target, then this is all the more true of Fundanius, who both signals Balatro's irony to the reader and who applauds the guests' decision at the end of the poem to run off and leave the final dish untasted, a dish that is itself an example of satiric irony: for in itself it was more than acceptable (*suavis res*), but only as it was reframed by the discourse of the host (*si non causas narraret earum et / naturas dominus*) did it become disgusting (92–3). Are we then to applaud the role the comic poet plays in his own story and are we to identify his role with that of Horace, or should we see it as both the subject and object of the poet's critique? The satirist leaves us in perplexity. There is no concluding conversation and we do not return to the initial frame of the dialogue; Horace neither endorses Fundanius' tale nor is he completely excluded from it.

But once the process of recontextualization begins, where does it stop? As we saw in *Satires* 2.7, Horace is by no means immune from the critique his own satires launch. By the same token, as we have already remarked, the poet himself envisions a process where external observation leads to internal critique and self-interrogation: precisely the ultimate aim of Socratic discourse, which more often ends in aporia or perplexity than dogmatic assurance (Hadot 1995: 105). The ironic frame of Horatian satire, thus, each step of the way, retreats to include an ever-wider swathe within its endless questioning, and this bottomless nature of the discourse is one of the most effective lessons it teaches, as the reader ultimately becomes both the questioner and the questioned, both mocker and mocked. And this, in the end, is one definition of the kind of infinite internal freedom that the satires cultivate, as opposed to the finite external liberty of the Roman aristocrat who seeks to impose his will upon the world, who 'notes' the behaviour of others to expose them to ridicule and bring them into conformity with his norms. This is the freedom not to be the great man, not to impress others with our power, our birth, our money or our knowledge, all of which are forms of servitude to objects that lie beyond the bounds of our nature, but the freedom to cultivate a self and a community in which thoughtfulness is valued, friendship appreciated and we can ride our mules wherever we wish.

II

GOING SOFT
ON CANIDIA

THE EPODES, AN
UNAPPRECIATED CLASSIC

AT THE TIME that Horace was composing the *Satires* (42–30 BCE), he was also engaged in another genre traditionally associated with invective, iambic poetry, which resulted in the publication of the *Epodes* at roughly the same time as *Satires* 2 (Johnson 2011: 23; Mankin 2010: 101). From a strictly formal point of view, iambic and satire are unrelated. The Roman genre of *satura*, as practised by Horace and those who came in his wake, is written in hexameters, and claims its legitimacy as a genre based on the work of Lucilius. It is the sole genre that was, as Quintilian notes, wholly Roman (10.1.93). Iambic, on the other hand, possesses its own unique pedigree, which is of equal age, if not prestige, to that of the Homeric epic, tracing its origins to Archilochus of Paros and finding expression in a variety of metrical forms, all of which have the iambic foot ˘ ¯ at their base. Archilochus' successors in the Greek tradition were Hipponax and Callimachus, and Catullus in Latin.

Horace acknowledges this genealogy, referring in his later work to the *Epodes* as *iambi* and acknowledging Archilochus as the founder of the genre (*Odes* 1.16, *Epistles* 1.19.23–5, 2.2.59–60). His metrical practice in the *Epodes* follows Archilochus closely, and there are a number of passages where he seems to quote either directly or indirectly from his great predecessor (Mankin 1995: 6–9, 14–22; Mankin 2010: 94–7; Watson 2003: 43–6; Harrison 2007: 126). At the same time, the *Epodes* are no mere translation or slavish imitation of Archilochus. As in the *Satires*, Horace makes the genre his own through adapting the themes and targets of attack to the realities of Rome at the end of the Republic, a polity wracked with political conflict and the ever-present dangers of civil war, proscription or assassination. Horace thus claims to be the first Roman poet to have written Parian iambics (i.e. in the fashion of Archilochus), but his are iambics with a difference:

> I first brought forward Parian iambics
> in Latium. I followed the metre and spirit
> of Archilochus, but not the matter nor the words that hounded Lycambes.
>
> (*Epistles* 1.19.23–5)

Horace's iambics may be the metrical and spiritual heirs to Archilochus', but their content and the violence of their style will be different.

The Lycambes mentioned in the *Epistles* had been the target of Archilochus' ire. He was, we are told, the poet's future father-in-law. When Lycambes broke off Archilochus' engagement to his daughter, Neoboule, the poet responded with such violent invective that both father and daughter hanged themselves in shame. This is not an isolated incident; we are also told the same of Bupalus, the target of Hipponax's iambic poetry. In both cases, we are dealing less with a set of historical facts than a traditional claim concerning the power of invective (Miller 1994: 21–9). The iambic poet is by definition a wielder of devastating verbal violence.

Horace in the *Epodes* shows himself to be well aware of these traditions surrounding the genre. In poem 6, he responds to an attack from another poet: the 'cowardly dog' should beware lest Horace, like a 'wolf', respond as did the 'scorned son-in-law to faithless Lycambes or the bitter enemy to

Bupalus' (1–2, 13–14). Iambic is a weapon with the power to shame, humiliate and destroy: a stance Catullus had adopted in the previous generation and that was clearly known to Horace (Mankin 2010: 94). Nonetheless, as the later poet is quick to add in the passage from the *Epistles* quoted above, although he followed Archilochus in metre and spirit, he did not follow him in the words that hounded Lycambes to his death. For, as we saw with the *Satires*, in the volatile political environment of the 30s unrestrained personal invective could be hazardous to one's health. Cicero's assassination after the *Philippics* – a series of speeches designed to destroy Marc Antony's public image – had shown only too well that, if you spoke freely, you could pay for it with your life (Johnson 2012: 56). Nonetheless, Quintilian a century after Horace still considered *libertas*, the satiric virtue *par excellence*, one of iambic's defining characteristics (10.1.94–6). He describes Archilochus as possessing 'The greatest force in his speech, with pronouncements that were as strong as they were concise and threatening, full of blood and sinew' (10.1.60; see Watson 2003: 29; Gowers 1993: 284–5).

Horace, then, is mindful of both genres' shared commitment to *libertas*: free, frank speech that can function as a weapon. In the *Epodes*, he refers both to his *liberrima indignatio* in *Epodes* 4 and the *libera consilia* of his friends in 11. At roughly the same time as Horace was writing these very poems, he was also contrasting the *libertas* of Lucilius and the poets of Greek Old Comedy with his own quieter *Sermones*, or 'Conversations'. The correspondence between the two genres at times becomes explicit. In *Epodes* 6, immediately before citing the precedent of Archilochus and Hipponax, Horace seems to quote directly from 1.4 (or is it the other way around?): 'Beware, beware: for I wield ready horns against evil men' (11–12). In the parallel passage from the *Satires* we are told that members of the public fear the satirist, shouting at his approach, 'His horns are wrapped in straw. Run far away. So long as he can raise a laugh, he does not spare any friend, not even himself' (1.4.34–5). The poet claims the charge is unfair and responds that he is not like that, that he is not even really a poet, and besides his father had taught him to internalize the examples of others for his own edification rather than use them as weapons. The image of the bull with his horn wrapped in straw, however, is clearly that of a dangerous animal against whom measures must be taken to ensure the public's safety. The satirist may disclaim all cause for fear, but his iambic doppelganger brags about his horns and asks threateningly, 'if someone has attacked me with a black tooth, shall I cry like a boy who has not been avenged?' (*Epodes* 6.15–16; see Freudenburg 1993: 79).

Nonetheless, as in satire so in iambic, by the late 30s the good old days of public character assassination had passed in favour of quieter, more internalized and more ironic forms of discourse. The offending poet threatened in *Epodes* 6 is never named. There is no Lycambes in the *Epodes* who is hounded until hanged. Indeed, in *Epistles* 2.1, Horace offers a brief genealogy of how the *libertas* of the early Romans was first transformed from the rustic abuse of ritualized Fescinnine verse (a sanctioned form of public raillery) into savage jokes that menaced respectable households with mad abuse (*rabiem*). 'And the poets changed their tune from fear of the cudgel, having been led back to speaking well [*bene dicendum*] and delighting' (2.1.145–55). This change from lawless licence in the composition of verse and the violence it wields ('the bloody tooth') to proper speech that delights the reader parallels the shift chronicled in *Satires* 1.10 from Lucilian *libertas* to Horatian restraint in terms of form and content:

> But that one [Lucilius], if his life had been stretched by fate into this our current age, would erase a lot himself, and he would cut back everything that went beyond the perfect, and in making verse, often he would scratch his head and gnaw his nails to the quick.
>
> (*Satires* 1.10.71)

The violence of unfettered *libertas* or *licentia* is subtly turned back on the poet himself, scratching his head and biting his nails, as he strives for the formal, aesthetic perfection of *bene dicendum*. In much the same fashion, as we saw in the previous chapter, *Satires* 1.4 chronicles how the genre's power in the hands of Lucilius to expose the vices of others (*multa cum libertate notabant*, 'they marked them out with great freedom', 5) becomes internalized by Horace as a tool for the shaping of both an ethical self (*ut fugerem exemplis vitiorum quaeque notando*, 'so that I might flee vices by marking out each of them with examples', 106) and an artistic ideal.

These lines cited from *Satires* 1.4 and 1.10 may be addressed to a fan of Lucilius, but they apply equally well to the practitioners of iambic, among the most prominent of whom was Catullus. While today most widely known for his love lyrics, Catullus freely insulted the politicians and others of his era with vivid and violent obscenity. In poem 28, a squib written in the hendecasyllabic metre, the poet addresses his two companions, Veranius and Fabullus, who have just returned home from a turn in the provinces with a certain governor Piso. Such stints in the retinues of provincial governors were thought of as gateways to larger political careers, during which young men from good families learned the administrative ropes and made valuable connections. They were also ways for these same young men to enrich themselves, generally at the expense of local inhabitants. Catullus and his friends, however, had the misfortune of landing with governors who did not allow their staff such opportunities, whether out of scruples or simply because they kept the loot for themselves. Either way, Catullus asks his comrades if they feel they got screwed as royally as he did with Memmius:

> Does whatever is paid out appear in your account books as a small profit,
> as with me, who after I followed my praetor marked anything given as
> gain? Oh Memmius, you laid me out long and slow with your whole
> beam. But, as far as I can see, you two were in the same situation. You
> were stuffed by no lesser prick. Seek out noble friends!   (28.6–13)

Such frank political speech is hardly rare in Catullus. In the very next poem, this time in iambic trimeters, Mammura, one of Julius Caesar's henchmen, is indicted for his insatiable greed and termed the general's *mentula diffututa* ('fucked-out prick', 29.13). Later poems simply refer to him as 'Mentula', including this gem in elegiac couplets:

> Mentula moechatur. Moechatur mentula? Certe.
> Hoc est quod dicunt: ipsa olera olla legit.

> Prick's a fucker. The fucker's a prick? Sure. You know what they say:
> the pot itself gathers the herbs.   (Poem 94)

The abuse we find in the *Epodes* is often tame by comparison.

While we have examples of Catullan invective in elegiac couplets and properly iambic metres, the hendecasyllabic is among the most common metres in Catullus for these poems. Technically a lyric metre, it is reminiscent of the first lines of the Sapphic stanza. Nonetheless, it is rarely attested in the archaic and classical periods outside of dramatic dialogue. The second half of the line is substantially iambic in rhythm, and the tone was generally thought to be conversational and appropriate for use in comedy (Halporn, Ostwald and Rosenmeyer 1980: 88, 100; Garrison 2004: 178; Sheets 2007: 200). It is a line the poet from Verona made his own.

Catullus effectively treats the hendecasyllabic as a species of iambic at several points in the corpus. On three occasions, he refers to his hendecasyllabic poetry as *iambi*, using the term less as a metrical marker than as what David Wray calls a name for 'invective poetry of the dangerously aggressive kind' (2001: 177; cf. Lorenz 2007: 430). In poem 54, after running through the deformities and faults in grooming of a string of unidentifiable louts, who are presumably Caesar's cronies, we are told that the 'general' will once more be angry at the poet's 'innocent *iambi*' (6). In poem 40, a certain Ravidus is warned to expect the assault of Catullus' *iambi* as just retribution for stealing his beloved. Wray has demonstrated this poem's reliance on a poem by Archilochus, in which Lycambes too is threatened with becoming a laughing stock by virtue of appearing in the angered poet's verse (2001: 178–80). Lastly, in poem 36, the poet commits to the flames the 'shitty pages' (*cacata carta*) of the poet Volusius, in ironic fulfilment of his girl's vow to burn the writings of the 'worst poet', if only Catullus would cease to threaten her with his *iambi* (1–8). For Catullus, then, *iambi* refer less to a metre than generically to abusive poetry, often aimed at specific, identifiable individuals, some of great political prominence (Johnson 2012: 47–8).

On at least two occasions, the poet treats his hendecasyllabics directly as a weapon for ensuring social conformity synonymous with *iambi* in the Archilochian sense. In poem 12, Catullus threatens a napkin thief with 'three hundred hendecasyllabics' (10) if he does not return the missing linen. Poetry, here, is a weapon of public shaming, analogous to what we have seen in *Epodes* 6, whose power to immortalize its object is as much to be feared as sought (cf. 6.16–17). Likewise, in poem 42, Catullus fully personifies his verses as an angry crowd, calling upon them to surround a girl who has stolen the poet's notebooks and, in a form of popular justice known as the *flagitatio*, demand their return:

> Moecha putida, redde codicillos,
> redde, putida moecha, codicillos!

> Foul slut, give back the notebooks, give back the notebooks, foul slut!
>
> (42.11–12)

After repeating this playground chant a second time with no better results (19–20), the poet tries a different tack in the final line: *pudica et proba, redde codicillos* ('prim and proper girl, give back the notebooks', 24).

Catullus 42 is directly imitated by Horace in the last poem of the *Epodes*, the final confrontation with his chief female antagonist, Canidia, to whom we shall return later in this chapter. There, after a beginning that decries her witchcraft and her lack of mercy toward the poet, and that describes her as 'greatly beloved by sailors and peddlers' (17.20), Horace too suddenly changes tack and all but directly quotes Catullus:

> Effare! iussas cum fide poenas luam,
> paratus expiare, seu poposceris
> centum iuvencos, sive mendaci lyra
> voles sonari: 'Tu pudica, tu proba
> perambulabis astra sidus aureum.'

> Speak up! I will honestly pay appropriate penalties, I am prepared to make amends, whether you will have demanded the sacrifice of a hundred bullocks, or you wish to be sounded on my lying lyre: 'You are prim. You are proper. You will wander through the heavens a golden star.'
>
> (17.37–41)

It cannot be accidental that Horace closes his collection of iambic verse with a clear allusion to Catullus, his predecessor in iambic. Nor can it be mere coincidence that the same collection opens with 'an unmistakable gesture toward Catullus: his promise to accompany Maecenas to the ends of the earth (1.11–14) evokes the similar willingness that Catullus ascribes to Furius and Aurelius' (Tarrant 2007: 70). Other less direct echoes are strewn throughout the collection.

What then does Horace mean when he claims to have been the 'first to have brought forward Parian iambics in Latium', since he knew Catullus already had engaged in iambic abuse, had used iambic metres, and knew the poetry of Archilochus and Hipponax? Of course, as we have seen, only one of the poems we cited from Catullus was in an iambic metre, poem 29 in iambic trimeters, the same metre used by Horace in *Epodes* 17. And such metres are rare in Catullus: for, while the hendecasyllabic may have had a strongly iambic rhythm in the second half of the verse, it was, as we have noted, considered a lyric metre. This kind of formal imprecision was anathema to Horatian poetics, and it is telling that Horace never writes a poem in hendecasyllabics, despite his great facility in a variety of metres.

By the same token, Catullus' true iambics as well as the abusive poems in hendecasyllabic metres, to which he refers as iambics, are scattered throughout his polymetrics (1–60) among other properly lyric poems, the famous love poems to Lesbia and a variety of squibs and occasional verses in varying metres. Horace's collection is very different: every poem is written in a metre attested by Archilochus, and all but one are in properly epodic metres, which is to say a couplet consisting of two verses of different lengths, often a dactylic hexameter followed by an iambic line. The sole exception is poem 17, whose allusion to Catullus cites one of the few iambic metres used by Horace's predecessor. Thus Horace acknowledges his debt even as he corrects Catullus: the poem he quotes, while explicitly iambic in content, is lyric in metre, but Horace rewrites it into an iambic metre Catullus himself used, placing it in emphatic final position and separating it from the rest of the collection by having this be the sole poem not written in epodic couplets.

Lest this level of poetic subtlety be thought beyond Horace or mere critical fancy, we need to recognize a third major strand of influence in the *Epodes*, Callimachus' *Iambi*. This collection by the famed Alexandrian scholar and poet, which announced itself as a revival of Hipponax without Bupalus, cannot have been without influence on Horace's conception of reviving Archilochus without Lycambes. Moreover, although there is some dispute about how many poems were in the Callimachean collection and whether all of them can be considered to be in iambic metres, the collection as received by Horace almost certainly contained 17 poems, which is the same number as Horace's *Epodes* (Morrison 2016: 32). When we recall the predilection of poets in the period to arrange their collections in symmetrical groups of ten (Virgil's *Eclogues*, Tibullus 1, Horace *Satires* 1), or at least even numbers (eight in *Satires* 2), the choice of 17 seems oddly unmotivated without a specific precedent. The fact that the *Epodes* open with the word *ibis*, 'you will go', a homonym with the title of a famous invective poem by Callimachus in elegiac couplets, the *Ibis*, later imitated by Ovid, reinforces the impression of his following a Callimachean model. This impression is further strengthened when we note that the final word of the collection is *exitus*, demonstrating careful arrangement on Horace's part as we move from *ibis* to *exitus*. Moreover, both poems 1 and 17 also cite Catullus, Horace's Latin predecessor in the iambic genre at Rome (Cameron 1995: 164–70; Watson 2003: 12–16; Mankin 2010: 101–2). Catullus too, of course, knew Callimachus' work and not only alludes to it on several occasions (7.1, 65.16), including the *Iambi* (116), but also translates one of his poems (66), and he may have even been led to consider the hendecasyllabic an iambic metre by following the example of the Alexandrian poet's 14th iambic poem, which survives only in a single line, making us unable to judge whether it is a true hendecasyllabic or part of an epodic couplet.

Horace in the *Epodes* takes up the works of his Hellenistic and Roman predecessors. He purifies and refines them, simultaneously alluding to them and correcting them by returning to a stricter vision of metrical and thematic unity. Callimachus had already played a similar role in Horace's rewriting of Lucilius in the *Satires*. In 1.4, Horace writes of Lucilius:

[...] he was faulty: often, as though it were a great thing, he would dictate two hundred lines in an hour while standing on one foot: when

he would flow in this muddy fashion, there was stuff you would want
to pick out.   (1.4.9–11)

This image of sloppy poetic composition as a great muddy stream is a direct
quotation from Callimachus' *Hymn to Apollo*. There the god of poetry
responds to Envy's praise of the poet 'who swells like the sea':

> The river Euphrates has a powerful current
> But the water is muddy and filled with refuse.
> The cult of Bees brings water to Deo
> But their slender libations are unsullied and pure,
> The trickling dew from a holy spring's height.
>
> (106–12, translation by Lombardo and Rayor 1988: 10)

The Callimachean poet seeks purity and refinement rather than the great
muddy flow. Horace, then, repeats the charge at 1.10.50, 'but I said that he
was accustomed to flow in a muddy fashion', just before the image, which we
examined earlier, of a modern-day Lucilius scratching his head and gnawing
his nails as he seeks to correct his verse (1.10.71).

In the *Epodes*, however, Horace will do Callimachus one better, produc-
ing a truly Parian iambic poetry, but without Lycambes. It will be an iambic
poetry that like its Hellenistic cousin will be more amusing than cruel and
more Socratic than vengeful. As in Horace's Rome, in the Hellenistic monar-
chies of the East 'iambic freedom was not what it was in the Classical polis.
It was neither safe nor profitable to attack anyone really worth attacking'
(Scodel 2010: 253). The result in both the case of Horace and his Hellenistic
predecessor was complex and ironic poetry that, rather than prosecute a
partisan case, 'presents a discourse so multivalent that it defuses rather than
sustains the one-sided mind set evident in warring and division' (Johnson
2012: 229–30).

Having now set the stage, I want in the remainder of this chapter to turn to
a reading of selected *Epodes*, about which I will make two parallel claims.
The first is theoretical. It argues that Horace uses irony in the *Epodes* to both

discipline those he sees as inimical to the emerging political order and to create a sphere of indeterminacy, and hence potential freedom (*libertas*), for himself and ultimately for the self writ large. In seeking to discipline others, he follows his iambic predecessors Archilochus and Hipponax (but also Lucilius and Catullus). But by creating a sphere of indeterminacy, or multivalence, he goes beyond them to use irony to delimit an interior space that makes possible the cultivation of a private ethical self which is fundamentally different from the iambic personas of his archaic predecessors or from the literary construct of Callimachus' *Iambi*. This is a self that, while intimately connected to its symbolic community through ties of patronage, friendship and politics, always finds itself at one remove from that community, a self that folds back on itself to create a space of reflection and difference (Classen 1993: 117; Citti 2000: 127; McNeill 2001: 127; Reckford 2009a: 109–10).

The second claim I want to advance is more traditionally philological or even empirical. It argues that the so-called impotence poems, *Epodes* 8 and 12, can be read as suggesting that the *anus* of these poems be associated with Canidia, Horace's primary antagonist and the object of iambic attack in *Epodes* 3, 5 and 17, as well as in *Satires* 1.8, 2.1 and 2.8 (Armstrong 1989: 60–2). If this second claim is accepted, then, in this series of epodes (3, 5, 8, 12 and 17), attacks on the putative Other are shown to be inseparable from confessions of impotence, both sexual and otherwise (Gowers 2016: 103–4). Canidia as the ultimate target of Horace's iambic venom is less the symbol of his poetic power – as Lycambes is for Archilochus and Bupalus for Hipponax – than the ironic reflection of the poet's powerlessness and ultimately castration (Oliensis 2009: 174; Barchiesi 2009: 225). The collection ends with Horace's sudden surrender to the superior power of Canidia's *mala carmina* and with her declaration that she will not refrain from taking her vengeance lest all her power be held in vain (17.37–41, 74–81). This network of associations, in turn, extends beyond the series itself to the other poems in the collection, which are linked to the series through a variety of textual and thematic echoes as well through direct juxtaposition.

These two claims are, in fact, less independent than at first they may appear. Poems 8 and 12 feature some of the most violent invective of the entire collection, and yet they are poems of impotence. If Horace's invective against Canidia, the only woman to receive such sustained abuse in the *Epodes* (and indeed in the entire Horatian corpus), can be read as an inverted reflection of his own *impotentia*, then, I would contend, every moment of other-directed, disciplinary irony also has the potential to become a moment of self-ironization in which the aim and object of the invective, in its very separateness from the speaking subject, becomes problematized in the moment of its utterance (cf. Oliensis 2009: 176, 179, 185). Such self-ironization, in turn, establishes a necessary distance between the speaker *within* the poem and the speaker *of* the poem and forces us to confront their lack of coincidence. Moreover, poems 3, 5, 8, 12 and 17 – the Canidia and impotence poems – are interlocked with a series of political poems (1, 7, 9 and 16) as well as with the poem that features the most explicit example of invective irony being reflected back on the speaker himself, poem 4's attack on the social climber (Armstrong 1989: 63–4).[5] That same social climber is himself a symptom of the civil discord that forms the object of the more explicitly political poems, even as in certain key respects he recalls Horace himself.

The *Epodes*, then, while for many years the most neglected part of Horace's corpus, show themselves to be poems of subtlety and complexity. These poems feature some of the poet's most explicit invective and, in the impotence poems, some of his most disturbing sexual imagery. These are both features of the iambic tradition from Archilochus through Catullus. But in Horace's hands that tradition also becomes a complex means of refined artistry and ironic reflection, without losing its capacity to disturb and discomfit even as it is adapted to the realities of a new era (Watson 2007: 93; Henderson 2009: 409; Johnson 2012: 21, 36).

At this point, I need to define more precisely what I mean by irony, since it is often used in a vague and imprecise manner. While we can certainly point to the example of Socrates, as we did in the previous chapter, it is important as we progress to have a formal definition that also grounds it in the rhetorical theory of the period.

Quintilian at 6.2.15 defines εἰρωνεία as a form of speech that produces an *intellectum* or 'understood meaning' that is at variance (*diversum*) from what it says (*dicit*). Irony is, according to this definition, the production of an *intellectum* that does not coincide with the *dictum*, and hence is dependent on the simultaneous presence of at least two distinct levels of meaning: the literal and the ironic. In pragmatic terms, the ironic statement participates in this multiplicity of meanings not simply through the observed fact that multiple possible readings coexist within a given text, but specifically through a moment of performative self-awareness that signals a conscious act of doubling an initial literal sense with a second, divergent sense. As everyone from Quintilian to de Man recognizes, irony is the *intentional* production of multiple meanings, and the ironic speaker must signal that intentionality as such through a rhetorical wink or nod (Quintilian 8.54; de Man 1983: 220–3). Yet this performative moment of self-consciousness, as opposed either to the *dictum* ('utterance') to which it is joined or the *intellectum* ('understanding') to which it gives rise, falls outside the signification produced by the statement per se. That moment is not a property of the words themselves. Rather, it is a property of the enunciation, of the act as performed in a given speech or textual context. In any ironic speech act, there is a gap between meaning one and meanings two, three, four, et cetera, which must be made explicit. The ironist, who says one thing but means another, is ultimately, then, the master of nonmeaning, of the gaps between meanings, which must be recognized if the irony is to be perceived. Horace is, in this sense, a master ironist (Oliensis 1998: 17; McNeill 2001: 50–1; Henderson 2009: 410).

The motivations for seeking to deploy a moment of nonmeaning to create alternative registers of meaning are multiple. Irony in its most common and limited sense is used either to define – and hence enforce – an ideological norm, or to resist it. There is often little to separate this most aggressive form from sarcasm. Irony, however, also knows quieter forms. It answers the desire to create a defensive perimeter around the self, a zone of nonmeaning that allows the creation of forms of interiority discontinuous with the enfolding social whole.

What I want to argue, then, is that Horace in the *Epodes* uses irony as an other-directed disciplinary form which is consonant with a traditional understanding of the function of invective in the ancient world. In this usage, the moment of nonmeaning becomes a form of violence which is deployed against the other. The violence of other-directed irony is not a function of multiple meanings per se but of the gap between those meanings, of the moment in which we say so-and-so is not *x* but really *y*.[6] But I also want to argue that in the midst of this very use Horace also creates a zone of nonmeaning or aporia that defines a new space of interiority, a gap between the public and private self, between the speaking and spoken subject, between being and seeming, and that this new space of interiority is ultimately coterminous with what will become the new, ideal form of elite Augustan subjectivity and, as such, comes to serve as a distant ancestor of what modernity understands as the private sphere (Reckford 2009a: 38; Miller 2018). Irony becomes a kind of wall that makes possible the formation of what Pierre Hadot would term, when referring to the Stoic philosophy of the imperial period, the 'citadel of the self' (1992).

Before examining in more detail the connections between the Canidia poems and the impotence poems, and their collective relations with the more political poems, however, I want to begin by reading closely *Epodes* 3, in many ways the ironic core of the collection. Canidia appears by name in three poems in the *Epodes*. On one level, poem 3 seems the least significant. It is primarily concerned with the gastric distress caused the poet by Maecenas' serving a dish heavily laced with garlic. Yet, this seemingly minor poem on an off-colour subject is, in fact, of particular importance since this is the only one in which Canidia and Maecenas both appear. Poem 3, thus, from a structural point of view, represents the nodal point where the political sequence and the Canidia/impotence poems come together.

 The poem begins with an exclamation on garlic as an appropriate punishment for parricides: a potion more noxious than Socrates' hemlock. The hyperbole is so over the top that it is impossible to take literally. We have all eaten garlic, but few of us have died. Literal truth is not a viable option. Enter Canidia.

> Quid hoc veneni saevit in praecordiis?
> num viperinus his cruor

incoctus herbis me fefellit, an malas
Canidia tractavit dapes?

What kind of venom rages in my guts? Has viper's blood stewed into
these greens deceived me, or has Canidia trafficked in evil feasts?

(3.5–8)

While there has been much inconclusive speculation about Canidia's identity
from Porphyrion to the present, some of it quite suggestive of the way this
sole recurring female character in Horace's *Epodes* and *Satires* might have
been received by its initial audience, none of it is conclusive. Canidia has
no identity attested outside of the Horatian corpus in the same manner that
Maecenas, Augustus or Virgil do. Even if we assume her name represents a
pseudonym for a real person – a rather large assumption – that person is
never made clear in the same way that Mentula is clearly said to be Caesar's
Mammura in Catullus (29, 105) or Lesbia revealed as Clodia (79). Canidia
is a signifier without a clearly recognized signified, a kind of fantasy object
who, on the linguistic level, can receive whatever meaning the poet or reader
wishes to attribute to her. She is, in the end, the sum total of the poetic
contexts in which she appears.

Canidia's initial role in *Epodes* 3 is to serve as the object of gratuitous
invective. She is the iambic target par excellence. There is no reason intrinsic
either to the poem itself or to her extra-poetic 'reality' why the name Canidia
should be associated with poison, vipers or severe gastric distress. Canidia did
not serve or prepare the offending dish, nor was she present at the meal. If
this poem were read outside the collection, you could substitute almost any
name and it would be just as effective. If, however, we look at Canidia in the
context of the lines coming before and after this passage, as well as the larger
collection, a more complex and interesting set of associations appears. In many
ways, Canidia functions as the placeholder of the ironic. She is the moment of
joining between separate, sometimes even opposed, but nonetheless intertwined
sets of meanings. It is through her presence that Horace's impotence becomes
associated with both his role as an iambic blame poet and with Maecenas
as metonym for the larger political world depicted in poems 1, 7, 9 and 16.

Let us try, then, to describe more precisely the context in which Canidia takes her shape within this poem. If we look just a line above our quoted passage in *Epodes* 3, we find the expostulation *o dura messorum ilia!* ('oh, the tough guts of reapers!', 3.4). On one level, this phrase simply acknowledges garlic as a peasant food and contrasts Horace's refined (Callimachean) innards with the intestinal fortitude of the typical agricultural labourer. On another, however, it implies that Horace suffers from *mollitia*, the opposite of *duritia*, implying not only refined softness but also effeminacy and even impotence (Gowers 1993: 293). This association whereby the *dura ilia* ('tough guts' but also 'hard loins' – *ilia* can mean both) of the reapers contrasts with the implied *mollia ilia* ('tender guts' or 'soft loins') of the poet of course provides a subtle linkage between the present text and poems 8 and 12, which as we have already noted above deal explicitly with sexual impotence, and which as we will argue below are to be read in conjunction with the Canidia poems, 3, 5 and 17. Thus a poem whose primary object, when read in isolation, appears to be to unleash a torrent of presumably good-humoured invective against Maecenas for serving Horace an over-spiced dish, and whose secondary object is to inveigh against Canidia, takes on a self-ironizing edge in which Horace becomes an impotent self-reflective, rather than a violent other-directed, iambist. This set of associations in turn implicates *Epodes* 3 in a much broader field of associations – or *intellecta*, to borrow Quintilian's term – that spreads throughout the collection.

Horace, it turns out, is a softy, an odd pose for the wielder of iambic venom, who is normally associated with masculine sexual aggression (Richlin 1992). Who precisely is being made fun of here? Maecenas? Canidia? The poet himself? The answer of course is 'yes'. This iambic dart swerves to penetrate its thrower and inflicts no small amount of collateral damage on the way. To the astute reader of the collection, this turn of events will come as no surprise. The poet's *mollitia* was already highlighted in *Epodes* 1. There, in a poem that looks forward to Actium, the poet contrasts Maecenas' willingness to undergo any danger for Caesar (1.3–4) with Horace's own nature as *imbellis ac firmus parum* ('unwarlike and none too firm', 1.16; Bather and Stocks 2016: 10). Of course, for the reader familiar with the conventions of elegy, such a pose has nothing surprising. *Mollitia* is almost an occupational hazard for many of Horace's contemporary poets, all of whom are followers of Callimachus (Kennedy 1993: 31–3; Edwards 1993: 63–6, 93). Nonetheless, the image of softness and refined passivity (*inertia* in Tibullus 1.1) sits ill alongside that of the hypermasculine poet of iambic, often priapic, violence. All the same, it is a recurring pattern within the *Epodes*. Thus, in *Epodes* 14, Maecenas directly accuses Horace of *mollis inertia*: there, it is for his failure to complete the *Epodes*, but echoes the charge of sexual impotence made against the poet just two poems earlier, as well as in *Epodes* 8 (Oliensis 2009: 182–3).

Now neither lines 1.16 nor 3.4 deal explicitly with Horace's sexual inadequacy, as we will see in poems 8 and 12, but we need not wait until poem 8 before the topic rears its head (or fails to): for at the end of poem 3, the next time Maecenas is mentioned after the opening of poem 1, Horace wishes on his friend and patron sexual failure, although admittedly of a different sort:

> at si quid umquam tale concupiveris,
> iocose Maecenas, precor
> manum puella savio opponat tuo
> extrema et in sponda cubet.

> But if ever you will have strongly desired any such thing, Maecenas you joker, I pray that the girl will ward off your kiss with her hand and will sleep at the very edge of the bed.   (3.19–22)

Thus the poet who begins this epode with the image of a criminal who strangles his father using his own *impia manus* concludes it with bad breath and an image of frustrated desire. Maecenas' mouth replaces the paternal *guttur* (3.2) and the courtesan's *manus* that of the tough-minded criminal (3.1). This ironic doubling both implicitly softens the opening image and places the poet's hand on his symbolic father's throat (just kidding, *really*). In the end, though, it is only the tough peasants of the Italic countryside who have hard loins *and* the ability to use them. Horace's are soft, and Maecenas' might as well be. In between, we find Canidia and the question of whether she is in some way responsible for the poet's discomfort: *an malas / Canidia tractavit dapes?*

At no point, however, does this question represent an actual request for information. It can only be read rhetorically and never truly literally, except to the extent that the literal meaning must be present for the other figurative levels – the levels on which the *intellectum* remains *diversum* from the *dictum* – to come into view. Horace knows that Maecenas served the dish, and he explicitly chooses to name Canidia so as to evoke the contexts in which we have either already met her (*Satires* 1.8) or will soon, *Epodes* 5 and 17. The poet's ironic rhetorical question is at once irrelevant to the basic information *Epodes* 3 ostensibly seeks to convey ('damn you Maecenas and your spicy cuisine') and enfolds that information in a much larger associative field that requires us to reread this seemingly simple poem in an ever expanding set of contexts. By the same token, however, it is only the presence of a moment of performative nonmeaning, of the actual difference between these possible meanings, exemplified in the very gratuitous nature of Canidia's naming, that ensures that these various levels of signification are neither collapsed into a single 'true meaning' (i.e. Horace really meant *x*, the rest is just rhetorical window dressing) or sublimated into some kind of grand synthesis (e.g. the political, the sexual or the biographical as the master reading).

But in fact there is another associative chain that further implicates Horace, Maecenas and Canidia in the same field. Immediately after line 8, there is a lengthy comparison between the person who confected the offending dish and Medea's poisoning of Creusa, as well as her subsequent escape on a winged serpent or dragon (*serpente* [...] *alite*; 3.14). The appearance of the winged serpent pulls through an earlier reptilian image implicit in the viper's blood. At the same time, the image of the fire consuming Creusa evokes the burning sensation searing the poet's innards and prepares for the next couplet's image of the Dog Star baking Horace's native Apulia (3.15–16). Each of these associative chains creates an alternative *intellectum* that both reinforces the structure of the poem and reveals it as always meaning more than it says. At the same time, the dissonance between the lowly content of the epode – indigestion caused by overly spiced food – and the high-flown mythological exempla creates still another level of metapoetic irony.

The shift back into an autobiographical register when Horace writes *nec tantus umquam siderum insedit vapor / siticulosae Apuliae* (nor ever did so great a heat/exhalation/warmth/ardour of the stars settle on parched Apulia) is particularly sharp, then, and forces the reader to re-engage with what they know about the historical Horace, not as something external to the poem but as an integral part of its structure. *Siderum*, moreover, is poetic plural for the *sidus fervidum* or the Dog Star, in Latin the Canicula, the brightest star in the constellation Canis (Mankin 1995: ad loc.; Watson 2003: ad loc.). Thus *siderum* by evoking Canicula echoes phonetically (on the level of the *intellectum* but not the *dictum*) the Horatian neologism *siticulosae*. Likewise, the Canis and the Canicula themselves evoke Canidia, who is posited as the source of the heat melting the poet's soft innards, but whose scorching fire is on the level of diction transformed into 'thirsty Apulia', the poet's parched place of birth.

But the key word here is *vapor*, for insofar as one of its commonly accepted meanings is 'exhalation', then the burning heat of the Apulian Canis becomes the channel through which Horace's inflamed guts at the beginning of the poem metamorphose into Maecenas' frustrated loins at its end: a noxious vapour rising from within. Moreover, insofar as we know that the dog and the wolf were common figures for the iambist (Miller 1994: 28–9; Gagné 2009: 262–5; Morrison 2016: 48), then the *vapor* of *Canis/Canidia* becomes a figuration of the voice of the iambist himself, the foul exhalation of parched Apulia.[7] Horace's dyspepsia is transformed into Canidia's black magic, her *mala carmina* ('curses', but also 'libellous, personal attacks', an ambiguity that parallels the meanings of *epodē*, 'incantations' but also 'a form of iambus').[8] Those *mala carmina* which we see exhibited in *Epodes* 5 are then compared to the burning heat of Medea's poisoned gifts, which are in turn identified with the heat of the Dog Star in Apulia or the scorching breath of that other Apulian dog, Horace, who in turn prays that his own searing exhalation becomes the offending *spiritus* of Maecenas himself, from which his *puella* must shield herself with a hand (*manus*) that necessarily recalls the one that crushed the paternal throat (*guttur*) at the opening of the poem. What we end up with is no longer a clearly delineated set of speaking subjects and their respective objects of invective, but a kind of circulating irony in which the poet speaks against that which he himself appears to embody in his speech, becoming both one with and opposed to Canidia, and through her identified with Maecenas himself (Oliensis 2009: 162–3, 181–2).

There is no clearer example of this self-ironizing phenomenon than in the immediately following poem, *Epodes* 4. On the one hand, this is among the most strongly iambic poems in the collection. It has both a clearly delineated target of invective and a squarely made claim of the iambic poet's right to exercise his *liberrima indignatio* on behalf of, and as the voice of, the larger community of right-thinking Romans (4.10; cf. *libera bilis* 11.16). This is the same form of social correction he claims for Lucilian satire and Old Comedy at the beginning of *Satires* 1.4[9]: the stigmatizing value of public ridicule (Bailey 1982: 3). Poem 4 is an exercise in social discipline against a freed slave who has become wealthy and acquired social respectability in the form of a military tribuneship and hence equestrian rank, positions that by custom were not open to freedmen (Armstrong 1989: 9–13).

On the other hand, as almost every commentator has noticed, there are numerous resemblances between the unnamed object of Horace's wrath and the poet himself (Oliensis 1998: 67; Oliensis 2009: 170–1; Fitzgerald 2009: 150–1; Johnson 2012: 97–8; Bather and Stocks: 2016: 2–3). In some cases, these resemblances are acknowledged by critics only to be argued away, but the fact that such arguments need to be made clearly shows the possibility of the identification and hence the impossibility of definitively excluding it (Bailey 1982: 4).[10] Whatever details may be invoked to suggest the illegitimacy of the identification, they remain just that: individual details at variance with a perceived resemblance, a moment in which the understood meaning (*intellectum*) remains at some variance (*diversum*) with the letter of what has been said (*dictum*).

The opening sentence of the poem establishes *Epodes* 4 as the first fully fledged invective poem of Horace's iambic collection, the true heir to the Archilochian tradition, and reflects that tradition back against itself and the poet (Kiessling and Heinze 1999: 500; Johnson 2012: 99). While poem 3's assault on garlic and poem 2's revelation of the hypocrisy of Alfius' pastoral dream both set the stage for a more full-throated invective, poem 4 is the first that opens squarely with a declaration of personal enmity as well as an insult aimed at the social standing of the target:

> Lupis et agnis quanta sortito obtigit,
> tecum mihi discordia est,
> Hibericis peruste funibus latus
> et crura dura compede.

Discord as great as what has fallen to wolves and lambs obtains for me with you, you who are burned on the side with Spanish ropes and on the shin by the hard shackle. (4.1–4)

As noted in the previous poem, images of wolves and dogs were associated with the iambic tradition from the very beginning, with Archilochus' Lycambes or 'Wolf-stepper', and in the earliest traces of the oral tradition in figures like the tricky Dolon in *Iliad* 10 who wears a wolfskin (Cavarzere 1992: 140; Miller 1994: 28–36; Gagné 2009: 262–5). The wolf is the symbol of iambic aggression and the dog his domesticated cousin, the image of a possible taming of that aggression as a tool for social discipline – but the dog still bites and sometimes nips his master (on dogs and wolves, see *Epodes* 2.60, 6.1–10, 7.11–12, 12.26).

Nonetheless, the following question immediately arises as we read these lines: who is the wolf and who the sheep in this little parable? The animal imagery indicates a clear distinction between victim and aggressor, yet the human drama is more confused. Horace appears to be at best a wolf in sheep's clothing. For if the object of Horace's attack is cast as the wolf, then the poet is clearly a sheep that bites back. If Horace, however, is the wolf, then we are forced to imagine the object of the attack as the hapless victim of the iambist's predatory aggressions (cf. 2.60). The term *discordia* is particularly loaded in this context. It bears with it the concept of civil conflict and, depending on the date of either the writing or the reading of the poem, evokes the ongoing or recently concluded civil wars against Antony at Actium, Sextus Pompeius off Sicily, or Brutus, Cassius and Horace himself at Philippi (Mankin 1995: ad loc.; Watson 2003: ad loc.; Hellegouarc'h 1972:

134, 538; Goh 2016: 71). This wolf and this sheep, then, in all the instability of their relative positions – just who *is* preying on whom? – are emblematic of the ongoing social conflict and Horace's own ironic reflections thereon. In civil conflict, each side claims to have been victimized by the other. One side's aggression is always a justified retaliation for the wrong done by the other. This is the history of Rome in which the iambist seeks to intervene: an endless retaliatory cycle of sheep and wolves, predators and prey, political actors who are constantly shifting positions and ultimately consuming their own. And this is why irony is such a potent rhetorical tool in this situation, for it is not the case either that it is self-evident who are the wolves and who the sheep, nor that all the wolves are really sheep and vice versa and that hence there is no difference between them. It is rather the case that iambists and their objects are always both wolves and sheep, that the difference between them even so does not collapse into uniformity, and that the victims in any such narrative are in fact *always* and *necessarily* the original aggressors and therefore must be attacked mercilessly, even as they remain victims both in reality and in their own counter-narrative. In the words of Clint Eastwood's character William Munny in *Unforgiven*, when the young gunslinger asks him if the man he just gunned down had it coming, 'We all have it coming, kid.' The opening statement of *Epodes* 4 expresses both a literal meaning (its *dictum*) and the precise opposite of that meaning (its *intellectum*), but it also insists on maintaining the difference between those meanings as well as their potential commutability.

Similarly in poem 7, immediately before the first of the impotence poems, Horace denounces the recent history of political warfare and the possibility of its continuation into the future:

> Quo quo scelesti ruitis? aut cur dexteris
> > aptantur enses conditi?
> [...]
> neque hic *lupis* mos nec fuit *leonibus*,
> > numquam nisi in dispar feris.
> [...]

> sic est: acerba fata Romanos agunt
> scelusque fraternae necis,
> ut immerentis fluxit in terram Remi
> sacer nepotibus cruor.

Where are you criminals rushing off to? Or why are swords that had been put away now fitted to your right hand? [...] *Not even wolves or lions* act this way, never savage except against the different. [...] That's the way it is: harsh fates goad the Romans and the crime of fratricide, since the sacred blood of innocent Remus flowed on the ground for his descendants.   (7.1–2, 11–12, 17–20, emphasis mine)

There are wolves, there are sheep, and then there are humans: the lone kind to prey upon their own. This poem posits a third position between generic victim and aggressor, producing a kind of meta-irony that does not deny the previous opposition between wolves and sheep, iambists and objects, but resituates them on that third level of commutability. Were Caesar's assassins – who made Horace the son of a freedman a military tribune – wolves or sheep, victims or aggressors? Or were they just blind actors in a larger historical drama that they were powerless (*impotens*) to change: the heirs to Rome's original sin, the spilled blood of Remus? Not even wolves and lions are so savage to their own.

In such a context, what is the heir to Archilochus, the foe of Lycambes, the wolf dancer, to do? Who is he, and where does he stand? The speaking subject of the *Epodes* is himself surrounded by an ironic *cordon sanitaire*. As ever new levels of meaning unfold, it becomes impossible to say who he *really* is, what he *really* means, to be able to label and to categorize *all* his possible meanings, to empty him of *all* interiority, to render him a mere function of a describable social, political, personal or sexual position. Each new *dictum* produces a variety of *intellecta*, meanings that are at once intentional and resistant to reduction (they cannot be synthesized into a single coherent meaning separate from the performative structure that makes them possible).

Returning however to *Epodes* 4, the abstract notion of *discordia* in the poem's opening couplet is given more concrete form in the next two lines' images of bondage and enslavement. The forcible deprivation of freedom as both a cause and consequence of civil conflict is a recurring theme throughout the *Epodes*. The social wars, Spartacus' uprising, Sextus Pompeius' recruitment of slaves to man his navy and Octavian's propaganda against Antony, Cleopatra and their unfree oriental hordes are all specifically cited in poems 9 and 16 (cf. 9.9–16; 16.5; Kiessling and Heinze 1999: 501; Watson 2007: 97). These two poems round out the series of political epodes that began with poem 1 on Maecenas as the willing companion of Octavian, as he prepares to sail for Actium, and continued with poem 7's vision of Roman civil conflict (*discordia*) being the result of *acerba fata* and Romulus' murder of Remus. These political poems (1, 7, 9 and 16) are, then, intercalated with the series of Canidia and impotence poems (5, 8, 12 and 17). They find their point of intersection in poem 3, where the vile, parching *vapor* of Apulia serves to join Horace, Canidia and Maecenas into a singular comic knot, which is then given a distinctly iambic point with poem 4's opening image of sheep and wolves, before poem 5 repeats almost word for word *Epodes* 3's evocation of Medea's burning gifts for Creusa, in the final tirade of a boy about to be sacrificed to satisfy Canidia's lust.

Poem 5, in many ways, serves as a masculinist fantasy genealogy of the origin of iambic. In it, the combination of Canidia's sexual insatiability and disgusting physical appearance lead first to literal violence, when she and Sagana capture and bury an innocent boy to the chin. Their physical assault and grotesque torture then leads to a violent verbal riposte on the part of the boy, who offers his own iambic tirade in response to Canidia's *mala carmina*. The narrative of iambic violence always traces its origin to a prior moment of aggression: here, the boy is transformed into an iambic poet by the enormity of Canidia's crimes. The surest sign of that poetic transformation is the boy's own use of intertextuality, when he cites almost word for word passages from poem 3, the very passages in which Horace, Canidia and Maecenas – if they do not become identified – at least begin to share certain imagistic associations. Together, poems 3, 4 and 5, then, serve as both the nodal point between these two series, the political and the Canidia/impotence poems, and as the place in which the poet's iambic irony bends back most clearly to include himself. As such, these poems take on a particular importance in any understanding of the *Epodes*.

Returning once more to the beginning of poem 4, we should note that the image of 'burning' caused by the ropes and shackles (*peruste*) on the body of Horace's iambic victim provides an imagistic link between this poem and its predecessor. That linkage, unsurprisingly, is ironic, producing multiple and even opposed *intellecta* from the same *dicta*. In poem 3, we saw the fire that roiled the poet's tender guts transformed into the product of Canidia's witchcraft. It then became the dog's breath of the Canicula, which parched Horace's native *siticulosa Apulia*, before finally being metamorphosed into the breath of Maecenas himself, a foul vapour that will cause his *puella* to beat a hasty retreat. In this fashion, the poet's *mollitia*, of which he complains in his invocation of the *dura ilia* of the reapers, and which in poem 1 renders him *imbellis*, is transformed over the course of poem 3 into the source of Maecenas' own sexual frustration or *impotentia*. As Oliensis observes:

> What helps hold together the miscellaneous material of the *Epodes* is their common stress on masculine impotence, variously manifested as Horace's unwarlike shakiness, his sexual inadequacy, his emotional inconstancy, and also as the uncontrollable civil violence deplored in poems such as *Epodes* 7 and 16. (2007: 226; cf. Morrison 2016: 44)

Thus, the fire of Horatian halitosis, which is also the iambic breath of the dog, becomes the inflammation that rubs raw the slave-turned-military tribune of *Epodes* 4, branding him with the sign of social transgression, the cause and the consequence of *discordia*. The fire of Horatian *liberrima indignatio* in poem 4 becomes at once a force of rage turned against the other, whose very existence threatens the emerging Augustan settlement, and an impenetrable wall between the poet and the social world, a wall that obscures his position in the moment he appears to reveal it. Horace is the fiery voice, the barking dog, the wolf whose anger gives voice to the outrage of the community, *and* he is the soft poet, the unwarlike sophisticate, the object of Canidia's wrath and, as we shall see, of her disappointed lust. He is the son of doubtful origins, raised to the rank of military tribune in a time

of discord, as well as the poet who decries that discord and the spilled blood
of the innocent grandchildren of Remus. The fire that burns the shin and
sides of the social climber in *Epodes* 4 is both a fire that has burned Horace
himself and the flame his iambic persona embodies.

Canidia within this complex ironic constellation not only becomes an
archetypical witch-figure and poisoner who serves as a stock object of the
invective poet's wrath, but is also a vehicle through which the poet's power as
a bestower of blame, as an iambist, is reflected back on itself. Asking in *Epodes*
3 whether Canidia has 'trafficked in foul feasts' is not only ironic in the sense
that it equates the dish proffered by Maecenas with a meal prepared by someone
whom we learn in *Epodes* 5 is a sexually frustrated and murderous practitioner
of black magic, but it also implicates the poet himself in a larger pattern of
sexual frustration and inability to perform. Thus in poem 5 Canidia is burying
a young man up to the neck and starving him to death so she can extract his
liver and make a philtre that will cause her wandering lover, Varus, to return:

> 'maius parabo, maius infundam tibi
>> fastidienti poculum,
> priusque caelum sidet inferius mari,
>> tellure porrecta super,
> quam non amore sic meo flagres uti
>> bitumen atris ignibus.'

> 'I will prepare a more powerful cup. I will pour on your disgust a greater
> cup, and the sun will not set beneath the sea, above the outstretched
> earth, before you burn for my love with black flames, like bituminous
> pitch.'   (5.77–82)

The dark flames of lust roused by Canidia's magic, of course, recall the
flames of Medea's magic exercised in vengeance against Creusa, flames which
were evoked earlier in this poem (5.61–4) and in poem 3 as well. At the
same time, Canidia's need to overcome her erstwhile lover's disgust looks
forward to poems 8 and 12, where the poet cites the woman's repulsiveness
as the reason he is unable to rise to the occasion. And while the clear points

of resemblance between Canidia, whose lover has fled, and the hag, who provokes impotent disgust in our poet, have been noted before (Armstrong 1989: 60–3), it will repay our effort to look more closely at these poems in concluding this chapter.

Indeed, we need not prove the absolute identity of the frustrated hag with Canidia – an impossibility in any case, since Canidia is not named in poems 8 and 12. We need only demonstrate the possibility, indeed the invitation, to make that identification. And that invitation comes in the opening lines of poem 8. There, Horace describes a grotesque old woman who provokes disgust in him, much as Canidia, the *obscena anus* whom the innocent lad-turned-voice of iambic rage curses in 5.98. Having dared to ask why Flaccus is flaccid, the woman in *Epodes* 8 is anatomized in grotesque detail: old age, wrinkles, a gaping anus, drooping breasts, a paunch and swollen ankles. There is an almost erotic luxuriance in this blazon of revulsion, leading up to the final command that if she wishes the poet to come to attention, she will have to work on him with her mouth (*ore alloborandum est tibi* 8.20). No other woman of similar description is named in the corpus, and with poem 8 coming shortly after poem 5, the longest poem in the collection, the allusion to Canidia is hard to deny.

Yet the resemblance with Canidia goes beyond generic disgust with an ageing female body. In line 3 of poem 8, we have a direct verbal recollection. Canidia's *dens lividus* ('black-and-blue tooth', 5.47) is recalled in the image of the *dens ater*, or single 'black tooth', of our archetypical hag. That tooth in turn recalls both the black flames of Varus' rekindled lust (*atris ignibus*) and the *dens ater* of traditional iambic vengeance cited at the end of poem 6. There the poet asks, if someone should attack him *atro dente* ('with a black tooth'), should he weep like an unavenged boy (6.15–16; cf. Hawkins 2014: 78)? That boy in need of vengeance, of course, calls to mind none other than the *puer* of 5.82, who fell prey to Canidia's own *dens lividus*. This same 'iambic' tooth in turn is associated in *Satires* 2.1 with both the fierce bite of the wolf (*dente lupus*, 2.1.52) and the carping of Horace's detractors ('envy [...] will hurt its tooth trying to strike against the solid with the weak', 2.1.77–8). Many years later, as we saw at the beginning of this chapter, Horace will present his genealogy of satire and invective in *Epistles* 2.1;

there, he will refer to the 'bloody tooth' of uncontrolled invective verse as what would eventually necessitate a law against *mala carmina* and a return to the care for speaking well or *bene dicendum* (2.1.148–55).

Thus, we have a complex multivalent web of associations surrounding the black-toothed hag of *Epodes* 8. She both provokes Horace's momentary impotence or *mollitia* and actualizes a potential softness within him, the presence of which was acknowledged from the very first poem. At the same time, her black tooth is associated with Archilochus and Hipponax, who are cited at 6.13–14, immediately before the line on the black tooth of abuse. She is, then, simultaneously the cause of the poet's impotence, the object of his abuse and his iambic doppelganger. That same black tooth of abuse, which recalls the *dens lividus* of Canidia, is commanded in poem 8 to call Horace's flaccid phallus back to life. But that very tooth is identified throughout the Horatian corpus, as we have seen, with the iambic poet in his most archetypical incarnations as the biting mouth of the wolf, the barking mouth of the dog and the voice of both protection and disgust. One way or the other, it seems, we all get bad-mouthed in the end.

That same unclean, iambic mouth, described and commandeered in poem 8, talks back in poem 12. There the lady in question responds to Horace's blazon by retailing the poet's sexual shortcomings, launching her own iambic attack on the soft poet: 'you were less limp for Inachia than for me / you were up for Inachia three times in one night, for me it's always one / *soft* job' (12.14–16). As Watson cautiously observes,

> It is possible that, in her gracelessness, old age, grotesque ugliness, and obscenity of word and deed, we are meant to see in the *vetula* an analogue of Iambe (Baubo), the eponymous deity of iambic, who encompassed all these attributes. (2003: 83; cf. Barchiesi 2009: 245)

This view that the hag who is Horace's nemesis in poems 8 and 12 is also his generic double – which as we have seen is consonant with both the structure of poem 3 and the image of the savage tooth of iambic abuse – is further reinforced by Mankin's suggestions concerning the import of Canidia's name and the significance of her activities:

Her name seems to point to two associations, with 'the dog' (*canis*) and the furiously 'dogged' genre of iambus (cf. *Ep.* 6), and with 'old age' (*canities*) and the decrepit impotence not only of the poet but of Rome as it collapses into ruin (*Ep.* 16, 1–12) under the weight of its ancient curse (*Ep.* 7, 17–12).

(Mankin 2010: 100; cf. Oliensis 2009: 163, 167)

This same image is recalled in inverted form at the end of poem 12, when Canidia/Baubo/the hag exclaims, *o ego non felix, quam tu fugis ut pavet acris / agna lupos capreaeque leones!* ('Oh how unhappy I am whom you flee as the lamb flees fierce wolves and she-goats flee lions!', 12.25–6). The image of the wolf and the dog have been part of the iambic genre from its earliest manifestations, but this passage specifically recalls the opening lines of poem 4, where the relation between wolf and lamb is peculiarly overdetermined: who is the aggressor and who the victim? Who is the attacker and who the attacked? Iambic poison is always a response to aggression, and hence the roles depend in their very nature on a potential reversibility. Thus the iambic poet at the end of poem 12 not only becomes the object of attack (i.e. the wolf becomes the lamb) but also the masculinist poet in his passive impotence becomes the she-goat, the penetrated prey: a role he assumes *as* iambist, *as* poetic ironist. Oliensis has succinctly summed up the case:

> Invective originates as a compensation for impotence. But impotence remains a part of the story. What distinguishes the *Epodes* is precisely the failure to erase the origin of invective in impotence. The failure is luridly obvious in *Epodes* 8 and 12. (2009: 175)

Iambic violence becomes the sign of weakness in an age of instability. Canidia becomes the double and the antagonist of Horace: the iambic subject and object simultaneously. She, like the social climber of *Epodes* 4, is the evil twin of the iambic dog (Barchiesi 2009: 241; Oliensis 2009; 169–70; Hawkins 2014: 72–3).

And so it is only appropriate that she be given the last word in the collection. Rather than ending with the triumph of the iambic poet over his adversaries, with the death of Bupalus and Lycambes, the *Epodes* ends with a cry of triumph by Canidia, the poet's ostensible object of iambic aggression and persistent doppelganger:

> I will be a rider carried on the shoulders of my enemies and the land will yield to my insolence. Or shall I, who can make waxen images come alive, as you yourself know from your spying, and tear down the moon from the pole with my chants, who can bring back to life the cremated dead and mix the cups of desire, weep that my art is of no avail against you? (17. 74–80)

The Horace of the *Epodes* then is not the triumphant enforcer of masculinist or aristocratic social discipline. Nor is he the herald of a new Augustan settlement after Actium's end, though clearly all of these elements are in play. He is not given – or more accurately does not give himself – the last word. Rather, Horace as we see him in *Epodes* 3, in the Canidia poems, in the political and in the impotence poems, is both the subject and object of iambic invective, the perpetrator and the victim of sexual aggression, the voice of social norms and of their enforcement as well as the embodiment of their breach. The ironic voice of Horace's *Epodes* leads us less to the adoption of any one definite point of view, a doctrine or explicit ideology, than to the creation of the subjective space from which the personal, the political, the sexual and aesthetic contradictions of the emerging Augustan settlement can be both sharply interrogated and immediately experienced. The Horace of the *Epodes* may not directly confront us with the question that opens the *Satires* – *qui fit, Maecenas* – but he no less forces us to interrogate our own position in regard to a variety of problems that concern our personal, political, sexual and aesthetic commitments in the very act of trying to understand his. If the unexamined life is not worth living, then the first step in any authentic examination is always, as Socrates recognizes in the *Apology*, aporia, a moment of separation and the moment when you finally *know* you know nothing (Hadot 1995: 55–7, 105; Blondell 2002: 100, 124). Horace's iambic poetry offers us a bracing dose.

III

EXEGI MONUMENTUM

HORACE'S TWO-EARED ODES

IN A PASSAGE we have already examined from Horace's final epode, the poet writes:

> Effare! iussas cum fide poenas luam,
> paratus expiare, seu poposceris
> centum iuvencos, sive mendaci lyra
> voles sonari: 'Tu pudica, tu proba
> perambulabis astra sidus aureum.'

Speak up! I will honestly pay appropriate penalties, I am prepared to make amends, whether you will have demanded the sacrifice of a hundred bullocks, or you wish to be sounded on my lying lyre: 'You are prim. You are proper. You will wander through the heavens a golden star.'   (17.37–41)

As noted before, this passage features a recollection of Catullus 42, a poem written in hendecasyllabics, which is considered a lyric metre, but in this instance functions to create an essentially iambic poem. Catullus was Horace's predecessor both in iambic and in lyric, a fact that makes the decision to cite him in the final poem of Horace's iambic collection, when he was already at work on the *Odes*, doubly significant. By dividing his lyric from his iambic poetry into two separate collections, Horace creates a distinction that, while classical and ratified by the poets and scholars of Alexandria, Catullus does not seem to recognize; nor do any of Horace's other Latin predecessors. Indeed, Catullus may be one of the greatest lyric poets the West has known, and, as I have argued before, he is the first lyric poet in the modern sense, that is a writer of short poems 'of personal revelation, confession or complaint' that project 'the image of an individual highly self-reflexive consciousness' (1994: 1). Nonetheless, Horace would not have recognized him as a lyric poet: only a small portion of Catullus' poetry was written in the Aeolic and glyconic metres that make up the majority of the *Odes* and which are validated by the precedent of the canonical Greek lyrists, nor are those poems formally differentiated in Catullus' collection from his iambic or hendecasyllabic poems (Tarrant 2007: 70–1).

Horace's choice, then, to allude to Catullus' hendecasyllabic poems at the close of his own iambic collection tells us as much about the way Horace conceived of the lyric project upon which he is already embarked as it does about the iambic collection he is finishing. As we shall argue throughout this chapter, picking up a metaphor that Horace uses in *Odes* 1.9, Horace's *Odes* are fundamentally 'two-eared'. On the most basic level, this refers to their profound cultural bilingualism: for the *Odes* are a very Greek project, founding themselves on a conception of Greek metres and genre in way that was unthinkable for the *Satires* and more rigorous than in the *Epodes*. Every ode is at once a Latin and a Greek poem. On a more profound level, however, Horace's *Odes* are 'two-eared' in the sense of doubly signifying, of engaging in a profoundly ironic discourse that never quite means what it says, and whose *intellecta* never seamlessly align with their *dicta*. Indeed, as we shall see, it is this articulated polyvalence of meaning that often serves as the principle of unity within the poems themselves.

Thus, it is hardly surprising that this passage from the *Epodes*, which on a programmatic level is designed to point the reader toward the *Odes*, can be read in more than one way. Moreover, it is not only the fact of this polyvalence that should be observed, but rather the attentive reader should also note the way in which the passage comes to function as a commentary on the difference between the lyric and iambic genres. Therefore, in the first line of the passage, we have translated *cum fide* as 'honestly', literally 'with good faith'. This is the standard translation and certainly the primary way in which the line should be understood. But another translation is possible. *Fides* can also be the third declension noun for 'lyre', the actual Latin word as opposed to the Greek loan word, *lyra*. Horace promises then to pay the penalty for his assaults upon Canidia both 'honestly' and 'with his lyre', the appropriate instrument for the performance of lyric verse, the genre upon which he has now formally embarked (Mankin 1995: ad loc.).

Of course, the reason this phrase is not normally translated 'with the lyre' is that it seems redundant: for, just a few lines later, Horace promises to expiate his crimes toward Canidia, whether she demand a sacrifice of Homeric proportions or that he render her immortal on his *mendaci lyra*, 'lying lyre'. Now why would Horace mention the lyre twice in three lines for essentially the same purpose? Clearly the ambiguity is only apparent and *cum fide* should be translated 'honestly'. But before we accept this imminently reasonable position, we should perhaps first ask ourselves why this second lyre is itself a 'liar'? Did it lie in poems 3 and 5, when it accused Canidia of being a witch and murderer, or will it lie now when it sings her praises (Cavarzere 1992: ad loc.)? In fact, the ironic doubling observed here reproduces that seen in *fides* above, but this double doubling is only perceptible in retrospect: the question of whether the penalty will be paid 'with honesty' or 'with the lyre' is only recognizable as such once we reach the *lyra* two lines later and understand it to be *mendax*. It is then that the force of the question of whether *cum fide* means 'honestly' and hence not *mendax* or *lyra* and hence *mendax* is posed. Moreover, the fact that the *lyra* can be *mendax* in two different senses, in turn, authorizes our reception of *fides* in two different senses. In addition, those latter two senses themselves correspond to a double genealogy since one of these lyres is Greek (*lyra*) and the other Latin (*fides*), the first being 'mendacious' and the second 'honest'. This passage is very much 'two-eared'.

More importantly, however, it is the problem of genealogy, of origins, that is in question in this final poem of the *Epodes*: for poem 17 is both a valedictory to iambic poetry and a hailing of Horace's lyric vocation and thus of the monumental three-book collection that is the *Odes*. Indeed, this passage, with its insistence on the lyre and its quotation of Catullus, directly problematizes what we mean by 'lyric'. The simplest answer to the question – what was a lyric poem in the ancient world? – is poetry sung to the lyre (Miller 1994: 78–84). According to Quintilian (10.1.44), there were nine canonical lyric poets established by Aristophanes of Byzantium, a scholar who became head of the library at Alexandria (circa 194 BCE). This list was widely accepted, and Horace seeks to become the tenth in the first poem of the *Odes*. There, after an introduction addressed to Maecenas, in which the poet discusses the activities that please various men, he gives voice to his own desire:

> Me doctarum hederae praemia frontium
> dis miscent superis, me gelidum nemus
> Nympharumque leves cum Satyris chori
> secernunt populo, si neque tibias
> Euterpe cohibet nec Polyhymnia
> Lesboum refugit tendere barbiton.
> quodsi me lyricis vatibus inseres,
> sublimi feriam sidera vertice.

The ivy crowns, prizes of the Muses' learned foreheads, will intermix me with the gods above; the cool grove and the graceful choruses of the Nymphs with the Satyrs will set me aside from the people, if neither Euterpe will deny her pipes nor Polyhymnia refuse to offer me the Lesbian lyre. But if you, Maecenas, would place me among the lyric bards, I will strike the stars with my lofty pate.   (*Odes* 1.1.29–36)

The image in the final sentence is of the poet's book being 'inserted' (*inseres*) among the scrolls of the lyric poets, of his becoming canonized and hence immortalized. He would be the tenth. It is a deliberate paradox. The canon has been closed and Maecenas has the power to open it and insert Horace's poetry, poetry written in Latin rather than the canonical Greek (Feeney

2009: 202–3). This is a profoundly self-conscious gesture on the part of the poet, every bit as much as the evocation of the *mendax lyra* and the *fides cum fide* in the final poem of the *Epodes*.

Traditionally, lyric poetry was poetry sung to the lyre or, in the case of choral poetry, the pipes (Gentili 1984: 41; Kurke 1991: 1). Horace, so far as we know, never sang his poetry or played the lyre, and while he often mentions the lyre, he never portrays himself as actually singing in the moment of performance (Barchiesi 2007: 148–9; Heinze 2009: 29–30; Rossi 2009: 359–62). As I and others have argued, Horace's *Odes* are very much a written and composed collection, one with a deliberate beginning, middle and end (Dettmer 1983; Santirocco 1986; Porter 1987; Miller 1994: ch. 8). He concludes the collection not with the image of ephemeral song but with the claim to have built something of lasting solidity, an artefact or object:

> Exegi monumentum aere perennius
> regalique situ pyramidum altius,
> quod non imber edax, non Aquilo impotens
> possit diruere aut innumerabilis
> annorum series et fuga temporum.

> I have raised a monument more lasting than bronze and higher than
> the royal site of the pyramids, which neither the corrosive rain, nor the
> raging north wind, nor the countless series of years and the flight of
> time is able to bring down. (3.30.1–5)

As with the *Epodes* themselves, these are poems that are meant to be read and reread, with new layers of subtlety and complexity revealing themselves with each rereading. True lyric in the Greek sense, performed lyric, sung poetry, was a dead genre every bit as much for Horace as it had been for Catullus (Lowrie 1997: 39). What then could Horace have possibly meant when he asks to be shelved (not sung) with the lyric poets?

On one level, he means that the *Odes* are poetry written in the metres and on the themes of the nine canonical lyric poets: Alcman, Sappho, Alcaeus, Anacreon, Steisichorus, Ibycus, Simonides, Bacchylides and Pindar. Of these,

Sappho, Alcaeus and Anacreon – the three so-called 'monodists', or solo singers – had the greatest influence on Horace. Although thematic allusions to Stesichorus, Simonides, Bacchylides and Pindar can be found throughout the *Odes*, the complex metres of later choral song do not appear in them, nor were any of Horace's *Odes* written to be performed by a chorus, with the exception of the *Carmen Saeculare*, which does not form a part of the three-book collection. Of the 88 poems in the *Odes*, 37 are written in the Alcaic strophe, named for the great Lesbian lyrist Alcaeus, who was known as much for his political themes as for what we today would consider the more common lyric themes of love and private meditation (Hubbard 1973: 12). Another 25 are written in the Sapphic stanza, named after the other great poet from Lesbos, Sappho. A third series of 25 poems is written in the predominantly glyconic (¯ ¯ ¯ ˘ ˘ ¯ ˘ ˣ) metres known as Asclepiadeans, whose first exemplars can also be traced back to Sappho and Alcaeus.

The only metre to appear both in the *Epodes* and the *Odes* is the so-called Alcmanic strophe, named after the lyric poet Alcman. It consists of a dactylic hexameter followed by a rare dactylic tetrameter and was thought to be typical of Alcman (see PMG frg. 27). The same metrical sequence is also referred to as an Archilochian, and it is attested in Archilochus' corpus as well (West 1989: frg. 195 and *testimonia*). This is one of very few metres to have both lyric and iambic attestations and the only one in Horace to appear in both the *Epodes* and the *Odes*. In *Epodes* 12, the metre is normally printed as epodic couplets (26 lines). The same metrical sequence appears in four-line strophes at *Odes* 1.7 (32 lines), in the course of what is known as the Parade Odes: a bravura performance in which Horace produces nine poems in nine different lyric metres to open the collection. The Alcmanic strophe makes one further appearance at *Odes* 1.28 (36 lines). Strophic composition (as opposed to couplets) is thought to be particularly characteristic of lyric verse, and, as Meineck's law demonstrates, all of Horace's *Odes* are divisible by four in their number of lines, while all the *Epodes* are divisible by two. Nonetheless, aside from this one example, and the possible shared genealogy of a single lyric and iambic metre, which traces its origin both to Alcman and to Archilochus, Horace keeps a strict metrical separation between the 'sung' poetry of the lyre and the recited poetry of iambic invective (Nisbet and Hubbard 1970: xlv–xlvi; Quinn 1980: xvi, 117, 135; Halporn, Ostwald and Rosenmeyer 1980: 16, 26, 81–2, 94, 103–4; Mankin 1995: 22).

Horace's citation of Catullus, then, in the final poem of the iambics, a collection that begins with a citation of Catullus as well, is not only a reflection on iambic but also on lyric. Catullus was Horace's predecessor in both genres, and because of that the *fides* of his *lyra* is questioned and simultaneously acknowledged in this one gesture. Horace chooses to cite a poem in hendecasyllabics, a metre he avoids in both collections. It is considered a lyric metre and yet not attested among the canonical lyric poets; it is also remarked on for its proximity to spoken language and hence able to be treated as an iambic form. Likewise, it is also the metre most closely associated with Catullus. From a strictly classical point of view, this makes Catullus' *lyra* doubly *mendax*: both lyric and iambic, and consequently neither fish nor fowl. Many years later, at the beginning of the *Ars Poetica*, Horace would warn explicitly against precisely this kind of mixing of forms:

> If a painter should join a horse's neck to a human head and cover limbs drawn from every quarter with feathers of various colours – so what begins as a beautiful woman's head above finishes as a hideous black fish below – were you brought in to take a look, my friends, would you not consider it a joke? [...] Let [your composition] be whatever you wish, so long as it is simple and one.   (1–5, 23)

This is not the place to parse all the subtleties of this passage, but the surface meaning is clear. For Horace, genre mixing is not a virtue. Catullus may have written stinging invective and achingly beautiful lyrics in hendecasyllabics (and elegiac couplets), but from the point of view of an Alexandrian librarian or a rhetorical writer like Quintilian, he was a mess. On one level, Horace, in the *Odes* and *Epodes*, is here to clean things up; on another, the very 'mendacity' or doublespeak of the Catullan lyre can itself in a poem like *Epodes* 17 become the foundation for a fertile Horatian ambiguity, an ambiguity and an irony that both acknowledges the power of the Catullan gesture and raises it to a higher level on which lyric and iambic will be distinguished in Latin verse. Only one exception will be allowed in this strict partition, and that one exception will be for a metre that is simultaneously said to be Archilochian and Alcmanic, epodic and strophic, lyric and iambic and, now, both Greek and Latin. This is two-eared poetry indeed!

In what follows, we will begin with a close reading of *Odes* 1.9, the poem from which the term 'two-eared', *diota*, is derived. We will argue that not only the word, but the way in which it functions in this poem is paradigmatic for the *Odes* as a whole. Indeed, we will read this poem with special care because its construction is emblematic of the craft with which the *Odes* are composed and of the near impossibility of translating these remarkably condensed artefacts of poetic craft. We will then turn our attention to a poem that has given rise to a great deal of critical controversy over the past fifty years, *Odes* 1.14. This is a poem in which scholars have striven mightily to deny its two-eared or ironic quality and to claim that there must be one single, true reading of the poem. Such a reading, I would contend, is fundamentally mistaken. In poem 1.14, as well as in 1.9, we shall also begin an examination of the relation between allegory and irony as 'two-eared' forms of speech, in which what is 'said' and what is 'understood' are necessarily divergent. The possibility of a political reading of *Odes* 1.14 will lead us then to look at a selection of other more directly political poems within the collection, including the so-called Roman Odes, before finishing with one of the most famous and artistically successful poems in the collection, the *Fons Bandusiae*, or *Odes* 3.13.

Odes 1.9 is a famously problematic poem. It starts inside in the winter and closes outside in the summer. It begins with old age and ends with youth. It starts with a quotation from Alcaeus and ends with Roman erotic play (Shields 1958: 171–3). In short, it defies all attempts to imagine or provide a single coherent context of enunciation, whether inside or outside, old or young, Greek or Roman, winter or summer (Fraenkel 1957: 177; Davis 1991: 150). The identity of the speaker seems to shift as well as his addressee. The place, time and theme all seem unstable. Perhaps it is just a failure. And yet this is a poem that occupies a crucial position in the collection as a whole. It comes at the end of the Parade Odes, Horace's tour de force of nine poems in nine metres, many of which to our knowledge had never before been used in Latin (Santirocco 1986: 23–4). It is the first poem written in the Alcaic strophe, the most used metre in the collection (Moritz 1976: 169–70; Santirocco 1986: 41). How is it possible that a poem serving such a key function in the collection could be so incoherent? We must be misunderstanding, the critics tell us. If only we were able to posit the correct context, then the ambiguities and ambivalences which seem to undermine its structural accord would be dissolved, and the poem would shine forth in its pristine unity (cf. Wilkinson 1946: 132; Connor 1972: 105; Catlow 1976: 76–7).

But what if the integrity of its structure were not founded on a unity of the speaking subject or of the dramatic scene but precisely on its ironic plurality (Quinn 1980: 139–40; Davis 1991: 152), on its refusal to posit any univocal totality while nonetheless vigorously asserting its structural coherence? What if its unity existed precisely in the multiplicity of its possible readings, readings that nonetheless formed a clearly discernible organization, that revealed a world of multiplicity? In many ways, this is the thesis of Lowell Edmunds' *From Sabine Jar* (1992), a book devoted to reading *Odes* 1.9 from a multiplicity of critical and theoretical perspectives, a book that demonstrates how each reading produces its own coherence while not denying the possibility of the other readings contained within the book. What our reading does, however, is consider less the possibility of these multiple readings, which we take as a given, than investigate the structure of the ode that supports those readings. What we propose to examine is precisely how such a 'two-eared' ode is possible, as a paradigm for the structure and style of the *Odes* as whole. Rather than view 1.9 as a failure, we argue it is one of the most fully realized of the *Odes* in its very ironic refusal of a singular identity while at the same time insisting on its structural integrity.

The poem begins with a scene of winter stasis. Everything is frozen. The reader appears to be addressed by the opening question – 'Do you see?' – and is asked to envision the scene. (Although, as will be made apparent in the next strophe, the reader is not addressed at all – but a character by the name of Thaliarchus.) But this kind of shift from one set of meanings understood from one particular perspective to a second set constructed from another is typical of both this poem and of the *Odes* as a whole. Moreover, we generally find out that these multiple readings are not so much mutually exclusive as reinforcing. Thus, while on one level we may discover in the next strophe that the 'you' addressed in *vides*, the first word of the poem, is in fact a fictive character internal to the poem, on another level, we, the readers, are individually addressed throughout the poem. We are hailed. The poem is directed to us, and it is we who are invited to imagine the scene or scenes described, to put ourselves in that position, and to reflect thereon, even as we are estranged from the situation, made to realize that what we thought we knew, in fact we did not, and in this fashion we are often reduced to an at once sublime and ironic moment of aporia or undecidability.

> *Vides* ut alta stet nive candidum
> Soracte, nec iam sustineant onus
> silvae laborantes, geluque
> flumina constiterint acuto?

> Do *you* see how bright Mount Soracte stands with deep snow, and how
> the straining trees do not now hold up under the weight and how the
> rivers are stopped with sharp ice?   (1.9.1–4, emphasis mine)

What precisely is the dramatic scene we are asked to envision here? Is the poet in his home looking out of the window? That seems unlikely. Soracte is 20 miles north of Rome and, while occasionally visible from the Janiculum on a clear day, the typical Roman house had few if any outward-facing windows, and these were thin slits (Rudd 1960: 391; Nisbet and Hubbard 1970: 116). Nor, despite the allusion to the Sabine countryside in the next strophe, is the scene likely to be the poet's farm, which is much farther away. In fact, we are asked to imagine a picture in our mind's eye which corresponds to no actually existing perspective.

We could, of course, posit a site somewhere from which the poet is asking an interlocutor to look at the mountain, but that is to miss the point (Quinn 1980: ad loc.); the scene is neither realistic nor dramatic but textual. The reader is asked to imagine a scene that at once strikes us with its realistic detail (hence past attempts to imagine the site from which it is envisaged) and yet converts itself almost instantly into a variety of figurative representations: most prominently an allegorical representation of wintry old age, which contrasts with the portrayal of sunny youth later in the poem (Wilkinson 1946: 131; Cunningham 1957: 101–2). But that is not all. The entire first scene also contains a substantial literary allusion: it is a virtual quotation of Alcaeus 338 (Campbell 1982), extending into the second strophe:

> Zeus sends rain, a great storm from the heavens, running waters are frozen solid [...] thence [...] Down with the storm! Stoke up the fire, mix the honeysweet wine unsparingly, and put a soft fillet round your brows.

We can, I would contend, safely assume that it is no accident that the first poem in Alcaics, the most common metre in the collection, begins with a citation of Alcaeus and that our recognition of the citation should in some way be determinative of our understanding of the poem.

The intertextual reading of Alcaeus continues in the second strophe, which features an analogous set of imperative verbs, with similar commands to build up the fire and bring out the wine:

> dissolve frigus ligna super foco
> large reponens atque benignius
> deprome quadrimum Sabina,
> o Thaliarche, merum diota.

> Melt away the cold by generously putting another log on the fire, and liberally decant the four-year-old unmixed wine, Thaliarchus, from the Sabine two-eared jar. (1.9.5–8)

So, what seems to begin as the literal description of a winter scene, on closer reflection actually produces at least two separate figural readings, which, while not inherently contradictory, cannot be reduced to a single unified meaning and which, consequently, will not allow us simply to dispose of the initial literal reading, since it is the ground from which these figurative meanings are conjured. In the first, figurative reading, we have the contrast between a frozen interior scene whose white stasis contrasts vividly with the picture of open-air, youthful erotic adventure at the poem's end. In the second, we have a metapoetic reading which sees the whole poem as a figure for literary commentary, quoting extensively from Alcaeus in the first ode to be written in Alcaic strophes and one placed emphatically at the end of the Parade Odes.

Each of these figural readings is essentially an allegory, which as Quintilian notes is a form closely related to irony. Both, he observes, are species of the tropic or the figural, in which one set of words is used in place of another, and in which a given form of speaking is transferred from its usual context into another where it is less familiar, where it is used to communicate an *intellectum* not commonly associated with this particular *dictum*. When this tropic irony is extended from individual words or phrases over the course of an entire narrative or even a life, Quintilian says, as in the case of Socrates, it becomes an extended metaphor, or what is known as an 'allegory' (9.1.4–5, 9.2.44–7; compare de Man 1983: 225–6). As in irony proper, we must again posit a moment of nonmeaning or what Quintilian terms 'obscurity', which separates the initial set of meanings from their figural possibilities (8.6.58; de Man 1983: 209; Lewis 2008: 166). Irony and allegory depend on the reader's recognition of the difference separating their literal from their figurative meanings.

In poem 1.9, we begin our reading with the problem that what appears to be a realistic description of a winter scene on Mount Soracte cannot, in fact, be one, since there is no place (almost literally) from which the poet can make this utterance and have it received as an actual description. Instead, that description, on a certain level, points to its own impossibility as a literal statement about the world, and so we must search for other possible contexts, other sets of meanings, that could allow this utterance to make sense. It is, moreover, precisely the gap between these words and their initially understood literal meaning that necessitates this secondary interpretive response, that signals that these words (*dicta*) do not mean what they say, but something more, something different (*allegorizein* means 'to say the other, the *allon*'; Nehamas 1998: 60). Indeed, the very foregrounding of this gap signals that we are dealing with the literary, that we are dealing with a set of statements that invite, indeed demand, poetic reinterpretation. Irony, allegory and the literary are in fact deeply intertwined concepts, sharing in common their transcendence of the literal. But this figurative movement is not simply a quality of literary language, for the demonstration that the meanings produced by what we say exceeds our understanding and intentions is at the very root of the Socratic philosophical impulse: the demonstration that what you say when you speak of the good, the just or the beautiful is something other, different and more than what you think. Mount Soracte, then, is in *Odes* 1.9 never simply a physical place and always gestures to both a set of meanings beyond itself and to the gap between its physical existence and those extended meanings.

If we return, then, to the text of the second stanza, the first thing we recognize is that we, the readers, are not being addressed. The switch to the imperative renders it unlikely that the person addressed in *vides* is in reality the reader being invited to imagine the scene put before them, even though that is exactly the effect of beginning the poem with the question, 'do you see?'. But let us also pause for a moment and understand that in recognizing this fact we also shift from the literal to the figural. The real *you* of the initial *vides* from the perspective of both the reader and the writer can only be the reader. Yet this *you* cannot be the same as the person addressed in the imperatives of the second strophe. In effect, this means that we have switched from a literal *you*, an actual person who can be addressed, to a literary construction, the image of a 'you', which makes possible a form of address no longer able to be interpreted as a simple question addressed to a person but as something that only makes sense within an imaginary field of representation. There are in fact two *you*s. The first *you* is the reader. And when you the reader are asked if you see the scene described, and you implicitly answer in the affirmative by continuing to read, with the scene now vividly imagined, that very act of imagination creates the dramatic scene in which the represented person, the second *you* addressed in the second strophe, is capable of acting on the command, *dissolve*.

Coming immediately after *geluque* [...] *acuto* the effect of this imperative is a juxtaposition of opposites. One moment we have the stasis of rivers frozen with sharp ice, the next a command to 'dissolve' the cold by placing more logs on the fire. The person addressed, however, is hardly even the representation of a real person, but an imagined Greek character, Thaliarchus, whose name means 'Master of the Revels'. Although the name is attested, it can only be ironic here, for any Greek in a Roman household who was commanded to build a fire and serve wine would hardly be the master but certainly a slave, and yet the name and the Alcaean citation ask us simultaneously to imagine an alternative Greek context in which Thaliarchus truly is the master of the revels, a context which must be denied as soon as it is evoked, since in the Lesbos of Alcaeus or the Athens of Horace's youth there was no Mount Soracte, either visible or imagined (Nisbet and Hubbard 1970: 117, 121; Connor 1972: 111; Quinn 1980: 141).

Mount Soracte, however, is not the only bit of local colour we are asked to envisage: Thaliarchus, for example, is commanded to bring forth a 'Sabine jar'. Again, this is no ordinary jar, and its unusual nature is emphasized by the substantial hyperbaton, or disturbance of normal word order, separating *Sabina* (end of line 7) from *diota* (end of line 8). *Diota*, however, is not only in an unusual position, being separated from the adjective that modifies it by the double-voiced *o Thaliarche*, it is also an unusual word. This passage is its sole occurrence in Latin (Nisbet and Hubbard 1970: 121; Mayer 2012: 110). *Diota* is in fact a Greek word and not one that had been naturalized into its Latin context, like *amphora*, which names the same kind of two-handled jug. The latter is commonly used by Horace and others, as well as other Latin words for various types of bottles and jugs (*cadus, testa*). *Diota*, then, is very deliberately chosen and placed in a position that highlights the poet's self-conscious choice. It literally means 'two-eared', and the word in itself names a non sequitur or a moment of nonmeaning that can only be recuperated on the level of allegory and irony: inasmuch as *diota*, with this one exception, is a Greek word, then by definition a *Sabina diota* cannot exist. 'Sabine' in Roman poetry refers less to a particular ethnic group than to deeply traditional italic culture. 'Sabine' in Horace is anything but a signifier for the cosmopolitan mixture of Greek and Latin artistry, and thus a Sabine Greek two-eared jar can no more exist than can a master (*archos*) who is a slave. They are both oxymorons. And indeed the phrase *Sabina diota* only becomes meaningful owing to the hyperbaton that separates the two words from one another and into which the paradoxical *o Thaliarche* intervenes, owing to the moment of nonmeaning created by the artistry of Horatian verse (Santirocco 1986: 156; Edmunds 1992: 11–12; Miller 1994: 158–61).

Sabina diota, in a strong sense, names the vessel that is the *Odes* themselves: old wine (Greek poetry) poured into new Sabine/Italic bottles, or perhaps new wine (Latin poetry) poured into old bottles (Greek lyric metres) (Moritz 1976: 171). This is a gesture that repeats one already cited from the close of 1.1 in which Horace asks Maecenas to insert him among the *lyricis vatibus*. Again, there is literally no such thing: for *lyricus* is a Greek word that names a Greek genre, while *vates* is an exclusively Latin word in place of the more common Greek *poeta* favoured by Catullus (Santirocco 1986: 22; Mayer 2012: 60–1). That Horace would be included in the fixed canon of Greek lyric poets is a literal impossibility. A *lyricus vates* is a new hybrid creation that names no existing thing; it is at once an act of imaginative daring and an ironic acknowledgement of that act's own impossibility. To return to the language of *Epodes* 17 and its complex allusion to Catullus, Horace's *lyra* may be *mendax*, that is, able to produce language that does not mean what it says and filled with doublespeak, but at the same time his *fides* is ultimately played *cum fide*, with a seriousness and good faith that is part and parcel of his ironic and literary intent.

The progression from stasis to motion that began with *dissolve* (5) and is continued through the second imperative, *deprome* ('decant', 7), accelerates with the third consecutive imperative addressed to Thaliarchus, *permitte* (9). But this is less a command to perform a specific action, one appropriate to a slave, than a philosophical recommendation. The basic meaning of *permitto* is 'to let go or send through'. It implies motion and a causative role on the part of the subject. But with the second word of the third strophe, we quickly switch registers from the physical to the metaphysical:

> permitte divis cetera, qui simul
> stravere ventos aequore fervido
> deproeliantis, nec cupressi
> nec veteres agitantur orni.

> Leave all the rest to the gods, who once they have calmed the winds
> battling with the boiling seas, aged cypresses and ashes are not shaken.
>
> (1.9.9–12)

Ironically, the recommendation to leave all things to the gods takes what in its literal form is a verb of putting an object into motion, *permitto* (*per* + *mitto*), and transforms it into a figurative admonition to remain calm, to return to stasis, to abjure from motion. In effect, the poet says, 'do not worry about what is not within your power to control: drink your wine, enjoy your fire, and leave the rest'.

This same duality between what on one level is a depiction of motion or even agitation and on another a return to calm or stasis is repeated in the second clause. There the gods are those who have power 'to calm' the winds 'battling' with 'the boiling sea'. The imagery is both kinetic – winds howling and waves crashing – and still. Thaliarchus is not to be agitated but leave all things to the gods, who have the power to calm the most powerful storms. The same duality is repeated in the final two lines with the negation (*nec* [...] *nec*) of aged cypresses and ash trees bending before the winds. This entire strophe is two-eared. Each clause both has a specific literal meaning and invokes its opposite. In this plurality of meanings and contexts we are invited to imagine a variety of worlds that exist within the singularity of our experience: Greek and Latin, master and slave, agitation and calm, inside and outside, literal and figurative, real and imagined. They are not posited as mutually exclusive but coexisting planes of meaning, each reinforcing and interrogating the others.

But where do these storms, which the gods are said to calm, come from? In response to this question, Nisbet and Hubbard in their commentary write, 'It may be asked why [...] Horace should choose this relatively unimportant manifestation of divine omnipotence. The explanation surely lies in the ode's literary ancestry.' Such storms, as they point out, 'strictly speaking' do 'not suit the weather of the first stanza' (1970: 121). Indeed, we began with a description of a frozen winter scene and now we are invited to envisage storm-tossed waves. Yet while they are no doubt correct, as the quotation from Alcaeus itself underlines, and one function of the storm metaphor is to remind the reader of the literary nature of the exercise, nonetheless they miss something fundamental in the assumption that there should have been a unity of dramatic action, and that the lack of said unity must be explained by the intrusion of the literary. Rather, as we are arguing, the shifts between literal and figurative senses of the words in this poem are both fundamental to its structure and unity and explicitly thematized through the figure of the *Sabina diota*. Therefore, when the poet admonishes Thaliarchus to leave the rest to the gods, he signals a shift not only from the literal to the figurative (from verb of motion to an invocation of calm), and from the servile to the philosophical (from a true imperative to a virtual admonition), but also from the external to the internal. In a real sense, the only storms present are those of the heart. No wonder this has proved to be such a challenging poem.

Indeed, ultimately *Odes* 1.9 calls into question the very possibility of separating the literal from the figurative: in such a text, in which the very possibility of an indicative relation to a single external reality is called into question, what would literal sense mean? Who is asked to see – and to see what – in the opening verb? What is the status of the winter scene invoked at the poem's beginning? To what extent do the three evenly spaced imperatives in stanzas two and three name actions to be performed by someone as opposed to pointing to their status as constituents of a self-conscious poetic structure? There is an assumption, even in the work of such careful scholars as Nisbet and Hubbard, that there remains a baseline literal meaning of the language in a poem like 1.9 that can be distinguished from other, secondary, figurative, ironic, allegorical meanings. There is an assumption that we can know what these words really mean and use that standard to judge and subordinate all figurative senses thereto. But in a verb such as *permitte*, which is the literal meaning and which the figurative: the verb of motion that follows as a patterned response to *dissolve* and *deprome*, or the admonition to 'leave' all the rest to the gods? Both meanings are clearly present, both are clearly separable, and both are part of a larger pattern that structures the poem; in no sense are they random or incoherent.

Where each of the first three strophes are syntactically self-contained, the last three are enjambed, presenting images of movement and enjoyment that spill over from one strophe to the next and embody the opposite of the frozen stasis pictured in the opening:

quid sit futurum cras fuge quaerere et
quem Fors dierum cumque dabit lucro
appone, nec dulcis amores
sperne puer neque tu choreas,
donec virenti canities abest
morosa. nunc et campus et areae
lenesque sub noctem susurri
composita repetantur hora,
nunc et latentis proditor intimo
gratus puellae risus ab angulo
pignusque dereptum lacertis
aut digito male pertinaci.

Flee from asking what will be tomorrow, put down as profit however
many days Fortune will grant, and you, boy, spurn neither sweet loves nor
dances, so long as old age's irritable hoar is far from youthful verdancy.
Now, let the Campus Martius and the piazzas and gentle whispers be
sought at night, at the agreed-upon hour, and now the pleasing laughter
that betrays the girl hiding in the furthest corner and the pledge seized
from her arm or from a finger that does not try too hard to hold on.

(1.9.13–24)

The fourth strophe returns to the pattern of imperatives already noted
above: *fuge, appone, sperne*. Together they form a cycle. We begin with a
verb of motion that as with *permitte* is here used of mental rather than
physical action. It is followed by a verb of placing. The image behind *appone*
is taken from accounting. Each day is to be placed in the profit column.
But the image of placing is one not of flight but of moving toward stasis.
You *put* something down as profit. The move from flight to acceptance is
completed with the final *nec sperne*, where we return to the opening image
of flight and rejection but here under the sign of negation, as with the ash
trees and cypresses in strophe three.

With *puer*, however, we return to the question of who is being addressed.
Virtually all the commentators assure us that the word is nominative and

predicative rather than vocative, meaning something like 'while you are young' (Kiessling and Heinze 1999: 51; Nisbet and Hubbard 1970: 122; Mayer 2012: 113). Yet the very fact that this needs to be repeated indicates the possibility for confusion, for the term *puer* often refers to a slave, much as the word 'boy' did in the American South. Coming immediately after the imperative, *sperne*, which is the last in the series that began with the address to Thaliarchus in his capacity as builder of fires and fetcher of wine, a natural assumption would be that *puer* is a vocative of the person addressed by the imperative. It is only once we ask why a slave would be admonished not to neglect 'sweet loves nor dances' that we stop and revise (Garrison 1991: 216). But then the question becomes: who is this *puer*? If he is Thaliarchus, and he is a Greek in Horace's household told to do household chores, then he is surely a *puer* in both senses and the irony of naming him 'master of the revels' is only reinforced. If not, then in effect this is the same generalized you, 'the reader', who is asked to envision frozen Mount Soracte in the first strophe and, in so far as the movement of youthful dances outdoors forms a direct contrast with that frozen stasis, the whole poem becomes an allegory for the contrast between age and youth and a variation on the *carpe diem* motif's admonition to enjoy life while time allows. This allegorization becomes explicit in the pregnant juxtaposition of *virenti* ('verdancy, green youth') and *canities* [...] *morosa* ('irritable grey-white, hoar') in line 17 (Shields 1958: 168–9).

Nonetheless, these competing readings are neither compatible nor able to exclude one another. It is not a question of what *puer* really means. If it were, the commentators would not have to remind us not to make the wrong choice. The question instead is what kind of 'two-eared' poem generates such alternative readings that are both coherently articulated with one another by the verbal texture of the poem, and logically incompatible. Thaliarchus cannot be both master and slave. *Vides* and *sperne* cannot both address the reader and Thaliarchus. And yet the poem's coherence depends precisely on a structure that makes the coexistence of these readings possible. It is not the case then that 'apparent incongruity masks some deeper unity', as is often argued, but rather that the poem's profoundly ironic structure necessarily generates opposed understandings (*intellecta*), each of which is predicated on the continuing existence of the others (Ancona 1994: 64).

In the end, these are poems for readers and thinkers. The oral performance of traditional symposiastic lyric would not have easily accommodated the multiple possible readings necessary to uncover the basic structures of a poem like 1.9. This is poetry of the book and not song. Horace is very much a *lyricus vates*, a hybrid product of Greek and Roman culture, producing a form of lyric which is at once more deliberately classicizing than Catullus and yet in some ways even further removed from the original performance contexts of Sappho and Alcaeus. It is not surprising, then, that poem 1.9 ends with lovers pictured outside on the Campus Martius, the very place the lover Sybaris at the beginning of 1.8, the previous poem, is said to shun. The ring composition in miniature produced by these two poems is an effect that is predicated on their being written in a book, and it reveals another level of metapoetic irony. This is poetry that presents itself as a return to the conventions of archaic lyric while acknowledging its own studied artifice (Santirocco 1986: 39).

As we shall see, this same structure repeats itself in *Odes* 1.14. Here again we have a poem which seems to cite a specific Alcaean text. Here again we have an example of allegory. As in the previous poem, however, the text seems to support opposed readings which are logically incompatible and nonetheless dependent on an identical verbal structure. Likewise, as in 1.9, the poem has definite relations to the surrounding poems that form an integral part of its interpretive context. Lastly, as in 1.9, only to a higher degree, this poem has given rise to extensive modern interpretive controversy as critics strive to argue that the poem is not 'two-eared' but possessed of a single correct meaning.

> O navis, referent in mare te novi
> fluctus. o quid agis? fortiter occupa
> portum. nonne vides ut
> nudum remigio latus,
> et malus celeri saucius Africo
> antemnaque gemant ac sine funibus
> vix durare carinae
> possint imperiosius

aequor? non tibi sunt integra lintea,
non di, quos iterum pressa voces malo.
    quamvis Pontica pinus,
        silvae filia nobilis,
iactes et genus et nomen inutile:
nil pictis timidus navita puppibus
    fidit. tu, nisi ventis
        debes ludibrium, cave.
nuper sollicitum quae mihi taedium,
nunc desiderium curaque non levis,
    interfusa nitentis
        vites aequora Cycladas.

O ship, what new waves bear you back upon the sea? O what are you doing? Cleave powerfully to port. Do you not realize that your flank, naked of oars, and your mast and sail yards, wounded by the swift south-west wind, groan, and that ships devoid of ropes are scarcely able to endure the too-imperious deep? Your sails are not whole. There are no gods upon whom you might call when pressed hard again by injury. Pontic pine, daughter of a noble wood, although you vaunt both your name and clan, it is to no end: the frightened sailor trusts not in gaudy painted sterns. You, beware, lest you become the bauble of the winds. You, who recently were a source of troubled anxiety for me, now a source of want and not trivial care, should avoid the waters of the shining Cyclades.   (1–20)

Very few readers have seen this as a poem addressed to a literal ship. Nonetheless, while critical opinion is largely agreed on the necessity of an allegorical interpretation, there is currently great debate on what that interpretation should be.

    Among ancient commentators, however, there was little doubt about the correct interpretation of the poem. *Odes* 1.14 is exhibit A in Quintilian's discussion of allegory:

Allegory, which they translate as 'inversion' [or 'irony'[11]], either manifests one thing in words and another in sense or sometimes even the opposite thing. The first kind is produced from extended metaphors, such as:

> O ship, what new waves bear you back upon the sea? O what are you doing? Cleave powerfully to port.

That whole passage from Horace says 'ship' in place of 'republic', 'waves' and 'storms' in place of 'civil wars', 'port' in place of 'peace' and 'concord'.

We find the same self-assurance in the ancient scholia. Those transmitted under the name of Acron begin 'truly this ode points to civil war through allegory' (Havthal 1966a: 53). Likewise, the commentary of the third-century scholar, Porphyrion, discerns a clear allegorical construction, *manifestea allegoria est*. While highly questionable in its specificity and timeline, Porphyrion's reading agrees with all of the ancient commentators in contending that we are here dealing with an example of the 'ship of state' metaphor and that the storms are meant to suggest the possibility of a recrudescence of the recently concluded civil wars: 'In this ode he speaks to Marcus Brutus, who having been chased by Augustus to Philippi, a city in Macedonia, seemed about to prepare himself again for the fight' (Havthal 1966a: 56). Considering that the battle of Philippi occurred more than ten years before the earliest ode we can date, this reading seems unlikely in its particulars. Nonetheless, while there was debate among the ancient commentators about which actual or potential civil conflict Horace may be referencing here, there is unanimity in considering this poem to be an allegory, an example of the 'ship of state' motif, and referring to the civil wars (McNeill 2001: 166n43).

As modern commentators have been quick to point out, the interpretation of 1.14 as political allegory by the earliest critics seems to be seconded by what seem to be quotations from Alcaeus, who was one of the earliest exemplars of the 'ship of state' motif (Lowrie 1997: 129; Lowrie 2009: 343–4). Horace appears to combine references to two different poems by Alcaeus (6 and 208[12]), both of which describe a ship about to suffer a peril similar to what it had suffered before, and both of which are described by the Homeric scholar, Heraclitus, as 'exemplary models of allegory' (Clay

2010: 139). The first (6) describes a new wave about to overcome a ship unless it beats a hasty retreat to port (Page 1955: 183–4; Nisbet and Hubbard 1970: 179). In the second fragment, there is direct reference to the *stasis* of the winds, a word commonly used to describe civil conflict, and according to the commentary in which the text is transmitted clearly referring to 'the stirring of a tyrannical conspiracy' against Alcaeus' fellow citizens (Page 1955: 188). Moreover, the 'ship of state' as an allegorical motif was not limited to Alcaeus; examples can be found in Theognis, Plato, the tragedians and the scholia to Aristophanes' *Wasps*, where an ancient commentator states that 'the poets are always comparing cities to ships' (29; Nisbet and Hubbard 1970: 180; Quinn 1980: 150–1). In this context, it is not hard to see why Horace's early readers interpret the poem as an allegory of civil conflict, and indeed it is almost impossible to imagine how such a reading would not suggest itself.

Nonetheless, in modern times the poem has been subject to a variety of revisionist interpretations. Most of these do not contest its allegorical nature, but many reinterpret that allegory in an erotic light.[13] Most of these readings base this contention on two objections: points of detail in Horace's poem that seem at variance with the Alcaean texts, and elements in the poem that lend themselves to an erotic reading, most prominently the 'naked flank' of line 4. The first article to suggest the alternative erotic reading was W. S. Anderson's 'Horace *Carm.* 1.14: What Kind of Ship?' (1966). Anderson voices two primary objections to the traditional reading. First, in the Alcaean and other Greek examples of the 'ship of state' allegory there is an emphasis on the ship's captain (or pilot) and on his ability or inability to control the vessel. The allegory is in fact a critique of the existing political regime. The captain does not appear in Horace's ode, and one has difficulty imagining the poet launching a critique of Augustus' ability to pilot the ship. The second objection is to the implied personification of the ship, which is directly addressed and treated as if it were an autonomous being. Again, this is not found in Alcaeus, Theognis or Plato; Anderson thus concludes that an alternative allegorical context must be found. After going through a variety of understandings of the poem, all of which can find some ancient precedent, including the 'ship of life' and the 'ship of poetry', Anderson proposes his reading of the poem. Focusing on Horace's description of the 'naked flank' and his later description of the ship as the object of the poet's 'care' and 'desire', Anderson not unreasonably concludes that the ship is not the state but a person who has been the object of the poet's erotic desire in the past and who is about once more to launch herself upon the stormy waters of love. Indeed, Horace even refers to the ship as the noble 'daughter' of the forest.

While Anderson's reading has been far from producing universal acceptance, it has found followers nonetheless, and it has an undeniable cogency that makes it difficult to disregard the erotic elements in the poem once they have been noted (Garrison 1991: 224; Thomas 2007: 58–60). Most recently, this reading has found a strong advocate in the person of Ortwin Knorr (2006). Following Anderson, Knorr offers a careful catalogue of various ways in which Horace's poem seems to be at variance with the 'ship of state' allegory, adding to Anderson's list the observation that where in the earlier Greek tradition the ship is at the beginning of a new journey, in Horace, the ship is at the end of its journey and approaching the harbour – although *referent* may mean to 'to take out again', making this the beginning of *another* journey, and hence the admonition is to return to port (Mayer 2012: 133).

Knorr's argument, however, is not precisely the same as Anderson's. Knorr wants to argue that the context is that of a love triangle and that the safe port to which the ship should return is the warm embrace of Horace the mature lover, basing this reading largely on the place of 1.14 in the collection. His arguments here are essentially three. First, the image of love as shipwreck was already established in the famous Pyrrha ode (1.5) earlier in the collection. There, the context is clearly established of Horace being the older and wiser former lover now watching the younger lover about to head out onto dangerous seas and implicitly warning him. *Odes* 1.5 and 1.14 are both composed in the same Third Asclepiadean strophe and therefore invite comparison. Second, in *Odes* 1.13 Horace is portrayed as the older lover who is now outside looking in at the passion Lydia experiences for the young Telephus. Thus when the reader comes to 1.14, the context of the love triangle should be clearly in mind. On this reading, Horace would be the stable harbour to which Lydia could flee when the storms of passion abate, although it is not clear that Horace in any other poem envisions himself in any version of enduring domestic bliss (a stable harbour), but rather always portrays himself as moving on to the next erotic encounter. Finally, *Odes* 1.15, the sole strictly narrative poem in the collection, is itself often viewed as another allegory. In it, Nereus prophecies in response to the rape of Helen the entire course of the Trojan War in brief lyric form, ending with the destruction of Troy. This too, of course, is the story of a love triangle, and one that obviously ends badly when the beloved leaves the safety of her home port.

Knorr, then, has a case, and it is one that finds some support in Alcaeus as well, when a ship in fragment 73 is referred to as a woman, although even here the poem has been read as a political allegory (Page 1955: 188–90; Campbell 1982: 279; Clay 2010: 139). Knorr and Anderson are also correct that Horace's poem does not directly reproduce all the traits of the 'ship of state' allegory as seen in Alcaeus, Theognis or Plato. Likewise, there are undeniable sexual overtones to 1.14 that makes an erotic allegory possible, including but not limited to the ship's 'naked flank', the fact that it is referred as the 'daughter of a noble wood', and the fact that the ship is referred to as the object of the poet's 'care' and 'desire'. Just as every detail of Horace's poem cannot be made to correspond to Alcaeus' political poetry, however, neither can every detail be subordinated to an erotic reading; the nature of allegory is that the vehicle of allegorical communication must say something different from what the allegory understands. This is why, as we have seen, Quintilian saw allegory and irony as closely related modes: in each of them, the *intellectum* is *diversum* from the *dictum*; the two levels by definition can never correspond completely. Finally, Knorr is correct that poem 1.14 finds itself surrounded by other erotic poems in the collection, many of which portray love as inherently triangular, including poem 1.15, which also invites allegorical interpretation.

Knorr, then, has a case. But just as the erotic reading of the poem, once suggested, is impossible to ignore and does pick up on elements of the text, so the political reading of the text is equally hard to ignore. This poem, every bit as much as 1.9, is 'two-eared'. The recognition of allegory demands a bivalent reading, and insofar as the literal reading remains *different* from the figural interpretation, insofar therefore as there is a moment of nonmeaning that prevents one reading from supplanting and absorbing the other, then the literal reading remains both available in itself (this *is* a poem about a ship) and as a vehicle for other forms of figurative interpretation ('ship of state', 'ship of poetry', etc.), no one of which can be totalizing (Lowrie 1997: 125–6, 130, 136–7; Lowrie 2009: 346–7; Johnson 2012: 201–2).

Indeed, it strains credulity to claim that the dominant reading for nearly 2,000 years, a reading founded on allusions to the text of Alcaeus and one adopted by readers only shortly removed from the poet himself, was simply incorrect and that only in the 1960s in the United States did the true reading begin to be recognized. But this is what Knorr wishes to claim: not that his erotic reading is possible, not that the traditional political reading is incomplete or unable to account for all elements of the text, but that it and other readings (including Anderson's) are simply wrong and to be discarded (2006: 166). Yet it seems that to hold Knorr's position one must not only confront the fact that all allegorical readings are by necessity incomplete, but also, more fundamentally, one must offer a convincing explanation for why all previous readings were incorrect, for how so many knowledgeable people were misled for so long, and for how only a single reader some 2,000 years later in a faraway land was able to read the poem correctly.

In the end, the most persuasive arguments Anderson and Knorr advance against the traditional reading of the poem centre on the fact that in the traditional 'ship of state' allegory the speaker is on the ship, where Horace here is a detached observer on the shore. Often, as in the case of Plato's use of the motif in the *Republic*, it is the pilot of the ship who is directly put in question. Again, this is not the case in *Odes* 1.14, although of course, as we have already seen in the case of 1.9, Horace can make poignant use of his Alcaean models without reproducing them precisely and while turning them to his own account. More importantly, Horace's relation to power is profoundly different from that of Alcaeus or Plato. The Rome of the nascent principate was neither the archaic polis of Alcaeus' seventh-century Mytilene nor the democratic polis of Plato's fourth-century Athens (Lowrie 1997: 146; Clay 2010: 139–40), and we should therefore not expect political allegory at the beginning of the principate – in which the leadership of the state was no longer open to contestation – to function in the same fashion as it did in archaic or classical Greece. Horace in effect was much more a political spectator during this period than an active participant in the contest for power.

To refuse the political reading, then, is to invite anachronism, but to ignore the erotic is to neglect both manifest elements in the text and the context of the poem within the collection. The relation between these competing contexts of interpretation is of necessity unstable with each ironizing and relativizing the other. Yet I am not simply arguing for a kind of deconstructive undecidability as a formal principle here; I would contend that this aporia is precisely the point. The poem itself forces us to pose the question – as in many ways does the entire collection – of what is the relation between the erotic and the political, both in terms of civilization itself and the emerging order of Augustan Rome (Miller 2004). The ironic allegorical structure of the poem forces the reader to pose this question without ever allowing either pole of the aporetical structure to becomes the dominant principle from which the other is either simply deduced or to which it must be subordinated. But rather, quietly, with humour and with elegance, *Odes* 1.14 forces us to pose the question as a question and to guard against its premature closure or reduction to a singular reading.

It is to some of the more overtly political odes that we will now turn our attention. While we have already concentrated most of our attention on Book 1 of the *Odes*, owing to the programmatic nature of the poems found there, no treatment of the political odes would be complete without an examination 1.37, the 'Cleopatra Ode'. The poem, like many others, begins with a tag from Alcaeus (frg. 332), and at first appears to be a straightforward and even strident celebration of Octavian's defeat of the Egyptian queen and her unnamed Roman consort at Actium:

> Nunc est bibendum, nunc pede libero
> pulsanda tellus, nunc Saliaribus
>   ornare pulvinar deorum
>   tempus erat dapibus, sodales.

> antehac nefas depromere Caecubum
> cellis avitis, dum Capitolio
> regina dementis ruinas
> funus et imperio parabat
> contaminato cum grege turpium
> morbo virorum, quidlibet impotens
> sperare fortunaque dulci
> ebria.

Now is the time for drinking, now the earth should be pounded with a free foot. Now was the time to decorate the couch of the gods with Salian feasts, comrades. It would have been wrong before to decant the Caecuban from the ancestral cellars, so long as the queen was preparing mindless ruin for the Capitoline and death for our rule with her herd of perverse men contaminated with disease. She was drunk on sweet fortune, mad enough to hope for anything at all. (1–12)

The poem opens with a call for long-postponed drinking and dancing now that mortal peril has been averted from Rome. The image of Roman *virtus* threatened by the feminine orient and the image of a queen drunk on power and surrounded by diseased eunuchs is meant to inspire disgust and draw a stark contrast with Roman masculinity.

Yet at this point the poem begins to make a turn and starts to question the too-neatly framed opposition that makes up its opening, with the initial hint of that shift seen in the word *impotens*, which possesses two almost opposite meanings. The first is simply 'powerless', a meaning that gives us the English word *impotent*. The second, however, is 'powerless to control oneself', hence 'mad', 'frightening', and thereby possessed of a not insignificant power.

Both meanings are appropriate to the context. The first chimes with the notion of Eastern effeminacy emblematized by Cleopatra's eunuchs, while the second is precisely what gives us cause for celebration. If Cleopatra (and Marc Antony) had merely been 'impotent', there would have been no reason to fear and hence cause for relief. But these meanings point in different directions, and it is precisely their 'two-eared' quality that makes possible their revaluation in the second half of the poem.

The central passage of the poem tells of Caesar's victory and transforms the Egyptian queen from the symbol of a perverse disease that threatens to engulf Rome to the helpless prey chased by the powerful hunter:

> Sed minuit furorem
> vix una sospes navis ab ignibus,
> mentemque lymphatam Mareotico
> redegit in veros timores
> Caesar, ab Italia volantem
> remis adurgens, accipiter velut
> mollis columbas aut leporem citus
> venator in campis nivalis
> Haemoniae, daret ut catenis
> fatale monstrum.

But the fact that scarcely a single ship escaped safe from the fires diminished her furor, and Caesar brought her mind soaked in Maerotic wine back to true fears, when he pressed her, as she was flying from Italy with her oars – just as an eagle chases soft doves, or the swift hunter chases a hare across the snowy fields of Haemonia – so that he might put this fatal wonder in chains. (12–21)

Where Horace's decorous drinking in stanza one had been replaced by Cleopatra drunk on fortune in stanza three, in these middle stanzas there is a process of sobering up. The reality of her defeat becomes apparent, and the earlier images of her plotting death and ruin have been replaced with that of the fleeing dove, an often erotic image (see Catullus 68.125–8), and of the soft hare bounding across the snow before the fierce hunter. This too is an erotic image, one that Horace had already used in *Satires* 1.2.105–8, having borrowed it from an epigram of Callimachus to characterize the erotic desire of the man who passes up easy satisfaction in favour of the difficult and the dangerous. Indeed, in these middle stanzas, the initial revulsion before the queen surrounded by her perverse crowd of eunuchs, as she plots the potential unmanning of Rome in a drunken frenzy, has been replaced with the image of her as a now sobered fleeing victim who is simultaneously an object of desire and fascination (Lowrie 1997: 151).

The duality of this characterization is nicely captured in the final phrase, *fatale monstrum*, in much the same fashion as *impotens* expressed the duality of her rage and impotence at the beginning of the poem. *Fatale monstrum* can be translated at least four different ways, each of which gives a different inflection to the poem. *Fatale* can mean either 'fated' or 'fatal', and *monstrum* can mean either 'wonder' or 'monstrosity'. If we accept the pessimistic view of the opening stanzas, Cleopatra is either a potentially 'fatal monster', from whom Octavian and now Augustus has saved us, or she is perhaps the 'fated monster' sent to Rome to atone for the sins of civil war and fratricide and to demonstrate the greatness of Caesar (compare *Epodes* 7). But she is also simultaneously – because the Latin does not force us to choose, unlike the English translation – a 'fatal wonder', a thing that is both amazing (and perhaps even attractive) yet offers a mortal danger. And she is likewise the 'fated wonder', a kind of miracle sent by the gods or fate itself, a thing that has about it the aura of divinity (Lowrie 1997: 153–4).

As noted above, while the darker, more pessimistic readings of this phrase point to the characterization of Cleopatra as mad, drunk and perverse, the awestruck tone of the alternative readings are consonant with the final stanzas of the poem (Garrison 1991: 256; Oliensis 1998: 145). Here Cleopatra is transformed into a figure of admiration, if not potential emulation:

> Quae generosius
> perire quaerens nec muliebriter
> expavit ensem nec latentis
> classe cita reparavit oras;
> ausa et iactentem visere regiam
> vultu sereno, fortis et asperas
> tractare serpentes, ut atrum
> corpore combiberet venenum,
> deliberata morte ferocior;

> saevis Liburnis scilicet invidens
> privata deduci superbo
> non humilis mulier triumpho.

Seeking to die more nobly, neither did she dread the sword, as women do, nor did she retreat to hidden shores in a swift boat. She dared to gaze upon her fallen kingdom with a calm face and bravely to draw to herself bitter serpents so that her body might drink in their black venom, having chosen to die without compromise, truly despising to be led back in cruel Liburnian galleys as a private, but not humble, woman in a proud triumph. (21–32)

The problem of Cleopatra's simultaneous monstrosity and miraculous nature is fully on display in these final stanzas. She is both noble (*generosius*) and one who behaves outside the norms of her gender (*genus*) by not acting like a woman (*nec muliebriter*). In a society whose highest virtue was masculine courage (*virtus*, the quality of being a *vir*), there could be little better than for your leader to act *generosius nec muliebriter*, but should your leader be a woman this is both monstrous and miraculous. Cleopatra, moreover, displays her nobility in the stoic calm with which she faces her defeat, choosing to die at her own hand rather than be led in Caesar's triumph. The final juxtaposition of *non humilis* with *superbo* establishes almost a momentary equality, as Cleopatra's proud refusal of public humiliation is compared to Augustus' pride, with a touch of arrogance (one possible translation of *superbia*), in Rome's triumphal procession. The ode ends not with the celebratory tone with which it began but with a sober recognition of the nobility of an enemy Augustan propaganda had sought to demonize as Eastern, effeminate and perverse, and with the implied possibility of Roman arrogance and overreach (Lowrie 1997: 154, 160–4; Oliensis 1998: 139–43).

Where that *superbia* had led is precisely the topic of *Odes* 2.1 on Pollio's history of the civil wars. The besetting tragedy of the previous hundred years of Roman history was self-slaughter as the leading men of Rome jockeyed for power in the senate, on the streets and on the battlefield. Pollio, Virgil's early literary patron and an accomplished tragedian and orator in his own right, had set out in his history to recount a portion of this series of conflicts, stretching from the First Triumvirate (Julius Caesar, Pompey and Crassus) to the battle of Philippi, a series that found its end with the defeat of Antony and Cleopatra in Egypt and the creation of the Augustan principate:

> Motum ex Metello consule civicum
> bellique causas et vitia et modos
> > ludumque Fortunae gravisque
> > > principium amicitias et arma
> nondum expiatis uncta cruoribus,
> periculosae plenum opus aleae,
> > tractas et incedis per ignes
> > > suppositos cineri doloso.

> You are writing the story of civic unrest from the time Metellus was consul as well as the causes, evils and strategies of war, the play of Fortune, the weighty alliances of the leading men, and arms soaked in blood not yet atoned: the full work of dangerous chance. You are treading on fires that lie just beneath painful ash.

The writing of history, Horace reminds us, can be a dangerous enterprise. The wounds of the recently concluded civil wars remain open, and within the poem they seem to be exacerbated by the ornately intertwined word order wherein *uncta* sits between *expiatis* and *cruoribus* (Quinn 1980: ad loc.). The flames of the conflict still smoulder just beneath a crust of ash. Pollio, the poet seems to warn, had best be careful lest he tread too heavily (Nisbet and Hubbard 1978: ad loc.).

The next stanzas, then, describe the power of Pollio's narrative, his vivid evocation of the sounds of battle, as well as the satisfaction with which Rome's enemies greeted this deluge of Roman blood. It filled the streams, the rivers and the sea, we are told. It washed upon the shores (2.1.33–6). Yet even this poem, seemingly in every way a study in gravity, is not without its final ironic turn, which makes us pause before assuming we understand its final message:

> Sed ne relictis, Musa procax, iocis
> Ceae retractes munera neniae,
>   mecum Dionaeo sub antro
>   quaere modos leviore plectro.

But, insolent Muse, lest you take up again the task of the Cean dirge,
with jokes and wit left behind, come seek with me in Venus' grotto
songs sung with a lighter pick.   (2.1.37–40)

This poem has a complicated structure, and it is not unambiguously clear
to whom and to what purpose this final stanza is addressed. The ode begins
as a dedicatory poem and a panegyric for Pollio's history, with due warning
for the perilous nature of the enterprise he has undertaken. Then through an
evocation of the force of Pollio's narrative, the poem becomes a dirge for the
civil war itself, complete with vivid evocations of a world awash in blood. In
the final stanza, *Odes* 2.1 is transformed once more, this time into a *recusa-
tio*: a refusal to write in a given genre while simultaneously demonstrating
the ability to do so. This last gesture is a recurring motif throughout the
Augustan period, as the writers of elegy, lyric and satire repeatedly disclaim
the ability to write in the so-called higher genres of epic and tragedy. Thus
in the final lines the epic and tragic tones of the previous stanzas are put
aside in favour of an admonition to seek lyric lightness. But this moment
of displacement is itself revelatory; Horace's lyric Muse does not so much
replace or gloss over the previous century of fratricidal conflict as become a
symptom of the very tragedy Pollio sets out to chronicle, creating in Venus'
grotto a fragile and momentary retreat from the temptations of the dirge
(Nisbet and Hubbard 1978: ad loc.).

Indeed, we might well ask in the end whose Muse is really 'insolent' and
in what sense? Is it Pollio's tragic Muse, who is here admonished to take
up lighter topics lest the poet break through the volcanic crust he treads
upon and sink into the flames of violence and self-slaughter? If this is the
case, Pollio's Muse is 'insolent' precisely in daring to take up dangerous
topics. However, if it is Horace's lyric Muse that is *procax*, then, the mean-
ing is exactly the opposite; she is insolent because she refuses to take up

weighty topics and concentrates on the joys of Venus, practising lyric in an Anacreontic vein. Here, then, insolence is synonymous with wantonness. Finally, there is a third option: Horace's Muse is 'insolent' not because she refuses to take up weighty topics, but because she has: she has strayed from her lyric mandate (Nisbet and Hubbard 1978: ad loc.; Quinn 1980: ad loc.; Garrison 1991: ad loc.).

Insolence, then, is very much in the eye of the beholder. The erotic and the political, the lyric and its other, are not so much mutually exclusive as separate but interpenetrating realms. Thus, in poem 1.9, the poet admonishes Thaliarchus to enjoy life, and specifically the possibility of its erotic charms, while time and climate allow. The *Sabina diota* of Horace's Romanized Greek lyric is copious enough to contain the oppositions of youth and old age, winter and spring, death and rebirth, within a single compass. And in 1.14, the allegory of the ship, erotic and political readings are both opposed to one another and yet exist side by side; neither is so totalizing as to be able to eradicate the traces of the other and indeed, insofar as the poem is universally agreed to be allegorical, such a totalizing reading is of necessity impossible. In 1.37, although Cleopatra is initially portrayed as a mortal threat to the state, drunk and surrounded by the enticements of perversity, she is then transformed into an object of desire, a fleeing dove, a bounding hare, before finishing as a figure of qualified admiration for her unwomanly virtue: a truly *fatale monstrum*. Finally, in poem 2.1, the powerful evocation of the tragedy of civil war at the poem's beginning leads in the final stanza to an admonition directed both to the poet and his addressee not to abandon the lyric Muse of poems such as 1.9 and hence not to abandon the refuge of desire (*Dionaeo sub antro*). The erotic and political throughout the *Odes*, thus, are shown to be interpenetrating realms of desire, each of which retains the potential to be allegorized in terms of the other even as each remains separate and capable of ironically relativizing the other.

The most famed political poems in the corpus are the so-called Roman Odes, 3.1–6. All written in Alcaics, these poems are generally thought to sing the praises of the Augustan regime and of its redefinition of traditional Roman virtues (Armstrong 1989: 99). Yet even here, these poems often offer odd or dissonant qualifications to the dominant panegyric tone, revealing ironic undertones that render the *dictum* at some variance from the *intellectum*, even if seldom directly opposed to it (Lowrie 1997: 265; Oliensis 1998: 132). Our primary example here will be poem 3.2, which offers what appears to be a redefinition of *virtus* for the new age, only then to call into question its ultimate justice if not its utility.

The poem opens with a very traditional definition of masculine virtue as Roman martial courage. The youth, we are told, should learn to endure deprivation and to live under the open sky as they prosecute Rome's conflicts with its long-time Eastern enemies the Parthians (3.2.1–6). This exhortation, then, gives way to Horace painting a scene strongly reminiscent of the *Iliad*, in which a young maid gazes out from the walls of an enemy town fearing her betrothed will anger the Roman lion who rampages across the field like Achilles (3.2.6–12). This opening section rounds off with a gnomic stanza that contains the formula immortalized by Wilfred Owen's poem on the futility of the First World War, 'Dulce et decorum est':

> Dulce et decorum est pro patria mori:
> mors et fugacem persequitur virum,
> nec parcit imbellis iuventae
> poplitibus timidove tergo.

> It is a sweet and proper thing to die for one's country: and death pursues
> the fleeing man and does not spare the youth with unwarlike knees or
> a timid back. (3.2.13–16)

Virtue in these first four stanzas is largely an external attribute. It involves performing certain actions, primarily of a martial nature, while exhibiting courage and a willingness to die for Rome. This would have been a definition of *virtus* familiar to the Roman Republic, the principate or the high empire. These are not the internalized virtues that a post-Christian world will associate with a spiritual vision that focuses less on the actual actions performed than on the attitudes exhibited toward those actions. For the early Roman Republic, much as for the Homeric world, the idea of practising virtue in isolation or in a strictly spiritual sense is a non sequitur: *virtus* is a quality of masculine action. A young woman exhibiting *virtus*, therefore, could only be a *fatale monstrum* (Edwards 1993: 174).

In the next two stanzas of 3.2, however, Horace attempts a redefinition of virtue, which, while not consonant with later medieval or modern notions of the term, is much more internalized and even spiritualized than that outlined in the first four strophes. It is, by the same token, one better suited for the new realities of the principate. The brave new world that Maecenas and Augustus were building was not one in which aristocrats competed with one another for military and political power as well as popular recognition; that was the world whose collapse Pollio was said to be chronicling in 2.1, and the world that breathed its last gasp with the Battle of Actium and the defeat of Antony and Cleopatra. This new world would require new virtues that would nonetheless be recognizable to the former inhabitants of the old. Augustus did after all claim to be restoring the Republic even as he laid the political, cultural and constitutional foundations for the empire (*Res Gestae* 34):

> Virtus, repulsae nescia sordidae,
> intaminatis fulget honoribus,
>   nec sumit aut ponit securis
>   arbitrio popularis aurae.
> Virtus, recludens immeritis mori
> caelum, negata temptat iter via,
>   coetusque vulgaris et udam
>   spernit humum fugiente penna.

Virtue, which knows not sordid electoral defeat, shines with undefiled honours. It neither takes up nor puts aside the axes that symbolize authority by judgement of the popular breeze.

Virtue, enclosing those who did not deserve to die within heaven, attempts the way there, even though the road has been denied. It spurns on fleeing wing the intercourse of the crowd and its humid soil.

(3.2.17–24)

This new, or updated, version of *virtus* was no longer dependent upon recognition by the Roman people through the electoral process. *Honor*, which in the past had been all but synonymous with electoral office, as in the *cursus honorum*, is now internalized and even spiritualized as it becomes purified, 'undefiled'. In the next stanza, this spiritualization is taken a step further: *virtus* here becomes synonymous with the state of the individual's soul or, to avoid anachronistic Christian overtones, with whatever part of the individual can be imagined as escaping death and mounting to 'heaven', a common Stoic theme (Quinn 1980: ad loc.; Nisbet and Rudd 2004: ad loc.). The final image of *virtus* rising above the crowd on the wings of the soul owes more than just a little to Plato's *Phaedrus* (Nisbet and Rudd 2004: ad loc.). On one level, this section seems an obvious allusion to the possibility of Augustus' own deification, but at the same time it opens up the field of virtue to the broad spectrum of individuals, who, insofar as they practice virtue in the Platonic and the Stoic sense, approach the immortality of the sage (Quinn 1980: ad loc.; Garrison 1991: ad loc.; Nisbet and Rudd 2004: ad loc.).

Yet even this process of redefinition is not wholly unidirectional or without its own ironic twist: for if *virtus* has become an internalized, spiritual value, then it should not be subject to the contingencies of accident or chance. A virtuous slave is not possible in Homer or in traditional Roman Republican ideology, but if, as we saw in the *Satires*, only the wise man is free according to Stoic doctrine, then many of those who pretend to be free are in fact slaves to greed, lust or the demands of public reputation. Likewise, since slavery is a merely contingent external state, then it is perfectly possible that the wise slave is far freer than his foolish master. All of this is compatible with a notion of *virtus* that frees it from public recognition and spiritualizes it as a set of undefiled honours bestowed on the potentially immortal portion of a given individual, the part that lifts him above 'the intercourse of the crowd and its humid soil'. Yet Horace warns in the end that the gods can be capricious or at least err. When they punish the wrongdoer, they may accidentally hit the innocent:

saepe Diespiter
neglectus incesto addidit integrum,

raro antecedentem scelestum
deseruit pede Poena claudo.

Often Jupiter, when slighted, includes the man of integrity with the
corrupt. Penalty, on its club foot, rarely deserts the crime that goes
before. (3.2.29–32)

Corruption is always punished in the end. But punishment is baulky and
often includes the innocent with the guilty. The safest way, therefore, is to
avoid the company of the corrupt, if you know them, although the possibil-
ity of random punishment – no matter how virtuous you may be – cannot
be excluded.

This final image is, on a certain level, comical. Divine vengeance is
portrayed as hobbling and lame, while Jupiter's thunder often goes astray.
Horace's ultimate picture of the divine reward for *virtus* is not the immortal
soul rising up to heaven in glory but a pratfall: a moment of quasi-comic busi-
ness that calls into question any neat opposition between the internal and the
external, the spiritual and the material, justice and its opposite. The irony here,
if actually dwelt upon, is potentially devastating: the virtuous man might at
any time be struck by Jupiter as punishment for an act he did not commit.
Such a world is arbitrary and capricious, authoritarian in the extreme; high-
lighting this fact seems an odd way to celebrate the birth of Roman autocracy.

What then is the answer to the possibility of the sheer contingency of our
lives, to the possibility that there is no larger meaning, at least not in a sense
that we can observe and trust in without fail? For Horace, on one level, the
answer is friendship. It does not cancel out the contingencies of the external
world, but it creates a moment of indeterminacy and potential refuge, a
moment in which the two-eared Sabine jar of 1.9 becomes the evocation of
a gap between levels of meaning – internal and external, public and private,
Greek and Roman – wherein a different form of selfhood, a different form
of mutual affection, a different form of freedom can be elaborated.

In *Odes* 3.8 Horace invites Maecenas to come and celebrate the anni-
versary of the poet's escaping death from a tree that fell on his Sabine farm
and nearly killed him. Random contingency had nearly taken his life and, in

this poem, Horace will take the recognition of that fact and use it to create new meaning, to make that moment resignify, and to convert the arbitrary into the overdetermined:

> Do you wonder why I, a bachelor, am celebrating the first of March, Mother's Day, why flowers and charcoal are placed on living turf with saucers full of incense, you who are learned in the speech of both languages? (3.8.1–5)

Why is this confirmed bachelor having a Mother's Day party, complete with incense, flowers and a simple rural altar? The imagery is at once hieratic and a bit silly. The addressee of the poem, Maecenas, we are told, is fluent in the two languages. These are most naturally taken to be Latin and Greek. Nonetheless, as the poem progresses, they could equally refer to the discourses of public and private affairs, and hence on what we have been calling internalized and externalized values: for the duality the poem hinges upon is not the opposition between Latin and Greek, but that between the arbitrary danger of the external and contingent (a tree falling on the poet, Jupiter's lighting striking the virtuous man) and the possibility of creating moments of meaning, moments of internal determination, that transcend the time of their articulation, that transcend the conditions of their possibility. This is indeed a two-eared poem.

The poet continues by answering his own question: he is celebrating the anniversary of his almost being struck and killed by a falling tree on his Sabine farm, a topic already treated in poem 2.13, a poem that featured a semi-comic vision of the underworld in which Sappho is shown charming the assembled shades and in which Alcaeus sings songs of war, exile and political conflict. The possibility of a meaningless death caused by a random act is transformed into an ironic vision of poetic immortality, even as the self-proclaimed successor of Sappho and Alcaeus narrowly escapes joining their ranks. Returning however to poem 3.8 and its invitation to Maecenas to celebrate this momentous (non-)event, we see the poet, in an echo of 1.9, urge the great man to put aside his cares and come enjoy a fine bottle of aged wine with the poet:

> Hic dies anno redeunte festus
> corticem adstrictum pice dimovebit
> amphorae fumum bibere institutae
>   consule Tullo.
> sume, Maecenas, cyathos amici
> sospitis centum et vigiles lucernas
> perfer in lucem; procul omnis esto
>   clamor et ira.

This feast day for the one-year anniversary will remove the cork fixed with pitch from the amphora put up in the consulship of Tullus to drink the smoked wine.

Maecenas, take up a hundred measures of wine for your friend's safety and burn the lamps all night till dawn. Let all anger and disruption be far away. (3.8.9–16)

The phrase *fumum bibere*, as the commentaries tell us, refers to a way of ageing wine in earthenware jars in the attic, near the chimney, where it was believed the smoke percolated through the porous clay and helped to mellow the wine. But in fact my translation, 'drink the smoked wine', is a bit tendentious. What the literal Latin says, almost incomprehensibly, is 'to drink smoke'. In the context of Horace's near-death experience, the literal rendering contains a haunting evocation of the funeral pyre.

Thus Horace's invitation to banish care with friendship and wine, not unlike what we have already seen in 1.9 and can be found in many other odes, is shadowed by the reality of our death. The symbol of our enjoyment, *fumum bibere*, is at the same time the recognition of its necessary negation, as the seemingly random contingency of the falling tree is viewed against the background of our inevitable demise, with the image becoming even more double-voiced in the seemingly innocuous temporal qualifier 'in the consulship of Tullus'. The Romans marked years with the names of the consuls, so on one level this is a simple date, a moment in time signifying that the wine is old, a rare and precious vintage. Tullus was consul in 66 BCE, the year before Horace was born (Quinn 1980: ad loc.; Garrison 1991: ad loc.). The choice of this vintage, as such, is anything but random; rather, it signifies the span of Horace's life plus one year, the exact amount of time that has passed since the near fatal fall, and thus also offers the hope of one more year before the moment Horace definitively will 'drink smoke'. Alternatively, that same Tullus' son was consul in 33 BCE, the year Horace received the Sabine farm from Maecenas (Nisbet and Rudd 2004: ad loc.). In fact, it could be either year; in the end, there is no need to choose which Tullus Horace means, as each adds an appropriate but different sort of resonance to the poem.

The irony of these stanzas is, then, at once subtle and stark, the signifiers pointing simultaneously in opposite directions. Nonetheless, this is not an example of sarcasm, but rather a subtle evocation of the way in which the poet's art converts the arbitrary and the meaningless (a tree falls on your head) into the overdetermined and the deeply felt. The opposition is not a negation. It is not the case that the poet *really* means either to drink finely aged wine or to inhale the smoke of the funeral pyre, but rather it is precisely the necessary fact of the latter that gives meaning to the former and that endows Horace's invitation to Maecenas with its emotional resonance. Maecenas truly is learned in both languages in the same way that the *Sabina diota* of 1.9 is in fact two-eared: Greek and Latin, life and death, inside and outside.

The final stanzas of 3.8 continue this double discourse as Horace proceeds to list a series of public dangers that Maecenas should not, at least for the moment, worry about: the Dacians, the Parthians, the Cantabrians and the Scythians (16–24). All of Rome's enemies have been defeated or have fallen into fighting among themselves. It is time to relax. *Nunc est bibendum.* And yet Rome from east to west is also here shown to be surrounded by dangers. All the things that Maecenas is admonished not to worry about constitute a list of precisely what he must worry about:

> Neglegens ne qua populus laboret
> parce privatus nimium cavere et
> dona praesentis cape laetus horae ac
> linque severa.

> Not caring whether the people are in difficulty, as a private citizen, do
> not be excessively cautious and happily seize the gifts of the present
> hour and leave behind serious matters.   (3.8.25–8)

The admonition not to care whether the *populus* is in difficulty can only
be double-voiced. Maecenas can only be a *privatus* for a brief moment, and
the admonition to be one contains the recognition that he is not. The gifts
of the present hour – wine, friendship, a moment without care – are only
possible and only meaningful because they are always haunted by respon-
sibility, struggle and death. In the end, we all drink smoke.

What matters is what we do with what is given to us. Poetry offers the
possibility to take the gifts of the present hour and the recognition of our
own mortality and to create possibilities of meaning that transcend the
narrow confines of the present, that transcend the pressing immediacy of
time, space and utility ('I have built a monument more lasting than bronze',
3.30.1). One of the most sublime examples of this claim to transcendent
creation, and yet one which is more modest than the grandiose claims that
cap the *Odes* in its final poem, can be found just before the halfway point in
Book 3, after the initial programmatic poems, the Roman Odes, the various
dedicatory poems and before the grand summation. *Odes* 3.13 is a poem
whose images and delicacy stay with the reader long after she puts aside her
volume of Horace and returns to the world of pressing things:

> O fons Bandusiae, splendidior vitro,
> dulci digne mero non sine floribus,
>   cras donaberis haedo
>   cui frons turgida cornibus
> primis et venerem et proelia destinat.
> frustra: nam gelidos inficiet tibi
>   rubro sanguine rivos
>   lascivi suboles gregis.

> O fountain of Bandusia, more sparkling than glass, worthy of sweet
> unmixed wine, not without flowers, tomorrow you will receive a kid,

whose brow swelling with his first horns destines him for love and
battles. In vain: for he will dye your icy banks with his red blood, the
child of the lascivious herd. (3.13.1–8)

The reader is asked to imagine a clear spring, a site of divinity in traditional
Roman religion, worthy to receive a sacrifice of wine and flowers (Quinn
1980: ad loc.). The Latin Camenae, analogues of the Greek Muses, were origi-
nally water nymphs, the divinities of springs, so this is almost by definition a
poetic location (Nisbet and Rudd 2004: 172–4). We see the wine swirling
into the cool clear waters and scattered flowers floating on the spring's glassy
surface. There is an implicit imagistic contrast between the wine and water,
which will soon become explicit with the warm blood of the kid about to
be swirled in where we imagined only wine and flowers before. The passion
and even the subtle eroticism of wine and flowers become explicit with the
description of the goat's swelling brow and the evocation of incipient sexual-
ity (*venerem*) and masculine aggression (*proelia*; Nisbet and Rudd 2004: ad
loc.). Love and war, wine/blood and water, hot and cold, youth and death
are all deftly evoked in a brief and delicate image that has its own sublimity
but is not easily susceptible to a final analysis.

Yet the spring, touched and even sanctified by the blood of the young
goat, remains a source of refreshment that resists even the most severe
summer heat, the withering rays of the Dog Star:

> Te flagrantis atrox hora Caniculae
> nescit tangere; tu frigus amabile
> fessis vomere tauris
> praebes et pecori vago.

> The angry season of the blazing Dog Star knows not how to touch you;
> you offer a beloved coolness to the bulls exhausted from the ploughshare
> and to the wandering herd. (3.13.9–12)

For readers who remember *Epodes* 3, the Dog Star (Canicula) in *Odes* 3.13
evokes images of both iambic heat and Canidia, only to banish them with

an evocation of lyric repose, but that repose has no saliency without the simultaneous strategic evocation of its opposite. The blazing of the Dog Star is balanced by the icy refreshment offered by the spring, just as the sparkling waters of the previous stanza gave rise to images of blood and wine.

Moreover, it is in that momentary, achieved balance that the poem's sublimity resides. For the corollary of irony's necessary duality is the possibility, however briefly envisioned, of pointing to a place beyond its oppositions, of pointing to a space of as yet unarticulated meaning that necessarily separates the *intellectum* from the *dictum*. It is the possibility of pointing simultaneously to the Dog Star and to the spring's beloved coolness, and indeed of Socrates pointing beyond any particular instance or action of the just man to the idea of justice itself. This is the space, if not of immortality per se, then, of beyond the merely mortal, of beyond the strictly time-bound as normally understood, of the soul on 'fleeing wing' that spurns 'the intercourse of the crowd and its humid soil':

> Fies nobilium tu quoque fontium,
> me dicente cavis impositam ilicem
> saxis, unde loquaces
> lymphae desiliunt tuae.

> You too will be made one of the famous springs, when I tell of the ilex
> planted in the hollow rocks whence your clear babbling waters leap.

> (3.13.13–16)

The poet's speaking immortalizes the spring as the images of its babbling waters become frozen in time – only to be given warmth with the return of sacrificial blood (this time our own), which, as in *Odyssey* 12, feeds the hungry ghosts of the underworld, giving them the power of speech. Poetic immortality, ironically, is always dependent on our death.

In the *Odes*, Horace reshapes lyric in his own image. On the one hand, as we showed in the opening of this chapter, he deliberately sets out to separate lyric from iambic and thereby separate his own *oeuvre* from that of Catullus, who had been the first lyric poet in Rome in both the ancient and the modern sense. Catullus had written poems in the traditional lyric metres established by the Alexandrian canon, and he had also written a collection of short poems 'of personal revelation, confession or complaint' that project 'the image of an individual highly self-reflexive consciousness' (Miller 1994: 1). But Catullus had not distinguished the lyric from the iambic elements in this collection with regard either to metre or to content; even some of the most famous love lyrics of the Catullan corpus contain a strongly invective element. One need only think of the final stanzas of poem 11, written in Sapphics, where the poet tells his companions Furius and Aurelius to convey to his beloved 'a few unkind words':

> Let her live and be well with her adulterers, whom she holds in her embrace three hundred at a time, loving none truly, but breaking the loins of them all again and again.
>
> Nor let her look back for my love, as before, which has fallen through her fault, just as a flower at the meadow's edge, after it is touched by the passing plough. (11.17–24)

Despite the aching lyric beauty of the final stanza, one can simply not find anything like the invective of the penultimate stanza in Horace's *Odes*. Canidia makes no appearances within their bounds. That is the province of *Epodes*, and to a lesser extent the *Satires*.

Nonetheless, the *Odes*, for all their classicizing tendencies, are anything but a straight reproduction of Greek lyric in Latin. They are a profoundly different sort of poetry from that produced by Alcaeus, Sappho, Pindar and Bacchylides. In the first instance, their content is deeply Roman, whether we are discussing the vision of Mount Soracte in 1.9, the civil wars which underlie the traditional reading of the ship of state in 1.14 and Metellus' chronicle in 2.1, the redefinition of *virtus* in 3.2, or Horace's tongue-in-cheek prayer that Maecenas shelve him with the other lyric poets in the temple of Apollo on the Palatine at the end of 1.1. Indeed, no collection like the *Odes* was ever produced by any of the Greek lyric poets. The Greek lyric poets did not write books; they sang their poems for defined audiences of communities of fellow citizens. The books of their poems that were shelved in the Palatine library were collected and edited by the same scholars in Alexandria who established the canonical list of nine lyric poets. The *Odes*, however, are a planned, written collection, with introductory and concluding poems for each individual book as well as for the collection as whole. They also contain repeated thematic motifs like the falling tree, and the thematic and metrical responsions that Knorr points to in his reading of 1.14 and which I have argued for in detail before (Miller 1994). These poems are also written in a more profound sense. They assume the possibility of rereading. Layers of meaning only become apparent when the reader returns to them again and again, when one stops and considers the multiple possible meanings of such seemingly simple phrases as *Sabina diota* or a slave named *Thaliarchus*. In this regard, Horace's classicizing *Odes* do owe much to the Catullan collection and to its various intersecting series of poems on his beloved Lesbia, on his companions Furius and Aurelius, as well as on Caesar and Pompey. These poems too play with metre, use clear responsions between groups of poems, and assume complex patterns of rereading. Horace's *Odes* are, as we have noted more than once, 'two-eared', both Greek and Roman, in a variety of ways.

Finally, as we have seen throughout this chapter, the presence of these competing frames of meaning, both within and between poems, produces a profoundly ironic discourse. These are poems that never quite mean what they say, but always mean something more and other. They point beyond themselves and their immediate literal meanings in deliberate and self-conscious ways that produce new possibilities of meaning whose immediate limit can never be fully established and recedes infinitely into the future.

The Roman Socrates is still very much with us. Thus a ship is never just a ship in a poem like 1.14 but also on one reading an allegory of the Roman state, and on another a present or potential erotic partner. Not only can these meanings never coincide with one another or even be fully reconciled with the direct literal meaning of the text, but they also gesture towards another possibility in which the erotic and the political rather than being two autonomous realms become able to be read in terms of one another. What is the desire that motivates our political life? What are the politics of erotic life? These are not only questions that contemporary life shows continue to be salient, they are also problems directly taken up in the Cleopatra Ode's evocation of debauched eunuchs, Octavian's pursuit of the Eastern queen who becomes a fleeing rabbit or dove, and Cleopatra's own final gender-bending transformation into a *fatale monstrum* who refuses to submit to Roman domination.

It is, as we have seen, these poems' capacity to resignify, to transform the arbitrary, the meaningless and the one-dimensional into the deliberate, the overdetermined and the complex that grounds their capacity to transcend the immediate context of their articulation. This is the foundation of Horace's claim in 3.30 to have created in these three books a monument more lasting than bronze. In doing so, he does not refer to the material existence of the papyri, nor to the physical contours of his collection, but precisely to that collection's continuing capacity to produce new meanings for new people in new contexts. He refers to the capacity of this given set of *dicta* to produce ever new sets of *intellecta*, in much the same fashion as the wine and flowers become the blood of the kid swirling into the icy-cold waters of the *fons Bandusiae*, creating a sublime image whose capacity for resignification validates the poet's claim to immortalize the spring. This immortality is achieved not through the spring's physical qualities or through their simple reproduction in verse. Instead, it is achieved through the *Odes'* capacity to take those qualities and endow them with ever new meaning, to swirl in the wine, flowers and blood that give the past's hungry ghosts the power to speak.

IV

FREEDOM, FRIENDSHIP AND THE TIES THAT BIND

SOCRATIC IRONY IN EPISTLES I

IN 20 BCE, Horace published his last major collection of poetry, the first book of the *Epistles*. Six years later, the second book of *Epistles* was published. It was not a planned collection, but a grouping of three long essays on poetry and criticism that appears to have been assembled after the fact, among them the *Ars Poetica*, which would go on to have a very substantial influence on the later history of poetry and criticism. In 13 BCE, a fourth book of *Odes* was published, but this is clearly a sequel to the great three-book original and represents an encore that reflects Horace's increased status as an official praise poet of the imperial family (Johnson 2007). *Epistles* 1, however, is a book of great originality and artistic finish. It is to our knowledge the first book of its kind, a planned collection of poetic epistles on philosophical themes, epistles whose composition was destined in large part if not *in toto* for publication as a unified work, not simply

collected after the fact (Kilpatrick 1986: xiv; Mayer 1994: 1–5, 10–11, 48; Ferri 2007: 122, 126–7). As we shall see, the collection is bracketed by two corresponding pairs of poems, 1.1 and 1.19 with 1.2 and 1.18, followed by a final envoi (1.20) that stands outside the structure of the collection as a whole. Within its bounds, in chatty and often informal verse that is nonetheless profoundly artistically structured, Horace returns again and again to what the duties of the friend, the poet and philosopher are, and how they relate to the concept of freedom and the obligations of daily life. Central to these concerns is *Epistles* 1.7, addressed to Maecenas.

The programme of *Epistles* 1 is laid out clearly in the opening:

> Maecenas, you who were spoken by my first Muse and who will be
> spoken by my last, even though I have already sufficiently been put to
> the test and given my wooden sword, you want to lock me up again
> inside the same old game. But I am not the age I once was, nor do I
> possess the same mind. (*Epistles* 1.1.1–4)

There is a tremendous amount happening in these opening lines. They invoke the poet's patron Maecenas. They announce the end of his lyric vocation and his turn to the more traditional philosophical topics of the true and the appropriate (Freudenburg 2002: 126). They bid farewell to the world of the *Odes* and announce a new undertaking that asks to be thought of as a form of retirement.

Maecenas may be the beginning and the end of Horace's poetic career, but the poet directly refuses the great man's request that he enter the poetic lists once more. This is not so much the typical *recusatio*, in which the poet playfully refuses to grant a request for promised verse, as it is a declaration of friendship and independence (Mayer 1994: 49). When Maecenas asks for epic verse from Propertius (2.1), the poet responds with a series of couplets in the high style that purport to explain the poet's inability to grant this request. When Horace in *Odes* 2.1 recalls his *procax Musa* to jokes, love and wine, it is only after he has described Pollio's histories and tragedies. Not so here, where the poet with his usual wit and charm nonetheless clearly refuses his friend and patron's request for a new instalment of the *Odes*, not claiming inability but fatigue and the desire to pursue new kinds of questions.

It is in fact the dialectic between freedom and the bonds of friendship (*amicitia*) that is at the centre of this collection of poems (Armstrong 1989: 119; Traina 2009: 303–4). *Amicitia* is a complex and much discussed term in Roman life and poetry. It often, though certainly not always, could be reduced to the bonds of clientage – that is to the obligations a lower-status individual might owe his higher status 'friend' and protector (McNeill 2001: 22; Bowditch 2001: 18–24; Cairns 2006: 36–8). Those bonds do not, however, exclude genuine affection. Likewise, friendship between equals of great distinction, such as Cicero describes in *De Amicitia*, while grounded in mutual respect and affection, does not exclude bonds of obligation that struc-ture and restrict the freedom and familiarity each owes the other (Kilpatrick 1986: xx; Armstrong 2010: 25). Indeed, as throughout Horace's work, it is the dialectic between external or contingent determinations – accidents of birth, class and circumstance – and internal character and cultivation, which is the most central occupation of the *Epistles*. And, as we have seen throughout the corpus, the frequent ambivalence and overdetermination of these relations can only be formulated and expressed by a multilevelled and self-conscious irony. What does Horace owe Maecenas? What does he owe his other friends? What does he owe those who serve him, and what does he owe himself? These are the bonds of obligation that consistently cross the *Epistles* and structure its investigations of such topics as how the wise man should live, what constitutes moral health and how we should define the term that was at the centre of the *Satires*, *libertas*, or 'freedom'.

More radically, the *Epistles* are concerned with the relationship between the possibility of self-determination and the necessary inscription of the indi-vidual into a social context of unequal power relations, a context in which the ability to be free, and hence truly be a friend in the fullest Ciceronian sense, is always threatened by the social constraints and conventions that make both freedom and friendship possible. For one is never simply free: one is always free somewhere, doing something, in relation to other people, who themselves exist in structured relations with one another. Hence the Stoic dictum that only the wise man is free is perhaps less of a paradox than it seems, even in a society of chattel slavery (McCarter 2015: 47). Likewise, friendship is never simply the recognition of a second self or the expression of spontaneous and unmediated affection or affinity. We are friends at work or in school. We are friends in relation to other friends, friends who occupy distinct social statuses. We are friends who share and sometimes betray financial interests, friends who share and sometimes betray erotic interests, friends who share and sometimes betray political and ethical commitments. But as these poems are only too aware, we are never just friends and we are never just free.

The *Epistles*, then, are self-consciously philosophical letters that return to the more discursive Socratic stance of the *Satires*. They often self-consciously refer to those earlier *sermones* or 'conversations', now without the fiction of the spoken word or the diatribe tradition, but firmly within the world of writing (Kilpatrick 1986: xv, 89–90; Braund 1992: 25; Johnson 1993: 3–4; Labate 2009: 120–1). Indeed, there is a deliberately retrospective quality to the *Epistles* that looks back on the poet's career and commitments and seeks to reframe and recontextualize them, not in order to draw a simple didactic lesson, but to force us to ask what is true, what we should care about, how do the truth and the objects of our concerns make us free, and to consider how we are always nonetheless constrained, often by the very bonds that make that reflection possible.

Before we go further in our investigation of *Epistles*, let us go back and look at these opening lines and see how the abstractions I have just now outlined are concretely enacted by the dense language of the opening of this last great book. The imagery of the first sentence is taken from the world of the gladiator:

> Prima dicte mihi, summa dicende Camena,
> spectatum satis et donatum iam rude quaeris,
> Maecenas, iterum antiquo me includere ludo.

> Maecenas, you who were spoken by my first Muse and who will be
> spoken by my last, even though I have already sufficiently been put to
> the test and given my wooden sword, you want to lock me up again
> inside the same old game. (1.1.1–3)

The wooden sword recalls the gift given to the successful gladiator upon his retirement. Horace has been fighting in the lists for Maecenas, and he has survived his various battles. Now it is time for him take his leave (Bowditch 2010: 68–9). Of course, the humour of comparing the effete world of the poet with the bloody work of the gladiator is evident, and the ambiguity of a word like *spectatum* is able to work on both sides of the comparison. I have translated it as 'put to the test', but the most basic meaning has got to be something like 'be the object of visual scrutiny', as in the English *in-spect*. Horace as the friend and the poet of the most powerful men in Rome has been put on display, and in that exposure he has been put to the test. That display we find out is like an arena itself, the object of a spectacle as surely as the gladiatorial *munera* ('gifts', but also 'duties') offered on the sand (*harena*) scattered in the Forum itself (Bowditch 2001: 2). The gladiator was not a free man, and the wooden sword signified not only his retirement but also his manumission. He is free no longer to be the object of the other's gaze, the other's judgement, the other's ability to constrain and even take his life. The loss of freedom is the submission to the possibility of death at the hands of the other, the loss of one's life, the reduction of the subject to the status of an object, a pure externality. Maecenas would be right both to smile at the drama of this comparison and also to feel slightly uncomfortable at the implication that his generosity had rendered Horace little better than a slave (Kilpatrick 1986: 101).

Both of these significations, in turn, find their full meaning in the final word of the opening sentence, *ludus*. As we saw in our reading of *Satires* 1.1, *ludus* is a word of multiple meanings. In that instance, we noted that it commonly referred to a primary school. *Ludus* also means simply fun and games. It is the opposite of *seria*, so as we noted there the juxtaposition *seria/ludo* offered a recapitulation of the Greek term *spoudaiogeloion* or 'serious laughter', which referred both to the satiric and the Socratic phenomenon of *ridentem dicere verum*, 'speaking the truth by or through laughing'. *Ludus* and its cognates were also favourite terms used by the neoteric poets, especially Catullus, for the act of writing poetry (Catullus 50.2; Grilli 1997: ad loc.; Fodyce 1961: ad loc.; cf. Virgil *Eclogues* 1.10), particularly in its iambic, lyric and elegiac forms, which were regarded, at least on the surface, as nothing serious, as *nugae*, 'trifles' (Catullus 1.4; Grilli 1997: ad loc.; cf. *Satires* 1.9.2, 2.1.73). The poetry designated by the semantic field of the terms *ludus*, *ludo -ere*, *lusus*, was the opposite of the 'real' world of business, law and the military (*negotium*) and of the generic world of tragedy and epic (Lyne 1980: 1; Habinek 2005: 111–12, 134, 142).

Nonetheless, in this passage from *Epistles* 1.1, while these other senses remain active, *ludus* has yet another meaning, one derived from that of 'school', which was always derivative from the fundamental meaning of 'fun and games', since school was the world of *otium* ('leisure') rather than *negotium*. But this is a very particular kind of school, a gladiatorial school or training facility, in which the participants were slaves and their pastimes could only with grim irony be termed 'fun and games'. It is this *ludus* from which Horace claims to have received the wooden sword of retirement. Only now, in a shift of registers, it is the *ludus* of light poetry that would appear to be the literal meaning rather than the figurative 'school' of the arts of death, although the tenuousness of any such distinction between the literal and the figurative in this context becomes increasingly clear.

In seeking to return Horace to the practice of light poetry, Maecenas is also returning him to the gaze, the judgement and the violence of the other: his fellow citizens, his fellow poets, his friend and protector, and ultimately the *princeps* himself. As the next sentence makes clear, he is seeking to return him to the arena from his rural retirement (presumably the Sabine farm), where he will once more be subject to the whims of his audience and need to plead for his life:

> Non eadem est aetas, non mens. Veianus armis
> Herculis ad postem fixis latet abditus agro,
> ne populum extrema totiens exoret harena.

> But I am not the age I once was, nor do I possess the same mind. The gladiator Veianus lays low having withdrawn to the country, his arms now fixed to the door of the temple of Hercules, lest he should beseech the people [for his life] at the end of the match again and again.

> (1.1.4–6)

Maecenas is subjecting Horace both to his own will and to the judgement of others. Of course this is all a joke, a mere figure, an example of the poet's over-the-top 'ludic' voice. And yet, as in the example from *Satires* 1.1, it is simultaneously completely serious, an instance of *spoudaiogeloion* (Moles 2009: 319).

In the next sentence, the metaphorical field shifts from the scene of the gladiatorial school to the pathos of an ageing racehorse with a distinctly Socratic twist:

> Est mihi purgatam crebro qui personet aurem
> 'solve senescentem mature sanus equum, ne
> peccet ad extremum ridendus et ilia ducat'.

> A voice often whispers in my well-cleansed ear, 'if you aren't crazy, kindly
> let the old horse go, so he doesn't make a fool of himself stumbling and
> wheezing to the end'.   (1.1.7–9)

The voice that whispers in Horace's ear recalls Socrates' *daimon*, the 'spirit' who in Plato warns the philosopher not to do something lest it put him in ethical peril (Mayer 1994: ad loc.; Préaux 1968: ad loc.; Plato, *Apology*: 31c4–32A3). This voice is in many ways the foundation of ethical thought, the internalized voice of the Other that admonishes us: the voice of conscience. If we recall the image from the end of *Satires* 1.4, where Horace describes himself putting into practice his father's past admonitions to look to others as exemplars of behaviours to be followed or to be shunned, we see the very image of the kind of internal ethical dialogue this voice represents:

> For I am not absent from myself, even when my writing couch or the
> shelter of a colonnade has received me. 'This is more proper; doing this
> I will have a better life; thus I will be a welcome sight to my friends; this
> indeed is not well done; would I ever foolishly do something similar to
> that?' I turn these things over with myself with my lips tightly sealed.
>   (1.4.133–8)

The internalized voice of the Other, whether imagined as the voice of god or of the remembered father, is both a form of self-presence and of self-doubling or alienation: the life of reflection is the opposite of unthinking spontaneity. It involves a separation from the self, the ability to take the self as an object of concern, but also a constant care for the self (Plato, *Apology* 29e–30b), a continued attention or self-presence. Freedom on this view is not simply doing what you want when you want: that is to be a slave to desire, the life of the tyrant in Plato's *Republic*. Freedom means exercising meaningful choice in the fullness of reflection: only the wise man is free (McLeod 2009: 266).

To hear the voice of the internalized other, however, requires the ability to listen, to have a well-cleansed ear (*purgatam* [...] *aurem*). The image is a common place for receptivity to advice (Mayer 1994: ad loc.; Lloyd-Jones 1990: 169), but it takes on a particularly philosophical colour in Persius, the Neronian and Stoic satirist who imitated Horace's *Satires* and *Epistles* (Hooley 1997; Reckford 2009b: 20). At the end of his first satire, shortly after claiming his place in the satiric lineage that leads from Lucilius to Horace (114–19), Persius writes that those who value the Old Comic poets whom Horace cites at the beginning of *Satires* 1.4 will get something a bit more boiled down (*decoctius*) from his work. He says that the reader with a well-steamed ear (*aure* [...] *vaporata*) should warm (*ferveat*) to him. While the imagery here is dense, Persius' philosophical satire is envisioned as having a cleansing function that leads the reader/auditor to pay heed to the voice of the other. The image of the *auris vaporata* owes not a little to Horace's *auris purgata*. The kinship becomes all the clearer when it is recognized that the image of the voice sounding (*personet*) in Horace's ear has a double lineage, on the one hand clearly descending from the Socratic *daimon*, on the other also deriving from the later Stoic philosopher Panaetius' theory of the *persona* as adopted by Roman thinkers such as Cicero. Specifically, this is the notion that one shapes a life or character (a *persona* in Latin is literally a mask) through the choices one makes and the roles one assumes within a given social nexus (age, gender, status, etc.). The Socratic *daimon* that 'sounds in' (*personet*) Horace's well-cleansed ear is an internalized voice of the Other that instructs the poet on how to adopt an appropriate role for his stage of life (Gill 1988: 175–8; Bowditch 2001: 167–8; Moles 2009:

316): to play the games (*ludi*) of children is unsuitable, he should retire from the race lest he be humiliated like a stallion past his prime.

Similarly in Persius 5, the satiric decoction that Persius in *Satires* 1 envisioned as steam-cleaning his reader's ear is described as a kind of Stoic vinegar that washes the ear and allows the reader to differentiate between two forms of *libertas*: the facile freedom to follow one's whims and the more substantive freedom to assume the responsibility of shaping a meaningful life. Again the Horatian subtext is critical to understanding the passage, and Persius 5 shines a light on how the image of the cleansed ear was received and understood a mere two generations later by a poet who claimed a direct affiliation to Horace and was writing in a cognate genre:

> Haec mera libertas, hoc nobis pillea donant.
> 'An quisquam est alius liber, nisi ducere vitam
> cui licet ut libuit? licet ut volo vivere: non sum
> liberior Bruto?' 'mendose colligis,' inquit
> *stoicus hic aurem mordaci lotus aceto*:
> 'hoc reliquum accipio, "licet" illud et "ut volo" tolle.'

> This is pure freedom. The freedman's cap gives us this. 'Or is anyone free of another unless he is permitted to live his life as he pleases. It is permitted to live as I please: am I not freer than Brutus [the founder of the Roman Republic]?' 'You put together a lot of nonsense,' *says the Stoic whose ear has been washed with biting vinegar*. 'I accept the rest just take away the "it is permitted" and "as I please".'

> (5.83–7; emphasis mine)

In this passage, the satirist's interlocutor initially defines freedom as no longer being subjected to the will of another, symbolized by the freedman's cap. This is *mera libertas*, 'pure freedom', a collocation also taken from the *Epistles*, which we will examine in 1.18. It also recalls *Satires* 1.4 in which there is much discussion of *libertas* and where satiric discourse is described as *sermo merus* ('pure speech', 'pure dialogue or conversation'). Freedom on the view of Persius' interlocutor is a lack of external compulsion, the ability to do what you want: sleep till noon, eat and drink as you wish, have as much sex as you desire. Freedom is the permission to follow your appetites, to be a slave to desire. The Stoic, whose ear has been cleansed with the strong vinegar of philosophical irony, however, steps in and raises his hand:

> Reason stands against and *prattles into the ear* that stands apart that it
> should not be permitted to do what anyone will do wrong by doing:
> the public law of men and nature contains that which is right.
>
> (5.96–9; emphasis mine)

Reason becomes the voice of the other, standing in for both the Socratic *daimon* and the homelier image of Horace's father and his satiric avatar, Lucilius. As Acron the scholiast glossed Horace's original line, *est mihi purgatam crebro qui personet aurem* ('there is a philosopher-teacher for me who sounds in my ear and makes it clean', Havthal 1966b: 356). To the ear that is prepared to listen, that has been properly purged, steamed, cleansed with vinegar, freedom is a complex dialectic between exemption from external compulsion – in the form of submission to another as a slave, a gladiator or a simple dependent – and a recognition of the demands of nature and civil life. Freedom becomes the opportunity to shape oneself, to assume a role that conforms to the demands of your condition (age, health, circumstances) and social station (gender, class, status): one that assumes its obligations. *Only* the wise man is free.

Returning to the text of *Epistles* 1.1, what precisely does this philosophical voice whisper into Horace's ear? That he should retire before he becomes a laughing stock (*ridendus*), like the racehorse that has been ridden too long and that is now panting and wheezing with the rider still on his back? That rider of course can be pictured as Maecenas, to whom the epistle is addressed, and so the question of freedom has both a strong philosophical pedigree and an immediate personal point. What are the obligations Horace owes his friend and patron, and when – if ever – do they come to an end? Moreover, if they have no end, in what sense can Horace consider himself a free man any more than his father was? Is the Sabine farm, which grants the poet his freedom from the hustle and bustle of Rome, in fact the emblem of his slavery (Bowditch 2001: 169)?

The only solution to the problem of freedom in this world of interlocking social obligations, of eternal exchanges of *officia* ('duties') and *beneficia* ('favours'), Horace says (Edwards 1993: 183; Bowditch 2001: 52), is to retire from the *ludus* in all its senses and get down to the serious business of philosophy:

> Nunc itaque et versus et cetera *ludicra* pono;
> quid verum atque decens, curo et rogo et omnis in hoc sum;
> condo et compono quae mox depromere possim.

> Now then I put away verses and other *games*, and instead I care for, and I ask, what is true, what is appropriate, and I am completely absorbed in this task: I put up and put together what I might be able soon to bring forth. (1.1.10–12; emphasis mine)

Of course, there is something profoundly *ludic* about this whole opening passage, and we should not take at face value the claim to put aside verse and *ludicra*, not least because the declaration is written in flawless hexameters. Moreover, there is something inherently comic and more than a little grotesque in the erstwhile lyric poet comparing himself first to an aged gladiator and then to a broken-down horse. Likewise, this is not the first time Horace has claimed not to be a poet. In *Satires* 1.4, a text we have already had cause to reference several times in this chapter, Horace makes a similar claim when he says that his *sermones* are no more to be considered poetry than the verses of New Comedy – although in both cases we should be careful not to take those claims at face value (Harrison 2009: 273). But now he will put aside all that is related to the *ludus* (the gladiatorial school, the grammar school, but also lyric play and childhood games; Moles 2009: 310) and (re)turn to the philosophical questions that have animated his work from the beginning (Johnson 1993: 56).

He will *care* and he will *ask* what is the true and what is the fitting, the proper, the decent (*decens*): what can we know and what should we do? For those who recall Plato's *Apology* of Socrates, there are no more basic philosophical activities than caring and questioning. Socrates defines his basic mission as the interrogation of his fellow citizens (28d10–30c1, 37e3–38b9). He stops them on the street and asks them what is it that they know and how they can show they know it (21b–23c1). His goal in every case is to demonstrate that their knowledge is far less than they assume and that because of their ignorance they are fundamentally mistaken in the things they should care for, mistaking their possessions for their being, their things for their soul (28d10–31c3, 39c1–d9). Socrates thus teaches a fundamental care of the self which requires an intensive self-awareness and that presumes an initial moment of self-alienation or aporia (the demonstration of the subject's ignorance and lack of self-knowledge) and a reorientation of the subject's gaze from the things of the world to the self, as a necessary propaedeutic for returning to the world with a new understanding of what is true and what should be done (*Alcibiades*, *Republic*, myth of the cave). Horace's claim that he is 'completely absorbed in this' (*omnis in hoc sum*) is a claim of philosophical self-presence (and hence self-alienation) that deliberately recalls his earlier claim from *Satires* 1.4, *neque* [...] *desum mihi* ('and I am not absent from myself'). The *decens* moreover, or *to prepon* in Greek, like the voice that *personet* in the poet's ear, also has a double lineage. It too was a recurring concern of Panaetius' moderate Stoicism as mediated through Cicero's *De Officiis*. Thus the passage continues the poem's mixing of Socratic elements with those drawn from more contemporary Roman philosophy (Johnson 1993: 38n.28).

The ironies of these opening lines of the *Epistles* abound. In hexameters, the poet announces that he will put aside ludic things, meaning both poetry and slavery, to take up matters philosophical. His choice of vocabulary is overdetermined at every turn by references to both his previous poetry and certain philosophical tropes; the declaration, therefore, that he is wholly absorbed in his new undertaking (which is simultaneously a reference to his previous undertakings) can only be accepted on the condition that it be understood that his current complete absorption must include a necessary lack of immediacy requisite both for the philosophical undertakings referenced and to the ironic overdetermination of meaning that every word demonstrates. In fact, the whole enterprise is described as a form of composition (*condo et compono*) preparatory to publication (*quae mox depromere possim*). If the verb *depromere* strikes a familiar chord in the reader, she has in fact seen it before: it is one of Horace's preferred verbs in the *Odes* for decanting and serving a favoured vintage, which in turn is often a metonym for poetry and its composition, whether in *Odes* 1.9.7–8, *deprome quadrimum Sabina, / o Thaliarche, merum diota* ('bring out the four-year-old vintage from the two-eared Sabine jar') or the Cleopatra Ode's *antehac nefas depromere Caecubum / cellis avitis* ('It would have been wrong before to bring forth the Caecuban from the ancestral cellars', *Odes* 1.31.5–6). Thus if Horace has put aside *versus* and *ludicra*, he has perhaps only done so in preparation to his bringing forth the new work we hold in our hands (cf. Bowditch 2001:178–9).

There are in these opening lines at least three interrelated claims: (1) a declaration of independence relative to the claims Maecenas can exercise over the poet, even as the poet declares his fealty to his long-time friend and patron by dedicating the new work to him; (2) a move away from lyric and towards a more explicitly philosophical and Socratic form of discourse; and (3) the announcement that the poet is bringing forth a new vintage, a new form and type of poetry, that will cause us to question the nature of poetry itself.

These claims of poetic and indeed philosophical originality look in two directions. First, they look towards the immediately following lines, in which Horace explicitly states that he is the adherent of no particular philosophical school:

> Ac ne forte roges quo me duce, quo lare tuter,
>
> nullius addictus iurare in verba magistri,
>
> quo me cumque rapit tempestas, deferor hospes.

> And don't ask me then by what leader, by whose household god I am protected, enslaved to swear by the words of no master, I am borne along as a guest, wherever the storm takes me. (1.1.13–15)

Looking in this first direction, Horace here asserts freedom of a different type, not that from a person or even a social condition, but from dogma, from the requirement to think a certain way about the world. If only the wise man is free, then only he is wise who has come to his own conclusions, who is not locked away (*includere*) in any school (*ludus*). He may not be a model of philosophical consistency, but he also is no retailer of pre-packaged cant.

Second, Horace's claims look to the history of poetry per se, for while the tradition of philosophical letters had been pioneered by Plato and Epicurus, while verse epistles had certainly been written before, and while the *Satires* share certain elements in common with *Epistles*, there had in fact never been a collection of verse epistles in the first person and on philosophical topics written before *Epistles* 1. Horace, here, is claiming literary originality and therefore freedom in yet another sense (Traina 2009: 303).

This topic returns in *Epistles* 1.19, another poem addressed to Maecenas and what is for all intents and purposes the final epistle of the book. The collection concludes with poem 1.20, but the latter makes no pretence to being a letter; it is instead an elaborate conceit addressed by the poet to the book itself. Imagined as a handsome young slave about to go to Rome for the first time, Horace's latest book is eager for the attentions his youthful good looks will attract but also naive about the dangers of being passed from hand to hand only eventually to be discarded or shipped to the provinces. The play on 'freedom' and its attendant dangers – the *liber* ('book') is now *liber* ('free'), but also a slave to its own and others' desires (1.20.1) – as well as the theme of the double-edged sword of fame are continued in this final poem, even as the reader assumes a wry smile about the ironic comparison of Horace's last book to a male prostitute (Kilpatrick 1986: 106; Macleod 2009: 202, 261). Poem 1.20, then, while in many ways an appropriate ending to the book, is not in fact the final epistle. That title goes to 1.19, which bookends 1.1's dedication to Maecenas and returns to many of the same themes. The collection is thus framed with two epistles addressed to the great man, providing a metapoetic gloss on its opening line: 'Maecenas, you who were spoken by my first Muse and who will be spoken by my last' (1.1.1–3).

Epistles 1.19 looks back over Horace's career, but it begins with questions of freedom and dependence, recontextualizing them within the literary problematic of originality versus imitation. Poem 1.19 also engages the perennial philosophical question of the accidental versus the essential. The opening lines recapitulate the proverbial dispute between poets who are drinkers of wine and those who are drinkers of water (Knox 1985). They ask: is it possible to be a poet and remain sober, or is drunkenness alone able to make one the next Homer? This same question – of what traits are accidental and what essential to a given genre or species of person or thing – is then reposed within a more traditionally philosophical context as: 'if I imitate your outward habits of dress and deportment, will I acquire your inner essence, will I acquire what makes you you?'

> Prisco si credis, Maecenas docte, Cratino,
> nullas placere diu nec vivere carmina possunt
> quae scribuntur aquae potoribus. ut male sanos
> adscripsit Liber Satyris Faunisque poetas,
> vina fere dulces oluerunt mane Camenae.
> laudibus arguitur vini vinosus Homerus;
> Ennius ipse pater numquam nisi potus ad arma
> prosiluit dicenda. 'forum putealque Libonis
> mandabo siccis, adimam cantare severis':
> hoc simul edixi, non cessavere poetae
> nocturno certare mero, putere diurno.
> quid si quis vultu torvo ferus et pede nudo
> exiguaeque togae simulet textore Catonem,
> virtutemne repraesentet moresque Catonis?

Learned Maecenas, if you believe ancient Cratinus, no song is able to please or to live long if written by a water drinker. Ever since Liber enrolled the poets, in their semi-sanity, in the ranks of the Satyrs and Fauns, the sweet Muses have totally smelled of wine from the crack of dawn.

> Homer shows himself a lover of wine through his praises of the
> grape. Father Ennius himself never leapt into the battles he was about
> to tell unless he was drunk.
>
> 'The Forum and the well-stone of Libo I will consign to the dry.
> I forbid the severe to sing.' As soon as I pronounced this edict, the
> poets never stopped vying in drink at night and never stopped stink-
> ing during the day.
>
> But if someone is fierce and has a wild face and a bare foot, and he
> imitates Cato in the cut of his narrow toga, does he also reproduce the
> virtue and habits of Cato?   (1.19.1–14)

The first line recalls the opening of *Satires* 1.4, 'The poets Eupolis and
Cratinus and Aristophanes': the reader who recognizes the intertext is
returned to the world of Old Comedy and satire that began the poet's career.
Poets here are slightly mad, and Liber – the Latin name for Bacchus – is
their sponsor, but also the sign of their freedom (McCarter 2015: 241–2).

The play on *Liber* and *libertas* is, of course, operative in *Satires* 1.4 as well.
There the poet insists that the satirist not be confused with the comic parasite
or *scurra* who, once he has drunk (*potus*), is liable to mock even his host,
significantly referred to there as the one 'who offers water' (*Satires* 1.4.88):

> condita cum verax aperit praecordia *Liber*
> hic tibi comis et urbanus *liberque* videtur.

> when truthful *Liber* opens the secrets of the heart, this one seems to
> you a good companion, elegant, and *free*.
>   (*Satires* 1.4.89–90; emphasis mine)

There, as in the later *Epistles,* the essential question is 'being' versus 'seem-
ing': is the rich man's comic companion really 'free', or does his drunken
ability to insult his host just make him seem to be? We will come back to
the problem of the *scurra* when we turn to *Epistles* 1.18.

The opening lines of 1.19 are overdetermined on the imagistic as well as
the thematic and intertextual levels. Plays on wine and water are ubiquitous

throughout them, representing a conflict (or perhaps more generously a dialectic) between inspiration and sobriety, seriousness and play, the ludic and the pursuit of traditional Roman *virtus*. All of these oppositions represent terms that have been central to the collection from its slightly absurd opening image of the poet as a retired 'gladiator of lyric', although many of these nuances are lost in translation. Thus in line 5, I have translated 'Camenae' as 'Muses', which is conventional, but, as Préaux observes (1968), the *Camenae* were originally Latin water sprites, and the humour of assimilating them to the Greek Muses by portraying them as soaked in wine is both part of the fun and fits into a larger pattern. Similarly, after assuring us that both Homer and Ennius had drunk deep before beginning their epic labours, the poet makes a pronouncement in the manner of a sober magistrate (*edixi*): 'The Forum and the well-stone of Libo I will consign to the dry. I will forbid the severe to sing.' The Forum as the legal and political heart of Rome was the central arena for duelling orators, not poets. In it there was a well-head (*puteal*), decorated in relief with lyres and laurels (symbols of Apollo in his role as god of poetry). It was the gathering place in the Forum for money changers and thirsty orators (Préaux 1968: ad loc.; Mayer 1994: ad loc.) and had been constructed (or reconstructed) by a certain Scribonius Libo (praetor 80 BCE), whose identically named kinsman in Horace's time was a former supporter of Pompey and the brother of Augustus' second wife, Scribonia. All of these are, of course, very sober people. But the passing resemblance between *Libo* and *Liber* in this context is hard to ignore, and the name likely means something along the lines of 'libation pourer' or 'maker of libations', a vinous-sounding office if ever there was one (Chase 1897: 111).

Still, the crux of the matter comes in the following lines, where we find that no sooner had Horace made his lapidary pronouncement consigning the sober and the dry to the *puteal Libonis* than all the poets in the city were drunk, fighting through the night and stinking of wine all the next day (*putere diurno*). The question Horace asks, however, is, 'did that make them inspired bards?' If the poets who seek to imitate Horace stink of wine in the morning, in the same ways as the Latin water sprites-turned-Muses, does that make them any more Liber, or *liber* (and remember Horace would have written without a distinction between upper and lower case), than Libo, the 'libation-bearing' founder of a well where thirsty orators and merchants were said to congregate? Does how you smell determine your degree of inspiration? The irony becomes all the richer when we recall that *liber* can mean not only 'free' but also 'book' (Freudenburg 2002: 137). If you imitate the outward manner of Horace and Homer, does that make you a poet? If you adopt the accidental and contingent qualities of the poet, does that make you one in your inner being, in your essence? Or does the distinction between water drinker and wine bibber, between *Liber* and *Libo*, point to something deeper, something more fundamental, which, while manifest through outward traits, is not identical to them?

> But if someone is fierce and has a wild face and a bare foot, and he imitates Cato in the cut of his narrow toga, does he also reproduce the virtue and habits of Cato?

Scholars are unsure to which Cato Horace is here referring. Cato the Elder (234–149 BCE) was popularly considered the image of stern, traditional Roman virtue, untouched by the refinements of the Greeks. He eschewed the lavish flowing togas of his Hellenizing rivals, the Scipios. Likewise, his great-grandson, the Stoic Cato the Younger, became a martyr and emblem for Republican *libertas*, committing suicide rather than submit to Julius Caesar. Like his great-grandfather, Cato the Younger was known for his rectitude and his personal abstemiousness (including going barefoot). To illustrate his larger point, then, Horace poses the question: if the would-be philosopher adopts the same outward fashion as the famous Catos, does he therefore accrue their inner virtue any more than the would-be poet would achieve a truly liberating inspiration by drinking himself silly? If we imitate the outward manner, do we achieve the inner essence?

While Horace's exemplum is intelligible on its own terms, there is, unsurprisingly, a Socratic subtext as well: barefoot imitators of philosophers, it turns out, are nothing new. For readers who recall the beginning of the *Symposium*, we meet there a certain Apollodorus. He has devoted the last three years to knowing everything Socrates does (172c). Nonetheless, this does not appear to have made him wise. Indeed, his unnamed companion, who initiates the dialogue by asking Apollodorus to repeat the speeches given in praise of Love during a party held at Agathon's house, calls him a 'madman' (173d). Those same speeches, we find out, were recounted to Apollodorus by another admirer of Socrates, Aristodemus, who tries to follow Socrates in every way, down to going barefoot (173b). Yet, despite their attempts to imitate Socrates, neither the mad Apollodorus nor the unshod Aristodemus have taken the appropriate lesson – and it is perhaps not insignificant that on the occasion of Agathon's party Socrates has chosen to wear sandals (174a). Wisdom and virtue, just like poetic inspiration, are not 'things', at least not in the normal sense of 'objects' that can be possessed and given to another in the way one might give a watch or a pair of sandals. The acquisition of wisdom and virtue requires an inner transformation that goes beyond adopting the outward attitudes or fashions of a Cato or a Socrates. It implies a concentrated care of the self that the philosopher Michel Foucault terms 'a spiritual practice': a set of 'practices, purifications, renouncements, and modifications of existence' (Foucault 2009: 17–18). As Socrates says to Agathon, when the poet asks him to share his couch so he may benefit from the philosopher's wisdom (175c):

> It would be great if wisdom were the kind of thing that flowed from he who was fuller into he who was emptier – should we happen to touch one another – just as water flows from the fuller cup to the emptier if you stretch a piece of wool between them (175d).

But wisdom, as Plato makes clear here and in the *Seventh Letter*, is not a 'thing' or a 'substance', something that can be transferred from one person to another like any other object, whether by sharing a couch or adopting a mode of dress. You can imitate Socrates in every way, but that does not mean you possess his wisdom. Likewise, simply because you wear a plain toga, go barefoot and present a fierce countenance, it does not mean you possess the virtue of Cato, any more than drinking lots of wine makes you a poet.

Horace draws the poetic moral a few lines later:

> decipit exemplar vitiis imitabile; quodsi
> pallerem casu, biberent exsangue cuminum.

> The exemplar, imitable in its vices, deceives us; but if by chance I should
> turn pale, they would all drink bloodless cumin.   (1.19.17–18)

The binary opposition of the accidental versus the essential, which began the poem as the wine bibber versus the water drinker, is here analogized to that of the imitative versus the original. The imitator can only emulate that which is inessential and hence directly transferable, whether in the model's fashion of dress, manner of speech, or habits of drink, but in themselves these easily transferable traits make us neither wise, nor virtuous, nor poetically inspired. It is the acquisition of traits that are both harder to acquire and more difficult to define which is in question: *Libo* and *Liber* may share more than just three letters, but it is neither by drinking water nor wine that one becomes free.

The relation between these philosophical questions and literary practice is in turn taken up in the following lines, addressed to those who have sought to imitate Horace:

> O imitatores, servum pecus, ut mihi saepe
> bilem, saepe iocum vestri movere tumultus.

> Oh servile herd of imitators! How often have your disturbances and
> lack of restraint moved me to anger! How often to mirth!
> (1.19.19–20)

Yet even here appearances are deceiving and each seemingly simple statement is undermined by its own ironic counterstatement. Liber and Libo are indeed closer than one might think, just as the lovely Latin water sprites are transformed into the wine-soaked Muses. Indeed, the poet who at the end of the *Odes* had claimed to have erected a monument 'more lasting than bronze and higher than the pyramids', in the form of a collection of lyric poems which, based on a refined study of ancient precedent, had more clearly distinguished between the lyric and iambic modes than had his predecessor, Catullus, could hardly disparage imitation per se. Moreover, it is on the basis of this distinction that Horace will claim in the following lines to have been both the first to have written iambics in the manner of Archilochus and the first to have written lyric in the manner of Sappho and Alcaeus. His imitation of his models was at once more faithful and systematic than any of his predecessors (hence he was the first) and strikingly original (there was no precedent for the way he followed his models).

For Horace, and indeed for all ancient poetry, there was no simple binary opposition between originality and imitation: the very possibility of poetry X depended on tradition and precedent. The Muses in Hesiod are the daughters of Memory, not romantic inspiration, and the whole notion of free verse would have been a non sequitur in the ancient world. Horace asked Maecenas to shelve (*inseres*) him with the nine lyric poets of the Alexandrian canon, and he based that request on the Muse Polyhymnia's offer of the 'Lesbian [...] lyre' (*Odes* 1.1.34), signifying mastery of lyric poetry in the manner of Alcaeus and Sappho. He could do all this and still claim not to be a servile imitator in the manner of those he ridiculed in this poem. Indeed, the very predicate of ancient poetic achievement, in almost every case (with the notable exception of Lucilius, who nonetheless appears to have cited Old Comedy and Archilochus for precedent and to have read Callimachus), is a direct reference to the tradition in which that achievement is to be understood. The *Epistles* themselves, while on one level unprecedented, on another build upon the tradition of the philosophical letter from the time of Plato and Epicurus, previous poetic missives, including examples from Catullus, as well as the publication of Cicero's correspondence.

The full ironic complexity of the Horatian claim to originality, and to separating himself both from the herd of servile imitators and the insufficiently rigorous Catullus is made clear in the immediately following lines from *Epistles* 1.19:

> Libera per vacuum posui vestigia princeps,
> non aliena meo pressi pede. qui sibi fidet
> dux reget examen. Parios ego primus iambos

ostendi Latio, numeros animosque secutus
Achilochi, non res et agentia Lycamben.

ac ne me foliis ideo brevioribus ornes
quod timui mutare modos et carminis artem,
temperat Achilochi Musam pede mascula Sappho
temperat Alcaeus, sed rebus et ordine dispar,
nec socerum quaerit quem versibus oblinat atris,
nec sponsae laqueum famoso carmine nectit.
hunc ego, non alio dictum prius ore, Latinus
vulgavi fidicen.

I am the first person to have placed free tracks through the emptiness,
tracks pressed by no other except by my own foot. The leader who has
faith in himself rules the swarm.

I first displayed Parian iambics in Latium, following the numbers
and spirit of Archilochus, not the subject matter and not the words
that drove out Lycambes.

And lest on this account you honour me with a smaller laurel
crown, because I feared to change the metres and the craft of song,
masculine Sappho tempered her Muse with the foot of Archilochus
[or 'tempered the Muse of Archilochus with her foot/metre'], Alcaeus
tempered his Muse with the foot of Archilochus [or 'tempered the Muse
of Archilochus with his foot/metre'].

But he is dissimilar in subject matter and arrangement: he neither
goes after the father-in-law, whom he besmirches with black verses, nor
does he tie a noose for his betrothed with defamatory song. I am the
Latin who made this lyrist well known, a poet spoken by no previous
mouth.   (1.19.21–33)

This is anything but a straightforward set of claims. In what sense precisely
were Horace's *vestigia libera*? Is it simply because Horace was stepping into
an empty place, a space like Plato's *chora* in the *Timaeus* that would faithfully
receive every impress because it has no characteristics of its own (*Timaeus*
50e)? Yet, in fact, this field was already rather crowded, no matter how one

cared to conceive of it. In claiming to have been the first to have brought Parian – which is to say Archilochian – iambics into Latium, the empty space in which Horace is said to have left free traces is significantly hemmed in. Not only did Archilochus' iambic poems have immediate successors in the works of Hipponax and Semonides, as well as more distant ones in the *Iambi* of Callimachus, but also, as we have seen, Catullus wrote poems in iambic metre while also deliberately and self-consciously producing poems of iambic content in other metres (see Chapter 2). Likewise, we know that Lucilius read Archilochus and that Horace in the *Satires* cites Archilochus as an inspiration for his own satiric work. What Horace did in the *Epodes*, however, was to purify the metrical practice of his predecessors while claiming to have captured the spirit of Archilochus and to have avoided the problematic portions of his content (Traina 2009: 303; Bather and Stocks 2016: 5): the hounding violence that drove its victims to suicide.

It is a very crowded *vacuum* into which Horace has stepped, and his *vestigia* can only be thought of as *libera* in a limited sense. Indeed, Horace's poetic *libertas* is a product of adhering to certain constraints. We never inscribe a truly blank slate; the condition of inscribing traces or tracks for others to follow is that they be recognized both as tracks and as ours, that they form part of a tradition in which their intelligibility is recognizable and imitable. The condition of our freedom is its determination within certain limits and hence its iterability. If there were no Archilochus and no history of iambic successors there would no *vacuum*, no defined empty space, in which Horace's *libera vestigia* could be inscribed. The condition of our originality is our ability to follow our predecessors, to imitate them in new and unexpected ways. We are far from the virginal space of Plato's *chora*.

In many ways, the problem with Catullus, from a Horatian point of view, is that he shows insufficient fidelity to those he imitates. He is entirely too free and therefore all the more servile, all the more superficial. Indeed, Horace goes well beyond the metrical practice of Archilochus by limiting himself to epodic metres. Archilochus, as Horace acknowledges in the immediately following lines, produced poetry in lyric, elegiac, and iambic metres, and did not limit himself to the epodic (Morrison 2016: 33). Thus Horace can claim to be the first to have brought forth 'Parian iambics' in

Latium only on the condition that we accept his restrictive understanding of what those 'iambics' mean, and only on the condition that we accept his betrayal of Archilochus' actual practice (and that of all subsequent iambists) as a truer or greater fidelity, that we accept his rigorous distinction between the accidental and the essential in his model, and that we accept that this distinction in fact constitutes his freedom and originality. One of the more amazing facts of literary history and one of the more singular testaments to the power of Horace's vision and astonishing originality is that we have in fact largely accepted these claims as fact for the past 2,000 years with very little equivocation, and indeed, I would contend, with a good deal less than Horace himself demanded or expected.

This passage, however, is not just about iambic but also about lyric. It looks back not just to the *Epodes* but also to the *Odes*. We slide almost imperceptibly from Archilochus to Sappho and Alcaeus. Horace argues that his glory should not be less because he did not seek 'to change the metres and the craft of song'. In short, he should not be taxed with being overly servile in his imitation, presumably of Archilochus, but the Latin does not specify; this could also be a more general observation on Horace's deep commitment to the tradition. And indeed, he cites as precedent Sappho's and Alcaeus' use of metres that Archilochus was thought to have pioneered. The argument is thus on a certain level: 'I am unlike the herd of servile imitators I have been criticizing because in my approach to Archilochus I follow strictly the precedent of Sappho and Alcaeus, who were my primary objects of imitation in the *Odes* after the *Epodes*.' But what exactly was the nature of that precedent? The Latin is capable of two polar readings, both of which I have included in my translation above. Either Sappho and Alcaeus tempered their respective Muses with the 'foot' or 'metre' of Archilochus (but we should also recall Horace's 'foot' pressed into the 'vacuum' and Cato's 'bare foot' as well), which is the reading preferred by Mayer, or they tempered the Muse of Archilochus with their own 'feet'. Either they regulated their sources of inspiration by bringing to them the metrical practices of Archilochus, in which case they followed precedent, or they regulated the harsh invective of Archilochus by bringing to it the lyric metres with whom their respective names are associated, in which case they altered precedent through their own original understanding. As Mayer observes, while the second reading possesses the more natural word order (1994: ad loc.), and hence would probably be the first to come to the reader's mind (Fraenkel 1957: 341–6; Préaux 1968: 209; Morrison 2016: 36–7), the first seems more logically consistent with the claim not to change the metres of iambic song.

Yet, as we have just seen, Horace in fact does temper Archilochus' metres, reducing them to the epodic couplet and putting that forth as the essence of Parian iambic. At the same time, he also explicitly moderates Archilochus' harsh content. Moreover, in the *Odes*, Horace will strictly avoid both epodic couplets and the Catullan hendecasyllabic, creating clearer formal and generic distinctions between lyric and iambic than existed in either the practice of his archaic models – Sappho and Alcaeus use metres found in Archilochus (Clay 2010; Davis 2010) – or his Roman predecessors. Horace is both truer to his models than they were to themselves and strikingly original.

It is in this context, then, that he can make the claim in *Epistles* 1.19.33, 'I am the Latin who made this lyrist (*fidicen*) well known.' In the first instance, this statement refers to Alcaeus, but at the same time puns on his earlier claim that 'The leader who has faith in himself (*se fidet*) rules the swarm' (1.19.22–3). This play on the two senses of *fides* ('faith' and 'lyre') is something we saw in *Epodes* 17 as Horace looked to the *Odes*. Nonetheless, in *Epistles* 1.19's play on *fidicen* and *se fidet*, the emphasis is less on the formal qualities of the verse than on the poet's self-presence, his faith in himself: a theme we have traced throughout Horace's work and one that resonates with the Socratic mandate that knowledge begins with self-knowledge.

In the end, the issue addressed in *Epistles* 1.19 is not which aspect of Archilochus to imitate nor how to distinguish lyric from iambic, but whether the poet's clear-eyed self-awareness allows him to fashion an authentic work that is neither a slavish copying of the external and the accidental nor an unrepeatable journey into the vacuum. Irony in its inherent doubleness is always the recognition that we are most self-present and most authentic when we find ourselves reflected in others, even when – especially when – we hold them and ourselves up to criticism. As we noted in our reading of *Epistles* 1.1, the life of reflection is the opposite of unthinking spontaneity. It requires a separation from the self, the ability to take the self as an object of knowledge, but also a continued attention or self-presence. Freedom, in this light, is not simply doing what you want. Freedom means exercising choice in the fullness of reflection: only the wise man is free (Foucault 2009: 58). Having faith in yourself means knowing yourself as reflected in others. Nonetheless, as poem 1.19 pursues the implications of the distinction between the accidental and the essential while also problematizing the same in terms of poetry and imitation, *Epistles* 1.18 examines these same problems in terms of the more properly philosophical questions of what is freedom and what is virtue, but poses those questions specifically with regard to the relationship between a young man and his social sponsor, a 'friend' or 'patron' (Oliensis 1998: 171). Like 1.19, it is paired with a poem at the beginning of the collection, 1.2. Together these four poems bracket and define the basic issues of the collection (Kilpatrick 1986: 18). *Epistles* 1.18, while one of the longer poems in the corpus (112 lines), articulates its essential themes in its opening lines:

> Si bene te novi, metues, liberrime Lolli,
> scurrantis speciem praebere, professus amicum
> ut matrona meretrici dispar erit atque
> discolor, infido scurrae distabit amicus.
> est huic diversum vitio vitium prope maius,
> asperitas agrestis et inconcinna gravisque,
> quae se commendat tonsa cute, dentibus atris,
> dum vult libertas dici mera veraque virtus.
> virtus est medium vitiorum et utrimque reductum.
> alter in obsequium plus aequo pronus et imi
> derisor lecti sic nutum divitis horret,
> sic iterat voces et verba cadentia tollit,
> ut puerum saevo credas dictata magistro
> reddere vel partis mimum tractare secundas.
> alter rixatur de lana saepe caprina,
> propugnat nugis armatus: 'scilicet, ut non
> sit mihi prima fides, et vere quod placet ut non
> acriter elatrem! pretium aetas altera sordet.'

If I know you well, free-spoken Lollius, you want to avoid giving the
appearance of being a great man's comic hanger-on, when you have
claimed to be a friend. As different and disparate as the respectable wife
is from the courtesan so will the friend be from the faithless jester. The
opposite vice is almost even greater: rustic, inelegant, plodding harshness,
advertising itself with close-cropped hair and black teeth, it wishes to be
called undiluted freedom and true virtue. Virtue though is a midpoint
between vices and pulls back from both. The one tips over into excessive
obsequiousness and is the mocker of the host's couch, he shivers so at the
nod of his rich friend, repeating his sayings and gathering up the words
that fall from his lips, so that you would think him a boy repeating the
dictations of a cruel master or a mime performing the second part. The
other causes a row about goat wool. Taking up arms, he fights about
trifles. 'Truly, how could I not be immediately believed? And indeed,
how could I not bark sharply at whatever I please? Another lifetime
would be a trifling reward.'   (1.18.1–18)

Lollius, it seems, is a satirist. The first thing that is emphasized is his
libertas: the vocative *liberrime* recalls the phrase *liberrima indignatio* in
Epodes 4 (10), which we discussed in Chapter 2. *Mera libertas* in line 8 is
a phrase we have already seen referenced in Persius 5, where we know the
poet is composing with his copy of the *Epistles* in hand. And in *Satires* 1.4,
one of the continuing reference points for the *Epistles* and its discussion
of *libertas*, Horace describes his style not as poetic but as *sermo merus*,
'pure conversation'. In the same poem, as we saw above, he contrasts his
behaviour as a satirist with that of the rich man's *scurra*, or comic parasite.
Lollius runs the same risk of being labelled a comic hanger-on. Yet if the
black tooth of invective is to be avoided, so is the easy compliance of the
courtesan. Freedom, like virtue, is a midpoint between extremes. It is
neither the ability to say the first thing that pops into your head, nor is
it servile repetition, the abdication of the subject's right to speak in his
own name, whether the words be of one's patron (*amicus*) or his teacher
(*magister*; cf. 1.1.14; Moles 1985: 36; Kilpatrick 1986: 50–1; Johnson
1993: 96–7).

Yet in fact servile complaisance to the words of the master, the poet's *dives amicus* (1.18.24), is exactly what Horace advocates for Lollius, if he wants to be successful. While Mayer's commentary (1994) reads these instructions very literally, taken in the wider context of both the *Epistles* and the body of Horace's work it is difficult not to see them as ironic, indeed as a thinly veiled satire of Lollius' eagerness to please in return for material reward. On the level of the 'said', of the *dictum*, Horace appears to advocate that Lollius completely submerge his identity beneath the prospect of a fine dinner:

> Neither will you praise your pursuits or blame those of others, nor when he wishes to hunt will you compose your poems.
>
> Thus the goodwill between the twin brothers Amphion and Zethus was torn asunder when the lyre, which had been mistrusted by the severe brother, fell silent. Amphion is considered to have yielded to his brother's way of life.
>
> You, yield to the gentle commands of your powerful friend, when-ever he will lead out into the fields draft horses weighed down with Aetolian nets and dogs, get up and put to one side the peevishness of the unsociable Muse, so that you too may dine on the sauces bought with your labours. (1.18.39–48)

There are a number of indices that this passage is not to be taken at face value. The emphasis on submerging the poet's identity in favour of the 'rich friend's' amusements recalls nothing so much as Tiresias' advice on legacy hunting to Ulysses in *Satires* 2.5 and Tibullus 1.4, where Priapus advises the pederastic lover that if his darling wants to go hunting he should shoulder the nets himself (1.4.49–50; Labate 1984: 203–4). If Priapus gives advice on how to behave as the *servus amoris* ('slave of love'), Horace gives advice on how to be *servus divis amici* ('slave of the wealthy friend'). In both cases, 'slavery' is proposed as a means to an end. It is perhaps no accident that in elegy the adversary of the poet is invariably the *dives amator*, whose wealth proves a more powerful lure to the beloved than the servile poet's poetry or his self-abasement.

In *Satires* 2.6, the poem immediately following Horace's send-up of legacy hunters, the poet makes it clear that while it can be bothersome to be known as a 'friend' of the great man, Maecenas, since everyone assumes the poet therefore has knowledge and influence that he does not, the benefit of that relationship accrues not from his ability to eat fancy sauces and relishes (*pulmenta, Epistles* 1.18.48) but from his possession of the Sabine farm, an oasis from the distractions of the city and a guarantor of his freedom. The farm is a place of calm where the poet can spend time with his books (2.6.60–2), eat simple fare (2.6.63–4) and discuss with his neighbours and household slaves perennial philosophical questions such as whether 'virtue or wealth makes men happy', whether 'habit or good behaviour leads us to friendship', or 'what is the nature of the good', and 'what is its highest form' (2.6.74–6). This is a long way from the image in *Epistles* 1.18 of a poet putting away his vocation to join the amusements of his wealthy patron so he can sup with great men. Indeed, 2.6 ends with the tale of the City Mouse and the Country Mouse, which recounts the dangers of seeking the dainties of urban sophisticates when simple country fare will do. Likewise, the obsessions of various gourmets are ridiculed throughout Book 2 of the *Satires*.

It is hard therefore to believe that Lollius, a fellow poet and presumably a satirist, could read Horace advising him to put aside his poems and go hunting with his wealthy friend so he can enjoy the sauces 'bought with his labours' as anything but ironic. There could not be a greater contrast with the image portrayed in *Satires* 1.6 of Horace, the son of a freedman, being introduced to Maecenas. There, we are told, Horace will win his place in the great man's circle not owing to his social standing nor his willingness to abase himself but to the recommendation of Virgil and Varius and a brief interview in which the poet says who he is (*Satires* 1.6.60). If Lollius had truly asked Horace for his advice and had taken what he received in this section of *Epistles* 1.18 literally, he would have been neither a very good poet nor a very good reader of Horace (Johnson 1993: 68–9).

Moreover, not only is the advice given at variance with what the poet advocates in his own satiric practice, it is also directly ironized by its prominent position within the *Epistles*. It should be recalled that the collection opens with Horace's refusal of Maecenas' request, whether literal or imaginary, that the poet return to lyric. This good-humoured but direct declaration of independence on the part of the poet is framed by 1.19's address to Maecenas on the nature of poetic originality, its relation to imitation, and the larger problematics of freedom versus servility and of the accidental versus the essential. In neither case are we presented with the image of the poet submerging his identity in relation to that of his *amicus* in the interest of immediate personal gain. Indeed, the entire problematic of the *Epistles* with its focus on questions of *libertas* and *amicitia* seems designed to call such behaviour into question. *Epistles* 1.18, moreover, is framed by poem 1.2, also addressed to Lollius, which specifically concerns the role of the poet and poetry. Likewise, *Epistles* 1.7 presents one of the most famous, seemingly frank and yet elusive discussions of the poet's complex relation with Maecenas found anywhere in the corpus, to which we shall turn at the end of this chapter. While there is much to debate about the exact nature and tone of this poem, no one would argue that it is a blueprint for toadyism or obsequiousness in service to the poet's stomach.

Indeed, from the perspective of the collection as a whole *Epistles* 1.2 can be read as both preparing for 1.18 and as its ironic gloss. It begins with the argument that poetry is a superior source for moral instruction to traditional philosophy, claiming that Homer better teaches us what is the 'fine' and what is the 'useful' than Chrysippus, the Stoic logician, or Crantor, the Academic philosopher (1.2.1–4). It continues with the question of what the nature of wisdom is and how it can be cultivated, and ends with the relation of the poet to his social superiors (Mayer 1986: 67). Its argument for the superiority of poetry to philosophy puts it in seeming contradiction with 1.1, which commences with Horace's announcement to Maecenas that he is putting aside poetic *ludicra* to focus on the philosophical questions of 'the true' and 'the proper' and ends with the ringing declaration that only the wise man is 'rich, free, honoured, handsome and, finally, king of kings; but especially healthy'. Of course, this pronouncement is immediately followed by an ironic deflation, 'except when he has a cold' (1.1.106–8; cf. Gold 1987: 126).

After this opening assertion that poetry is a better source for learning philosophy than syllogisms, *Epistles* 1.2 continues with a recounting of the *Iliad* and the *Odyssey* and the moral lessons to be gleaned from them. It then turns to the specific case of Lollius. Here study and the pursuit of wisdom are urged on the dissipated and youthful poet as key elements to his emotional and spiritual health, even if, as the previous poem observes, they will not prevent him from catching cold:

> Thieves rise in the night so that they can throttle a man, will you not bestir yourself so that you may be saved? But if you don't when healthy, you will when swollen with the dropsy.
>
> And even if you don't send for your book and the lamp before dawn, if you do not apply your soul to honest studies and pursuits, you will be awake through the night tortured by envy and desire.
>
> For why do you hurry to remove things that harm the eye, but if anything gnaws at your soul, you put off for a year caring for it? He who begins has done half the deed: dare to be wise! Start! (1.2.31–41)

The lesson here hardly reinforces 1.18's ironic instructions that the poet should put away his studies and join his powerful friend hunting so he can have a fine dinner later.

Indeed, Persius will take up this very passage in his third satire and make clear its implications by extending the basic conceit over the entire length of the poem (Kilpatrick 1986: 27–8). In Persius 3, the dissipated young man is the poet himself, who receives a severe address from his friend and philosophical advisor. The young man is told he needs to study, to care for his soul, and to stop sleeping his life away after drinking bouts at table the night before. The satire ends with the story of a man swollen and pale, recalling Horace's image of Lollius with the dropsy. In Persius' version, the patient continues his lavish lifestyle, dining with his rich friend and drinking in the baths until he is struck down with a seizure. As his teeth chatter and hands shake, the night's 'elaborate sauces' are expelled from his lips in his death throes (*uncta cadunt laxis tunc pulmentaria labris*) – recalling those same *pulmenta* that Lollius' labours had 'bought' in 1.18. Freedom, then, is both the necessary condition for the exercise of virtue and wisdom, and it is something one achieves through study and discipline (Mayer 1994: 45).

Subjecting oneself to one's most basic and immediate desires ultimately leads only to a grotesque demise.

Epistles 1.2, thus, returns us to the Socratic argument on the necessity of caring for the self and the importance of distinguishing the self from its possessions. The tyrant can have whatever he wants, but desire and fear go hand in hand in an endless cycle of anxiety and agitation. In consequence, the man who has no external bonds and has developed no internal shape or limitations, who seems the freest of men, is in fact a slave to his own endless obsessions:

> Non animo curas. valeat possessor oportet,
> si comportatis rebus bene cogitat uti.
> qui cupit aut metuit, iuvat illum sic domus et res
> ut lippum pictae tabulae, fomenta podagrum,
> auriculas citharae collecta sorde dolentis.
> sincerum est nisi vas, quodcumque infundi acescit.
> sperne voluptates: nocet empta dolore voluptas.
> semper avarus eget. certum voto pete finem.

You do not care for your soul. The person who possesses things needs to be healthy, if he intends to use the things he has amassed.

A house and fortune aid the man who desires or fears in the same way paintings do the man with conjunctivitis, poultices the man with gout, and harps ears painfully clogged with filth.

Unless the vessel is pure, whatever you pour in sours.

Remove pleasures: pleasure bought with pain harms. The greedy man is always in need. Seek a clear end to what you desire. ⅄

(1.2.49–56)

The vessel must be purified if what is poured in will not sour. The soul must be cared for and prepared. If the ear is not steamed or cleaned with vinegar, it will not be able to hear. Wisdom is not mere information. It is not a thing that can be transferred from one person to the next, as in the image from Plato's *Symposium* cited before. In this context, the divergence between what is said (*dictum*) and what is understood (*intellectum*) by poem 1.18's admonitions to Lollius only increases.

Together *Epistles* 1.2 and 1.18 constitute an ironic diptych that demonstrates the actuality of Horace's claim that poetry, as opposed to arid argument, offers the best and clearest way to achieve the discipline that wisdom demands through offering lessons on the 'fine' (*pulchrum*) and the 'useful' (*utile*). It should be remembered that Aristotle himself famously argued that poetry is more philosophical and more serious (*spoudaioteron*) than history, because poetry traffics in the universal, concerning itself not with what *has* happened but with what *could* happen (*Poetics* 1451b). In some ways, it is precisely poetry's power to produce enjoyment that makes it the superior medium for not only communicating but actually enacting the universal within the concrete particular: the individual story, image or striking formulation.

Horace's praise of poetry as a philosophic exercise in *Epistles* 1.2 is, then, no simple or one-dimensional panegyric to Stoic discipline. He is no ascetic saint; rather, he offers 'an art' or 'aesthetics of existence' which is neither the strict, unreflective adherence to a pre-existing moral code (*Epistles* 1.1.14) nor the naive refusal of all limitations, but the 'mindful practice of freedom' to create a worthy and memorable life.[14] Horatian discipline was a serious but hardly grim affair, undertaken in the spirit of reasoned and reflective enjoyment (Johnson 1993: 110); his ironic winks and nods are subtle and serious ways of presenting and understanding basic problems of human existence – what is freedom, friendship, the good, the useful, the fine? – and at the same time sly jokes, good humour and deflations of pretence. We should have a glass of wine and talk with friends.

Epistles 1.2 ends with a complex set of ironic puns that both brings a wry smile to the reader and asks us to recontextualize Horace's admonitions in the context of the collection and Roman culture generally. The multilayered nature of the poem's close has not generally been recognized, but it bears close reading.

> Nunc adbibe puro
> pectore verba puer, nunc te melioribus offer.

quo semel est imbuta recens servabit odorem
testa diu. quodsi cessas aut strenuus anteis,
nec tardum opperior nec praecedentibus insto.

Now, when still young, imbibe words with a pure heart. Now present
yourself to better people. The wine jar once it has been filled will long
preserve the scent.

But if you yield or you strive to get ahead, neither will I press hard
the slow, nor will I stand in the way of those moving ahead.

(1.2.67–71)

The translation of these lines offers the reader a number of seemingly opposed
choices, to which the rendering above does not do justice. First, we must
decide whether *puer* is vocative or predicate nominative. Wickham's 1901
Oxford Classical Text is printed above. The punctuation there, which would
not have been present in Horace's original, leads one to assume that *puer* is
to be taken as a predicate nominative meaning 'while you are young'. It is
unusual, however, to use *puer* in the nominative with an imperative, where
one might normally expect a vocative. The result since antiquity has been
a variety of notes that seek to explain the usage, ranging from Acron's gloss
'while you are an adolescent, a *puer*', which could be taken as a general
admonition rather than a specific command (Havthal 1966b: 381; cf. Mayer
1994: ad loc.), to Rolfe's 'now while still a boy', which makes little sense.
The problem with the latter is that Lollius is generally assumed to be M.
Lollius, the consul in 21 BCE, who, while younger than Horace, would not
in any normal chronological or social sense be a *puer* or 'boy'. Even if this is
a different Lollius, which no one has convincingly proposed, this must still
be someone of social prominence to receive two poems in such important
positions, and who in 1.18 is addressed as a mature poet seeking patronage
from a wealthy and powerful friend. While there are a variety of colloquial
uses, normally one ceases to be called a *puer* at around 15 to 17 years of
age when one assumes the *toga virilis* at the *Liberalia*, which celebrates the
young man's sexual maturity and his entrance into maturity as a free man
(*vir*) (Uzzi 2005: 24–7; Préaux 1968: ad loc.; cf. Foucault 1984b: 152–3).

Puer then presents an interpretive problem. It introduces a variety of possible meanings, none of which really fit, but which as a group and in the context of the collection as a whole present a complex and ironic commentary on the perils of patronage, the price of freedom and the nature of the poetic vocation. Another possible solution is simply to accept *puer* as a vocative, which Shackleton Bailey does in his Teubner text by adding a comma immediately before it (2008). This would be a more normal Latin usage. The problem is that the standard meaning of such a usage for a mature man would be to treat him as a slave, one of the common meanings of *puer*, especially in direct address. Although the usage has a variety of meanings, all have in common the notion of minority, that one is not fully in control of one's actions or one's body; hence all the slaves and children in a household could be termed the *pueri* of the *paterfamilias* (McCarter 2015: 211).

There is also an erotic connotation. It was universally assumed that young men were an object of sexual attraction to older men, and while there were prohibitions in the form of the *Lex Scantinia* and military regulations against older men sexually subjecting the sons of freeborn Romans, there was little debate about the desirability of such youths, and slaves were considered fair game. Social subjection and sexual subjection were assumed to go hand in hand unless special measures were taken.[15] To address someone as *puer* and then tell him that he should offer himself to his betters (*nunc te melioribus offer*) could easily be read as both a thinly veiled insult and as consonant with the advice in 1.18, which we have already seen assimilates, through intertextual echoes, the young client's subjecting himself to the desire of his patron to the figure of the *servus amoris*. As Horace says at the end of *Satires* 1.2, when your loins swell, rather than commit adultery with the wife of another free man, you should simply rape the nearest *ancilla verna* ('house-born maid') or *puer* (1.2.116–18). Horace, we feel, could not possibly mean *puer* in that sense in *Epistles* 1.2, hence the elaborate notes and explanations, the alternative punctuations deployed to keep such a possibility at bay; and yet there it is.

Of course, as we have seen throughout this book, this is how irony works. It is impossible to assimilate these various meanings into a single coherent message, but it is also impossible to forget them, hence the perceived need to 'explain' the passage, to warn readers away from thinking what they are already thinking. None of this is to say, however, that the web of various possible *intellecta* or meanings is incoherent or does not possess mutually reinforcing resonances. Let us take the word *melioribus*, for example. It has at least three different possible meanings, which have been the subject of commentaries and explanations over the centuries. Acron declares that we should understand *philosophiae magistris* ('teachers of philosophy') with it. This is not absurd in a poem that emphasizes the importance of study for the health of the soul. Nonetheless, Horace has already said in the previous poem that he is bound to no 'master/teacher', and this poem argues that poetry is a better medium for learning the lessons of philosophy than philosophy itself. Of course, if Lollius were in fact a boy, he might well need a teacher of philosophy, and why not a better one? Then again, as Mayer recognizes (1994), *melioribus* could just as easily be neuter as masculine and mean that Lollius should dedicate himself to 'better things', something roughly equivalent to the idea expressed at lines 35–6, that if 'you do not apply your soul to honest studies and pursuits, you will be awake through the night tortured by envy and desire'. Honest studies and pursuits would be 'better things'.

Nonetheless, *melioribus* can equally mean 'social superiors'. 'Offer yourself to your betters' could have two complementary meanings that seem opposed in modern English but which were practically homologous in the ancient world. On the one hand, the notion could simply be to make yourself of use: if you want to get ahead in the world, then you should make yourself available to your 'betters' in every sense of the word. In Rome's highly stratified society, one of the primary ways for a young man to move himself forward was to attach himself to the retinue of a wealthy and powerful man, as Lollius seeks to do in *Epistles* 1.18. There are thus numerous extant examples of letters of recommendation for ambitious young men to their social superiors, including in the present collection (e.g. 1.9).

On the other hand, the imagery is also distinctly sexual, and in Latin the social and the sexual are never far removed (Walters 1997). While it was normal practice for young Romans to attach themselves to their social superiors in the hope of advancement, that subjection, in turn, could either be literally imaged as a form of sexual submissiveness or imagined as such in barbs and jokes. Thus in Seneca the Elder (*Contr. 4 praef.* 10) we are told of a declaimer in court who remarked that sexual submission was a necessity for a slave and a 'duty' (*officium*) for a freedman. This, in turn, we are told gave rise to a spate of jokes about 'doing your duty' (Adams 1982: 163–4). The analogy between a potentially humiliating servitude in relation to a social superior and sexual subjection is vividly concretized in Catullus 28, which contains the ironic injunction *pete nobiles amicos!* 'seek prominent friends!' and which has already been quoted extensively in connection with the *Epodes*. There Catullus vividly compares serving under Memmius in Bythinia to being well and thoroughly screwed (cf. Oliensis 1997: 154–5).

Of course, Horace is not literally suggesting that Lollius offer sexual services to his social superiors. This is at most a humorous double entendre, which on some level is what irony always is: a singular *dictum* that gives rise to a variety of *intellecta*. But it is a double entendre that drives home Horace's point about the relation between freedom and the care of the self, and it is a point that only gains in saliency when the reader reaches *Epistles* 1.18. Thus after the poet has told Maecenas in 1.1 that he has put aside both the slavery and the game of lyric poetry (*ludus/ludicra*) in favour of traditional philosophical questions, in 1.2 he tells Lollius that he is rereading Homer and admonishes the younger poet to bend his spirit to study and to caring for the self. Such discipline is not necessarily a dry affair, but the clear message is that Lollius will face a series of choices that require him to both know and be present to himself through the disciplined study of others – of those who are better than him – and that the alternative is a form of slavery that differs little from sexual subjection. Slavery in this larger, more philosophic sense may be servitude to the desires of others or to the desires of the self. Likewise, the 'other' may be our master, our teacher, our friend, or our patron, or it may be any one of their figurations within us. But freedom only really exists in the moment of simultaneous distancing and self-presence that we call reflection: a moment whose constitutive doubleness and ambivalence, as Socrates knew, is best expressed through irony.

The complexity of this dialectic is taken up at many places throughout the collection. *Epistles* 1.17, which in part serves to introduce 1.18, famously includes an exchange between Diogenes the Cynic, a philosopher who believed freedom came from eschewing all forms of dependence, and Aristippus, the Cyrenaic hedonist and pupil of Socrates, who argued that pleasure was the end of life and enjoyment our goal (Mayer 1986: 64; Mayer 1994: 44; Traina 2009: 307; McCarter 2015: 198–9). In preparation for 1.18, the whole of this poem takes place under the sign of instructions to a certain Scaeva on how, if he wants to live better, he will need to approach a well-heeled patron. Diogenes is then quoted as saying that Aristippus would not need to know how to approach the great if he were content to live on vegetables, proverbially simple fare. Aristippus replies that Diogenes would not need to live on vegetables if he knew how to treat the great. But Aristippus goes on to claim that he in fact is the freer of the two because while he has to amuse his benefactor as his *scurra*, Diogenes plays the fool to everyone in the street, begging but often with no tangible benefit. Horace then continues by arguing that Aristippus would more easily be able to change positions with Diogenes than the other way around. Diogenes is thus not only the slave to many but also to his own limited conception of freedom, while Aristippus serves only one, one he can just as easily live without, and this indeed is the acid test (1.17.23–32; Moles 1985: 43–8; Kilpatrick 1986: 44–5).

It is not an ascetic life Horace envisions, but a free one within the bounds of pleasure and friendship, which brings us to the final poem we will examine, *Epistles* 1.7, the third epistle addressed to Maecenas. In this poem, Horace is often said to declare his independence from Maecenas, but what that means and how we are to understand it are matters of considerable dispute (Havthal 1966b: 407; Kilpatrick 1986: 8; Bowditch 2001: 181–4; McCarter 2015: 124). Poem 1.7 is thus considered one of the key poems in the collection for defining its governing themes, even as it is also recognized as a complex and ironic work of art (Armstrong 1989: 120–1; Labate 2009: 116; Bowditch 2010: 69–70). The poet begins the letter by acknowledging that he had promised to be away in the country only five days but had in fact been gone the entire month of August. He admits that this avowal makes him a 'liar' or *mendax*, but says that Maecenas should care about Horace's health, or at least about Horace's perception of his health, and with more than a little hyperbole he portrays August as a gift to undertakers. Of course, if Horace is a 'liar', then why should we believe him? The poem begins in doubleness and ambivalence.

Horace, it appears, thanks Maecenas for the gift of the Sabine farm by staying there rather than returning to Rome and fulfilling the obligations of *amicitia*. The farm (*rus*) thus stands simultaneously as the concrete symbol of Horace's freedom, of his ability to escape from Rome and of his obligations to his wealthy and powerful friend (McCarter 2015: 125). The problem for Horace is how to parse these obligations without rendering himself either a slave to his benefactor or an intolerable, ingrate boor. More profoundly, the question is this: how in a society of strict hierarchy and unequal power relations can one actually be a friend (Kilpatrick 1986: 71; McNeill 2001: 24; Labate 2009: 120)? Horace concludes the opening section of the poem by announcing that, if the weather turns bad, he may go to the sea and not return to Rome till spring. Five days has quickly become six months.

After these opening lines, there follows the first of three examples that purport to illustrate Horace's main point(s) in this text (Gold 1987: 127). These are just the kind of poetic exempla that *Epistles* 1.2 contends are a better means of understanding the 'fine' and the 'useful' than the strict dialectic of traditional philosophers, and such exempla function by pointing beyond themselves to that which is more 'universal' and 'more serious' in Aristotle's terms than the merely particular. That is to say that when we tell the story of Odysseus, or the fable of the City Mouse and the Country Mouse, we are never just talking about the Ithacan hero or various small rodents but what they could mean in a variety of contexts.

Moreover, as we have already discussed, there is a profound kinship between allegory and irony, first noted by Quintilian. Each figure depends both on its capacity to signify beyond itself and on our perception of the difference between what is said (*dictum*) and what is understood (*intellectum*). Even if the poetic exemplum may not in every case be able to be formally assimilated to the ironic or the allegorical, there is in the exemplum an analogous doubleness that both makes possible the production of meaning in concrete form and also guarantees that meaning's necessary incompletion. As such, the exemplum, like irony and allegory, requires of the reader ever more attention to its details and to their potential significance, and consequently those details produce ever more meaning: never reaching a final closure, never coming to the moment where the reader has learned all there is to know, where the poet has said all there is to say, and where reflection comes to an end. The exemplum becomes, in a very real sense, a bounded space of care and reflection, which is the essence of both Socratic irony and poetic signification.

Horace begins his first exemplum by contrasting Maecenas' generosity with that of a certain Calabrian host:

> Non quo more piris vesci Calaber iubet hospes
> tu me fecisti locupletem. 'vescere sodes.'
> 'iam satis est.' 'at tu quantum vis tolle.' 'benigne.'
> 'non invisa feres pueris munuscula parvis.'
> 'tam teneor dono, quam si dimittar onustus.'
> 'ut libet; haec porcis hodie comedenda relinques.'
> prodigus et stultus donat quae spernit et odit:
> haec seges ingratos tulit et feret omnibus annis.
> vir bonus et sapiens dignis ait esse paratus,
> nec tamen ignorant quid distent area lupinis.
> dignum praestabo me etiam pro laude merentis.

You did not make me rich in land in the same manner in which the Calabrian host orders his guest to fill himself with pears. 'Please, eat up.' 'That's enough for now.' 'But take as much as you want.' 'That's very kind.' 'You will take home not unwanted gifts for the small children.' 'I am as much obliged as if I were weighed down.' 'As you please. You will leave these behind to be fed today to the hogs.' A wasteful and foolish man gives away what he rejects and hates: that harvest has and will produce ingratitude, year after year. The good and the wise man says that he is ready for the worthy, and moreover is not unable to distinguish coins from lupines. I will continue to present myself as someone worthy before the praise of he who deserves it. (1.7.14–24)

This simple story brims with complexity. *Locupletis*, while often translated as 'rich', etymologically means 'rich in land', presumably referring to the Sabine farm. Of course, Horace here is making a distinction between Maecenas' gift and that of the Calabrian host. Nonetheless, the fact that he chooses to contrast Maecenas with someone who does *not* understand how to give a gift – even as Horace calls himself *mendax* and frustrates Maecenas' desire that he return from the country – makes the reader question whether this negative comparison does not also serve as a polite reminder not to let it become a positive parallel. Praise as a form of admonition and instruction is recognized by Aristotle in the *Rhetoric* (1368.9.35–7) and closely related to irony. When I say to my superior that her patience and good humour are second to none, am I stating a fact or making a gentle suggestion (Miller 2015)?

What precisely does the Calabrian host do wrong? The first indication is the verb *iubet*, 'he commands, orders'. One cannot order someone who does not owe you obedience. One cannot order someone who is free to tell you no. Of course, as the example shows, the guest does in fact refuse the gift, which means the host had misjudged the purchase his superiority has on his social inferior. What becomes clear as we read on is that these pears are anything but a delicacy. They are rotting, or soon to be, since the host will feed them to the hogs if the guest does not take them. We are told the host in fact hates and rejects (*spernit et odit*) the pears and that he should expect therefore to reap ingratitude.

In this context, the phrase *pueris* [...] *parvis* is particularly interesting. Are these the younger slaves or smaller children? As we have seen, *puer* can mean both, and its initial placement, especially following *iubet*, cannot help but suggest that 'slaves' are the reference, even if that suggestion is immediately qualified by the adjective *parvus*, which points to the meaning 'child'. From a linguistic point of view, however, this is a distinction that is more important in English than Latin. *Puer* means *puer* in Latin and bears with it all the semantic fields and contexts of usage that the word possesses. Only in translation are we forced to choose one meaning over another.

Maecenas is, of course, nothing like the Calabrian host. Certainly, he may want the poet to write lyric when Horace has moved on to another genre. Certainly, he may expect the poet to return to Rome and attend on him, when the poet prefers to remain in the country. But they are friends and they respect each other's freedom to make their own choices, do they not?

Still, if all that went without saying, then it would not need to be said. This poem would not need to be written. I do not mean that *Epistles* 1.7 is an actual letter and that the speech act we witness is primarily intended as a communication between poet and patron; the poem is best understood as a literary performance aimed at a variety of audiences (including Maecenas and us). *Epistles* 1.7 is a complex and multilevelled artistic artefact. It exists within a social, historical and biographical context, and that context determines in part the significance we can all agree to grant it.

Thus when Horace writes, 'The good and the wise man says that he is ready for the worthy,' it is generally considered that he is referring to a patron being ready to support a worthy client. But in fact the phrase itself cuts both ways. Indeed, the case of the Calabrian host suggests that each must be worthy of the other, that, while they would never be equals, if they are to be 'friends' each friend must be free to say no to the other. Each must find the other worthy. This reciprocal relationship is encapsulated, with all its ambiguity, in Horace's final declaration, 'I will continue to present myself as someone worthy before the praise of he who deserves it' (Bowditch 2001: 205).

Horace, in fact, makes it clear that they are well beyond the point in their relationship where Maecenas can expect Horace never to leave his side:

> Quodsi me noles usquam discedere, reddes
> forte latus, nigros angusta fronte capillos,
> reddes dulce loqui, reddes ridere decorum et
> inter vina fugam Cinarae maerere protervae.

> But if you do not wish me ever to leave, you will return my strong loins,
> my black hair on a narrow forehead, you will return my sweet talking,
> you will return my decorous laughter and my weeping at the flight of
> wanton Cinara amid the rounds of wine.   (1.7.25–8)

If Maecenas wishes Horace to serve as he once did, the great man needs to return Horace to his youth. But this is not just any youth, it is the youth of lyric poetry, the very genre from which Horace took his leave in *Epistles* 1.1 (Bowditch 2001: 207). The characteristics of Horace's youth evoked in *Epistles* 1.7 are virility, a full head of hair, courtship and the pleasures and sorrows of fleeting love. All of these are topics central to the *Odes* but touched on only briefly in the *Satires* and *Epodes*. Cinara is only known from her two appearances in Book 4 of the *Odes*, where she appears as the nostalgic sign of the poet's past youthful prowess (4.1.4, 4.13.21) and current decrepitude. Maecenas, or even Augustus, may be able to command a performance, but they cannot return Horace's youth or rekindle its lyric magic. If they do not want to appear like the Calabrian host, they should not insist, even with gifts.

Gifts, of course, are never really free. They enjoin one in a cycle of reciprocity and hence obligation. You should never accept a gift that you do not feel free to return (Bowditch 2010: 71). This lesson is drawn in the second exemplum, the fable of the fox in the granary:

> Forte per angustam tenuis vulpecula rimam
> repserat in cumeram frumenti, pastaque rursus
> ire foras pleno tendebat corpore frustra.
> cui mustela procul 'si vis' ait 'effugere istinc,
> macra cavum repetes artum, quem macra subisti.'
> hac ego si compellor imagine, cuncta resigno;
> nec somnum plebis laudo satur altilium nec
> otia divitiis Arabum liberrima muto.

Once upon a time a slender young fox had crept through a narrow crack into a granary and, having eaten, she was trying in vain to get back out, her body now full. A weasel outside said to her, 'If you want to get out of there, you will need to be as skinny returning through the narrow hole as when you came in.'

If I am accused by this image, then I sign over everything; neither do I praise the sleep of the common man, stuffed with fattened fowl, nor would I exchange my free leisure for the riches of Araby.   (1.7.29–36)

The surface meaning of this story seems clear: the gifts one receives are confining. The free person must be ready to give up all he has received. Horace recognizes that he can be seen as the fox: *hac ego si compellor imagine*. The verb *compellor* has two possible readings. As translated above, it is derived from *compellare*, 'to accost, reproach' or in a more technical, legal sense, 'arraign, indict'. Here, Horace would seem to say, that if others, including perhaps Maecenas, say he is like the fox, then he will 'sign over everything'. But *compellor* can equally be derived from *compellere*, in which case it means 'to be forced, compelled'. As Kilpatrick notes, while it may be difficult for literal-minded readers to understand how a fable could 'force' Horace to do anything, this was the way the ancient commentators understood *compellor* (1986: 11; cf. Havthal 1966b: 412, 416). Such a reading would seem to mean: if this way of imagining my conduct should force or compel me, then I would in fact 'sign over' everything.

Yet *compellor* is not the only verb in this line capable of multiple meanings; *resigno* is as well. On the one hand, it has generally been understood to mean something like *reddere* or *rescribere*. Thus Horace, like the fox, will return what has been given if he is accused of fattening himself on the grain of others, rather than be trapped inside a box (*cumera*), whether literal or figurative (Préaux 1968: ad loc.; Mayer 1994: ad loc.). But *resigno* can equally mean 'refute', so 'if I am accused by this fable then I refute everything', which is Kilpatrick's preferred understanding (1986: 12; Bowditch 2001: 190, 195–6). But who is accusing him? Horace himself introduces the fable without explanation, as if it explained his conduct, but if the fable 'forced him', he would 'return everything'. Nonetheless, there is no grammatical or textual way to decide between these competing meanings, and the belief that one of them must be the sole true meaning is just that: a belief. In fact, Horace's use of the exemplum is further ironized by the plurality of understandings he introduces about the possible relations that exemplum entertains with the situation he describes at the beginning of the poem: the poet as a *mendax* has told Maecenas that he will be back in five days, but he may well not return till the spring. If this fable of the fox indicts me, I refute it all, but I am also willing to return everything you gave me, but only really if I am forced: because it is precisely my possession of the Sabine farm that gives me the ability to be in the country and say no to returning to the city. It is in a concrete sense the essence of my freedom and I owe you for it, but it is a freedom I will not purchase at the cost of being a slave (Macleod 2009: 254). Thus the poet continues, 'I am no hypocrite. I do not praise the life of the common man, while stuffed with gourmet delights, nor would I exchange my *liberrima otia*, 'my most free leisure', for all riches of the east.' It is precisely Horace's ability to get away, his ability to escape from the demands and obligations of *negotia* ('business') that define his *libertas*, and this has been the essence of his claim since *Satires* 1.6, where he says that he is freer than the *praeclarus senator* because he can ride his castrated mule wherever he desires (104–11). *Liberrime*, it will be recalled, is the opening epithet given to the budding satirist Lollius in 1.18 where Horace ironically advocates that Lollius be willing to drop his poetic vocation and accompany his patron on the hunt in order to purchase his gourmet treats. But while Horace claims to have been loyal to Maecenas and to have praised him both when present and absent, and while he notes that Maecenas has praised his own modesty as well, nonetheless he challenges the great man, *inspice si possum donata reponere laetus* ('go ahead and see if I am able to put aside the things I have been given', 1.7.39). Of course, even here there is irony, since *reponere* may mean equally 'to give up' and 'to lay away (for later use)' (Préaux 1968: ad loc.; Kilpatrick 1986: 12; Mayer 1994: ad loc.). And the scene itself, of the poet who defends his friend even when absent, is meant to contrast with the negative image of the satirist and *scurra* in the paradigmatic *Satires* 1.4. There the poet moves directly from the image of the witty man who will insult his absent friend (1.4.81–5) to the *scurra* drunk on too much Liber who insults his host (1.4.86–91). Horace in *Epistles* 1.7 is merely the man who has lied (*mendax*) to his friend in order to preserve his *libertas*, a *libertas* which on one level is founded on the gifts provided by that friend but which on another he must remain free to return, if he is to enjoy them.

The final exemplum is the most complex of all, and as one reader noted, 'critics have tied themselves into knots attempting to unsnarl its complications' (Oliensis 1998: 164; cf. McCarter 2015: 137). A certain Philippus, who is a famous and high-status pleader in the courts, on his way home from the Forum spies a person sitting in the shade paring his nails and paying no attention to the grand man. Philippus sends his slave (*puer*) to find out who this person is, who his father is, who his patron is and what the size of his fortune is (*Epistles* 1.7.46–54). All of these, if we are to believe the beginning of *Satires* 1.6, are questions Maecenas considers unimportant compared to the nature of a friend's character (Freudenburg 2002: 130). Philippus receives the report that the man's name is Vulteius Mena. Like Horace's father, he is a *praeco*, or 'auctioneer'. He is of modest means, has no serious moral blemishes and is known both to work hard and to rest, to seek money and to spend it. He takes pleasure in his friends, his hearth god, games (*ludis*) and the pleasures of the Campus Martius, but only when his work is done (1.7.55–9). He is, in short, the contented model citizen of Augustan Rome.

Philippus wants to get to know such an extraordinary fellow better and invites him to dinner. He is shocked when Mena politely refuses the invitation (using the same formula the guest had used for refusing the Calabrian host's pears, *benigne*, line 16). Unwilling to accept the idea that the modest man might not long to associate with the great, Philippus begins to pursue Mena. He reverses social convention by showing up at the latter's humble place of business and greeting him with the morning *salutatio* normally offered by a wealthy man's clients in the atrium of his home before the day begins; although even here what appears to be a form of self-abasement is a subtle way for the great man to assert his power as he commands (*iubet*) Mena to be well (*salvere*), just as the Calabrian host had earlier commanded his guest to stuff himself with pears (1.7.14, 66). There ensues an almost instant restoration of normative power relations as Mena is subtly put in his place through Philippus' act of seeming generosity: Mena immediately apologizes for his failure to show up at the great man's house that morning, offering as an excuse the need to work and earn his fee (*mercennaria vincla* 1.7.67). This formulation is telling. The basis of Mena's freedom, his ability to earn an independent living, is now seen as the chains that bind him (*vincla*), at least from Philippus' perspective. Philippus assures Mena that all will be forgiven if he will come to dinner.

Mena soon becomes the great man's dependant, and at first he seems to prosper. After Philippus has observed Mena coming often to the morning salutation and attending him at dinner, the client is ordered (*iubetur*, 1.7.75) to accompany his patron to the countryside for the Latin holidays. The naive Mena, who has little experience of the country, praises the Sabine plough land without cease. Philippus is amused and offers to give Mena 7,000 sesterces and to loan him another 7,000 if he will use it to buy a small plot of land (*agellum*, 1.7.81), giving Mena what he thinks he wants while at the same time binding him in debt and dependence.

Immediately, Mena sets to work, throwing himself into viticulture and literally killing himself in the pursuit of possession (1.7.85). But reality soon sets in. His sheep are stolen. His goats die of disease. The harvest fails. His ox is killed off by the labour of the plough. Mena, the once contented auctioneer, wakes in the middle of the night, grabs a horse and rides back to Rome, where he bursts into the house of Philippus 'shaggy and scurfy' (1.7.90). The following exchange ensues:

> 'You seem to me, Vulteius, to be excessively frugal and harsh.' 'By god, patron, you may call me Wretch if you wish to give me my true name!' he says, 'but I beseech you and appeal to you, by your Guardian spirit, your own right hand, your household gods, give me back my previous life.'   (1.7.91–5)

The moral is then drawn quickly and cryptically, and this most important epistle draws to a close. 'Once a man has examined how much things lost excel those sought, he should at the right time go back and seek the things left behind. But it is true that each man measures himself by his own foot and measure' (1.7.96–7). What things has Horace lost, what things Maecenas? What were they seeking and how would they go back? None of this is specified, nor are they themselves even named. Each makes his own determination, whether in life or in deciding the import of a poem, especially one that opens with its writer laughingly, ironically – and thus ultimately seriously – calling himself *mendax*.

A double discourse pervades the poem. The Calabrian host is not like Maecenas, but if Maecenas wants Horace to be what he was in the past he should return to Horace his youth: a youth that is a lyric fiction. Likewise, the relation between the story of the fox in the granary and Horace is never specified, but if Horace is 'accused' or 'compelled' by this story then he will 'refute everything' and/or 'give up everything', or even, if *resigno* is used in the same sense as it is in line 9, 'unseal, open up everything' (cf. Bowditch 2001: 188). Maecenas is no Philippus; he did not force himself upon Horace. And Horace is no Mena; he has not begged Maecenas to take back the gift of his country estate. But at what point does that gift become a burden? At what point does the gift become, as in the story, a loan (*mutua*), something which must be paid back with interest, an obligation? At what point does friendship become patronage, and freedom a form of servitude? These are the questions this poem and its exempla force us to ask, not by making accusations, but through the ironic language of a *mendax* poet who tells a truth that each man must measure by his own (metrical?) foot.

The *Epistles* are a quieter form than the *Satires*, to which they are closely related. The diatribes of *Satires* 1.1–1.3 are unimaginable in the *Epistles*, as well as the constant need to position the poet vis-à-vis his great predecessor, Lucilius. The dialogues and long speeches featured in Book 2 of the *Satires* would be equally out of place in a genre whose operative fiction is the letter. Likewise, the engagement with formal philosophy is more direct in the *Epistles* than what is found in the *Satires*. By the same token, the *Epistles* do not have the invective edge and tolerance for the grotesque of the *Epodes*, nor the sheer technical virtuosity of the *Odes*. Nonetheless, with their formal polish, their extraordinary care in word choice and placement, their engagement with fundamental issues not merely of philosophy but of life, *Epistles* 1 has to rank as one of Horace's greatest achievements. They possess a subtlety and sureness of touch that is unsurpassed, impossible to translate and easily missed by the inattentive reader.

And it is this message of care, of mindfulness, that may be the *Epistles'* most important lesson. These quiet, often understated poems ask us to pay close attention to their words and structures, but also to ourselves as reflected in those words and structures, and they ask us to do so with all the complexity and ambivalence a poem requires. The self-presence that Horace demands, as we have seen, is both a form of alienation and attention. To care for the self means both to take the self as an object and to be attentive to it as a subject. Self-knowledge as Socrates knew is no simple task (*Phaedrus* 230a). The *Epistles* through the means of the poetic exemplum and through their gentle irony invite us again and again to ask who we are and what we really want. What is the true and what is the proper? What is virtue and what is freedom? What is the accidental and what the essential? They do this not by pounding us with syllogisms, not by trying to force us to think a certain way, but through poetry, through humour, through examples. We should talk among friends. We should share a glass of wine. But we should also take our obligations seriously, take our friends seriously, and within the constraints that existence in a multifaceted and unequal society imposes, cultivate freedom and reflection.

Epilogue

THE AFTERLIFE OF HORACE'S POETRY is long and complex. It could easily be the subject of several books. As we have already seen, in the next generation Persius was a close reader and imitator of the *Satires* and the *Epistles*, while Juvenal clearly saw himself as continuing a tradition established by Lucilius and Horace. The *Odes* left no direct poetic heirs in the ancient world, but the commentaries of Porphyrion and Pseudo-Acron, as well as mentions in Quintilian, assure us that they continued to be taught and read. The same is true of the *Epodes*, which were imitated by Martial in content if not in form. Horace became an instant classic, but his achievements outside of hexameter poetry were so monumental and seemingly final that they found few if any direct imitators.

In the Middle Ages, when Catullus was all but lost but Ovid and Virgil became the object of sacred exegesis, the pattern continued. There are many manuscripts from the ninth century onwards, so we know that Horace was read, but if we look at the characterization of Horace he is most often viewed as a moralist, with emphasis on the *Satires* and the *Epistles* and with the *Ars Poetica* seen as a source of authority for poetry's utility (Braund 2010: 367–8). The *Odes* remained surprisingly popular. Often seen as the poetry of youth, many were set to music in the twelfth century. While few imitators could rise to the challenge of reproducing their metrical complexity, music offered one avenue of approach.

In the Renaissance, we move beyond glosses and manuscripts to viewing Horatian poetry as a source of innovation. Petrarch, on the cusp of the Early Modern period, like his medieval predecessors, drew inspiration primarily from the *Satires* and the *Epistles*, seeing Horace as a philosopher similar in breadth and tenor to Cicero. Nonetheless, he certainly knew the *Odes* and alludes to them on several occasions in the *Canzoniere*, and indeed the recognition of these latter intertexts was key to Petrarch's early reception as a lyric poet. Nonetheless, the *Satires* and the *Epistles* were the texts that were easiest to read as a form of Christian reflection and those from which one could most easily extract the kinds of classicizing aesthetic doctrines that would become the foundation of Renaissance humanism.

Petrarch produced three books of metrical epistles in dactylic hexameters, written in some of the best classical Latin since antiquity (he also wrote prose letters modelled on Cicero). Like Horace's own, these poetic letters are addressed to friends and often have a relatively light tone. They include invitations to visit the poet at his retreat in the Vaucluse, which clearly recalls Horace's Sabine farm. The following passage from *Epistles* 1.6 to Jacopo di Colonna reminds the reader of both *Satires* 1.6 and a variety of passages from the *Epistles*. Petrarch has created a fusion of different intertexts to produce an imitation that it is at once clearly recognizable and yet never slavish:

> Now listen briefly to how I live my life on most days.
> I have a light dinner. Hunger, labour and fatigue are by far
> The best sauce for those who dine alone.
> The bailiff is my servant. I am my own companion and my dog,
> A faithful animal; this place has frightened off all the rest,
> Since pleasure armed with Cupid's darts runs riot
> And commonly inhabits rich cities.   (156–63)

The Horatian notes here are clear, but at the same time there is a tone of Christian asceticism that is alien to the Roman poet. He is both the Country Mouse and a kind of hermit, living alone with his books and meditations. Horace's irony and wit have given way to a tone of deliberate self-denial.

This pattern continued as the Renaissance progressed. In Du Bellay's sonnet sequence, *Les Regrets*, the great theorist of the Pléiade and the author of *La Défense et illustration de la langue française* created a radically new form of poetry that fused the Petrarchan sonnet form with imitations of Ovid's *Tristia* and direct quotations from the *Satires* and *Epistles*. In one of the most innovative works of the French Renaissance, Du Bellay brought together forms and conventions from opposed genres – lyric, elegy, satire and epistle – to create a work that claimed to speak immediately and from the heart so convincingly that critics for many years failed to recognize its dense intertextual weave, often mistaking Horatian subtlety for autobiographical confession (Miller 2013a). During this same period, Sidney's *Defence of Poesy* offered a fusion of Aristotelian rhetorical and poetic theory with lessons drawn from the *Ars*. Sidney defends poetry as a speaking picture (*ut pictura poesis, AP* 361) whose purpose is to teach and delight (*utile dulci, AP* 343), producing the first great work of literary theory in English (Golden 2010: 396–7).

The *Ars*, of course, as we observed in our Introduction, is anything but straightforward. It is a complex poetic work whose lessons are undermined and ironized within the text, a fact that many of its post-classical readers failed to recognize. But the kinship of the *Ars* with the *Satires* and *Epistles* was not lost on two of Horace's most famous early modern emulators, Boileau and Pope, both of whom produced literary criticism that was marked by its Horatian influence and biting wit. Boileau in seventeenth-century France is prompt to satirize poetic self-satisfaction in lines taken directly from Horace. In rhyming Alexandrines, he warns of flattery's seductions:

> The flatterer searches at once to exclaim
> Every verse he hears lights him aflame
> All is charming, divine, not a word out of place
> His feet stomp with joy, tender tears wet his face   (193–6)

In like manner, Horace had warned the wealthy poet not to ask the poor client's opinion of his work for fear of receiving a flattering response. He warns the overeager poetaster against taking the poor man's response as sincere:

For he will cry out 'beautiful, well done, rightly so!' He turns pale over
these verses. For his friend, he will drip dew from his eyes. He will leap
in the air. He will pound the ground with his foot.   (*AP* 428–30)

Likewise, Pope in his 'Essay on Criticism' imitates numerous passages from
the *Ars*, and he later published *Imitations of Horace* with the Latin origi-
nal on the facing page (Golden 2010: 398–403). In both cases, Horace's
poetry gave rise to works of originality and lasting influence which defined
the neoclassical style of seventeenth- and eighteenth-century Britain and
France.

The *Odes*, while widely admired, found fewer imitators. Their sheer
technical virtuosity made them difficult to approach. And while the *Satires*
and the *Epistles* often lost in the process of translation and imitation their
Socratic scepticism, these more prosaic works were nonetheless easier to
assimilate to an ethic that sought moral lessons and to a neoclassical aes-
thetic that sought regularity, grandeur and grace. Nonetheless, there are
moments of real beauty here, such as the beginning of Dryden's translation
of *Odes* 1.9:

> Behold yon mountain's hoary height
> Made higher with new mounts of snow:
> Again behold the winter's weight
> Oppress the labouring woods below
> And streams with icy fetters bound
> Benumbed and cramped to solid ground.

In the nineteenth century, Horace's lyric achievement inspired the work of
Tennyson, who as a schoolboy memorized all of the *Odes*, translating the
opening of the Soracte ode as follows:

> See! How Soracte's hoary brow
> And melancholy crags uprear
> Their weight of venerable snow:
> And scarce the groaning forests bear

> The burthen of the gloomy year
> And motionless the stream remains
> Beneath the weight of icy chains.

Imitations of the same ode would later make an appearance in the poet's *In Memoriam*. Tennyson recalls Horace in his metrical inventiveness, imitating a vast variety of classical measures in English verse.

Among the modernists, Robert Frost in his devotion to classical form and understatement has often been compared to Horace, and A. E. Housman's lyrics have also been shown to owe much to the *Odes* (Gaskin 2013). Likewise, W. H. Auden in a 1971 interview given at Swarthmore College acknowledged Horace as one of his most lasting influences.[16] Nonetheless, there is no single poet since the ancient world who has captured Horace's unique combination of the pursuit of formal perfection, metrical versatility and a sustained commitment to Socratic inquiry and the care of the self, although many have captured one aspect or another. Horace remains an elusive and unparalleled classic, but one who has also never left us.

NOTES

Except where stated, all translations are the author's own.

1   Although translating *curto* in this passage to mean 'bobtailed' remains common, this interpretation was refuted more than sixty years ago. The practice of bobbing tails is nowhere found in antiquity, whereas the castration of domesticated farm animals to render them docile was common. Likewise, the castrated mule as an emblem of the poet's impotence, relative to the powerful senator, has more point than would a bobtailed mule. See Ashworth and Andrewes (1957) and Freudenburg (2001: 59–60).

2   The irony deepens when we realize that one common meaning of *beatus* is not only 'happy' but 'rich'.

3   The hesitation between these possible meanings has left a trace in the textual tradition. Wickham's OCT prints line 6 as *ignotos, ut me libertino patre natum* ('humble people *like* me, born from a freedman father'). But also attested are *aut, aut ut, at ut* and *et ut,* 'humble people *or/or like/but like/and like* me born from a freedman father', hesitating between an exemplary, an alternative, an adversative and a correlative meaning.

4   Romans dined on a *triclinium*, a set of three couches surrounding a square table. The fourth side was left open for serving. Each couch normally accommodated three diners.

5   On the arrangement of the *Epodes*, see Carrubba (1969); Watson (2003: 15–16, 20–3); Mankin (2010: 101–3); Johnson (2012: 20n36, 229).

6   On the violence of satire, iambic and invective, see Schlegel (2005: 4) and Keane (2006: 49).

7   On the canine motif, uniting poems 1–7 as well as 12, 15, 16 and 17, see
     Watson (2003: 24) and Hawkins (2014: 58, 74n59, 79n74). When added to
     the Canicular motif in poem 3, Canis/Canidia becomes central to Horace's
     portrait of the iambic enterprise. On the Dog Star as associated with Archilochus,
     disease, female lust and male impotence – all motifs in the *Epodes* – see Hawkins
     (2009: 5–9).

8   See Oliensis (2009: 171).

9   The collocation *liberrima indignatio* is particularly interesting. Insofar as *libertas*
     is the banner under which Lucilian satire was perceived at Rome (Freudenburg
     1993: 87) and *indignatio*, Juvenal claims, is the origin of his satire, it is likely
     either that Juvenal had this passage in mind or, more speculatively, that *indignatio*
     played a role in Lucilius and the reference assimilates Lucilian social discipline
     to Horatian iambic (Morrison 2016: 45; cf. Johnson 2012: 97n41).

10   Mankin argues without proof that the object of the invective in this poem is not
     simply a freed slave but a criminal, yet the resemblance is too close for comfort
     and he feels compelled to go on to argue that the speaker is not Horace (1995:
     ad loc.).

11   See Cicero *De Oratore* 2.65.

12   All citations follow Campbell 1982.

13   For a survey of various readings, see Lowrie (2009: 343–44n20).

14   See Foucault 1984a: 90, 105; Foucault 1994a: 711–12; Foucault 1994b: 617;
     Foucault 1994c: 415; and McLeod 2009: 247.

15   The bibliography here is quite extensive. See *inter alia* Foucault 1984a: 82–3, 98,
     232–7; 1984b: 220; Edwards 1993: 75; Konstan 1994: 116–21; Veyne 2001b:
     112–13; Ormand 2005: 99.

16   See http://www.swarthmore.edu/library/auden/QandA_pt1.htm.

BIBLIOGRAPHY

Adams, James Noel. 1982. *The Latin Sexual Vocabulary*. Baltimore, MD.

Ancona, Ronnie. 1994. *Time and the Erotic in Horace's Odes*. Durham, NC.

Anderson, William S. 1960. 'Imagery in the satires of Horace and Juvenal'. *American Journal of Philology* 81: 225–60.

———1966. 'Horace Carm. 1.14: what kind of ship?' *Classical Philology* 61: 84–98.

———1982. 'The Roman Socrates: Horace and his Satires'. In William S. Anderson. *Essays on Roman Satire*, 13–49. Princeton, NJ.

Armstrong, David. 1989. *Horace*. New Haven, CT.

———2010. 'The biographical and social foundations of Horace's voice'. In Gregson Davis, ed. *A Companion to Horace*, 7–33. Malden, MA.

Ashworth, W. D. and M. Andrewes. 1957. 'Horace, Sat. i. 6. 104–5'. *Classical Review* 7: 107–8.

Bailey, D. R. Shackleton. 1982. *Profile of Horace*. Cambridge, MA.

———ed. 2008. *Horatius: Opera*. Berlin.

Baker, Robert J. 1988. 'Maecenas and Horace, *Satires* II.8'. *Classical Journal* 83: 212–32.

Barchiesi, Alessandro. 2007. '*Carmina*: Odes and Carmen Saeculare'. In Stephen Harrison, ed. *The Cambridge Companion to Horace*, 144–61. Cambridge.

———2009. 'Final difficulties in an iambic poet's career: Epode 17'. Trans. Maya Jessica Alapin. In Michèle Lowrie, ed. *Horace: Odes and Epodes (Oxford Readings in Classical Studies)*, 232–46. Oxford.

Bather, Philippa, and Claire Stocks. 2016. 'Introduction'. In Philippa Bather and Claire Stocks, eds. *Horace's Epodes: Contexts, Intertexts, & Reception*, 1–29. Oxford.

Beard, Mary. 2014. *Laughter in Ancient Rome: On Joking, Tickling, and Cracking Up*. Berkeley, CA.

Benedetto, Andrea di. 1981. 'Le satire oraziane II,8 e II,1: Epilogo e prologo "Luciliano" di un libro "non luciliano"?' *Vichiana* 10: 44–61.

Blondell, Ruby. 2002. *The Play of Character in Plato's Dialogues*. Cambridge.

Bowditch, Phebe Lowell. 2001. *Horace and the Gift Economy of Patronage*. Berkeley, CA.

——2010. 'Horace and imperial patronage'. In Gregson Davis, ed. *A Companion to Horace*, 53–74. Malden, MA.

Braund, Susanna H. 1992. *Roman Verse Satire: Greece and Rome: New Surveys of the Classics No. 23*. Oxford.

——2010. 'The metempsychosis of Horace: The reception of the *Satires* and the *Epistles*'. In Gregson Davis, ed. *A Companion to Horace*, 367–90. Malden, MA.

Brown, Michael P. 1993. *Horace: Satires I*. Warminster.

Brown, Wendy. 1994. '"Supposing truth were a woman ...": Plato's subversion of masculine discourse'. In Nancy Tuana, ed. *Feminist Interpretations of Plato*, 157–80. University Park, PA.

Cairns, Francis. 2006. *Sextus Propertius: The Augustan Elegist*. Cambridge.

Cameron, Alan. 1995. *Callimachus and His Critics*. Princeton, NJ.

Campbell, David A., ed. and trans. 1982. *Greek Lyric I*. Cambridge, MA.

Carrubba, Robert W. 1969. *The Epodes of Horace: A Study in Poetic Arrangement*. The Hague.

Catlow, Laurence. 1976. 'Fact, imagination, and Mercury in Horace: *Odes* 1.9'. *Greece and Rome* 23: 74–81.

Cavarzere, Alberto, ed. 1992. *Orazio: Il libro degli Epodi*. Venice.

Chase, George Davis. 1897. 'The origin of Roman praenomina'. *Harvard Studies in Classical Philology* 8: 104–84.

Citroni, Mario. 2009. 'Occasione e piani di destinazione nella lirica di Orazio'. Trans. [as 'Occasion and levels of address in Horatian lyric'] Maya Jessica Alapin et al. In Michèle Lowrie, ed. *Horace: Odes and Epodes (Oxford Readings in Classical Studies)*, 72–15. Oxford.

Citti, Francesco. 2000. *Studi Oraziani: Tematica e Intertesualità*. Bologna.

Classen, Carl Joachim. 1993. 'Principi e concetti morali nelle satire di Orazio'. In Scevola Mariotti et alii. *Atti del convegno di Venosa: 8–15 Novembre 1992*, 111–28. Venosa.

Clay, Jenny Strauss. 2010. 'Horace and Lesbian lyric'. In Gregson Davis, ed. *A Companion to Horace*, 128–46. Malden, MA.

Coffey, Michael. 1976. *Roman Satire*. London.

Connor, Peter. 1972. 'Soracte Encore'. *Ramus* 1: 102–12.

Cunningham, Maurice P. 1957. 'Enarratio of Horace *Odes* 1.9'. *Classical Philology* 52: 98–102.

Davis, Gregson. 1991. *Polyhymnia: The Rhetoric of Horatian Lyric Discourse*. Berkeley, CA.

——— 2010. 'Defining lyric ethos: Archilochus lyricus and Horatian melos'. In Gregson Davis, ed. *A Companion to Horace*, 105–27. Malden, MA.

De Man, Paul. 1983. 'The rhetoric of temporality'. In Paul De Man. *Blindness and Insight: Essays in the Rhetoric of Contemporary Criticism*, 2nd ed. rev., 187–228. Minneapolis, MN.

Dettmer, Helena. 1983. *Horace: A Study in Structure*. Hildesheim.

Duff, John Wight. 1936. *Roman Satire: Its Outlook on Social Life*. Berkeley, CA.

Edmunds, Lowell. 1992. *From a Sabine Jar: Reading Horace, Odes 1.9*. Chapel Hill, NC.

Edwards, Catharine. 1993. *The Politics of Immorality in Ancient Rome*. Cambridge.

Feeney, Denis. 2002. '*Una cum scriptore meo*: poetry, principate, and the traditions of literary history in the *Epistle to Augustus*'. In Tony Woodman and Denis Feeney, eds. *Traditions and Contexts in the Poetry of Horace*, 172–87. Cambridge.

——— 2009. 'Horace and the Greek lyric poets'. In Michèle Lowrie, ed. *Horace: Odes and Epodes (Oxford Readings in Classical Studies)*, 202–31. Oxford.

Ferri, Rolando. 2007. 'The Epistles'. In Stephen Harrison, ed. *The Cambridge Companion to Horace*, 121–31.

Fitzgerald, William. 2009. 'Power and impotence in Horace's Epodes'. In Michèle Lowrie, ed. *Horace: Odes and Epodes (Oxford Readings in Classical Studies)*, 141–59. Oxford.

Foucault, Michel. 1984a. *L'usage des plaisirs: Histoire de la sexualité II*. Paris.

——— 1984b. *Le souci de soi: Histoire de la sexualité III*. Paris.

——— 1994a. 'L'éthique du souci de soi comme pratique de la liberté'. In Daniel Defert and François Ewald, eds. *Dits et écrits: 1954–88*, vol. 4 (1980–88), 708–29. Paris.

——— 1994b. 'A propos de la généalogie de la éthique: un aperçu du travail en cours'. In Daniel Defert and François Ewald, eds. *Dits et écrits: 1954–88*, vol. 4 (1980–88), 609–31. Paris.

——— 1994c. 'L'écriture de soi'. In Daniel Defert and François Ewald, eds. *Dits et écrits: 1954–88*, vol. 4 (1980–88), 415–30.

——— 2009. Ed. Frédéric Gros. *L'herméneutique du sujet: cours au Collège de France (1981–82)*. Paris.

Fraenkel, Eduard. 1957. *Horace*. Oxford.

Freudenburg, Kirk. 1993. *The Walking Muse: Horace on the Theory of Satire*. Princeton, NJ.

——— 2001. *Satires of Rome: Threatening Poses from Lucilius to Juvenal*. Cambridge.

———— 2002. '*Solus sapiens liber est*: recommissioning lyric in *Epistles* I'. In Tony Woodman and Dennis Feeney, eds. *Traditions and Context in the Poetry of Horace*, 124–40. Cambridge.

Frischer, Bernard. 1991. *Shifting Paradigms: New Approaches to Horace's Ars Poetica*. Atlanta, GA.

Gagné, Renaud. 2009. 'A wolf at the table: sympotic perjury in Archilochus'. *Transactions of the American Philological Association* 139: 251–74.

Galinsky, Karl. 1998. *Augustan Culture: An Interpretive Introduction*. Princeton, NJ.

Garrison, Daniel H. 1991. *Horace: Epodes and Odes*. Norman, OK.

———— 2004. *The Student's Catullus*, 3rd ed. Norman, OK.

Gaskin, Richard. 2013. *Horace and Housman*. New York.

Gentili, Bruno. 1984. *Poesia e pubblico nella Grecia antica: da Omero al V secolo*. Bari.

Giangrande, Lawrence. 1972. *The Use of* Spoudaiogeloion *in Greek and Roman Literature*. The Hague.

Gill, Christopher. 1988. 'Personhood and personality: the four-*personae* theory in Cicero, *De Officiis* I'. In Julia Annas, ed. *Oxford Studies in Ancient Philosophy*, vol. 6, 169–99. Oxford.

Gold, Barbara K. 1987. *Literary Patronage in Greece and Rome*. Chapel Hill, NC.

Golden, Leon. 2010. 'Reception of Horace's *Ars Poetica*'. In Gregson Davis, ed. *A Companion to Horace*, 391–413. Malden, MA.

Goh, Ian. 2016. 'Of cabbages and kin: traces of Lucilius in the first half of Horace's Epodes'. In Philippa Bather and Claire Stocks, eds. *Horace's Epodes: Contexts, Intertexts, & Receptions*, 63–83. Oxford.

Gowers, Emily. 1993. *The Loaded Table: Representations of Food in Roman Satire*. Oxford.

———— 2009. 'Horace, Satires 1.5: an inconsequential journey'. In Kirk Freudenburg, ed. *Horace: Satires and Epistles (Oxford Readings in Classical Studies)*, 156–80. Oxford.

———— 2012. *Horace: Satires 1*. Cambridge.

———— 2016. 'Girls will be boys and boys will be girls, or, what is the gender of Horace's *Epodes*?' In Philippa Bather and Claire Stocks, eds. *Horace's Epodes: Intertexts, Contexts & Receptions*, 103–30. Oxford.

Grilli, Alessandro. 1997. *Gaio Valerio Catullo: Le poesie*. Rome.

Gurd, Sean Alexander. 2012. *Work in Progress: Literary Revision as Social Performance in Ancient Rome*. Oxford.

Habinek, Thomas. 2005. *The World of Roman Song: From Ritualized Speech to Social Order*. Baltimore, MD.

Hadot, Pierre. 1992. *La citadelle intérieure: Introduction aux Pensées de Marc Aurèle*. Paris.

———1995. *Qu'est-ce que la philosophie antique?* Paris.

Halporn, James W., Martin Ostwald and Thomas G. Rosenmeyer. 1980. *The Meters of Greek and Latin Poetry*, rev. ed. Norman, OK.

Harrison, Stephen John. 2007. *Generic Enrichment in Vergil and Horace*. Oxford.

Havthal, Ferdinandus. 1966a. *Acronis et Porphyrionis: Commentarii in Q. Horatium Flaccum*, vol. 1. Amsterdam.

———1966b. *Acronis et Porphyrionis: Commentarii in Q. Horatium Flaccum*, vol. 2. Amsterdam.

Hawkins, Julia Nelson. 2014. 'The barking cure: Horace's "anatomy of rage" in Epodes 1, 6, and 16'. *American Journal of Philology* 135: 57–85.

Hawkins, Tom. 2009. 'This is the death of the earth: crisis narrative in Archilochus and Mnesiepes'. *Transactions of the American Philological Association* 139: 1–20.

Hellegouarc'h, Joseph. 1972. *Le vocabulaire latin des relations et des partis politiques sous la république*, 2nd ed. Paris.

Henderson, John. 2009. 'Horace talks rough and dirty: no comment (*Epodes* 8 and 12)'. In Michèle Lowrie, ed. *Horace: Odes and Epodes (Oxford Readings in Classical Studies)*, 401 – 17. Oxford.

Heinze, Richard. 2009. 'Die Horazische Ode'. Trans. [as 'The Horatian ode'] Maya Jessica Alapin et al. In Michèle Lowrie, ed. *Horace: Odes and Epodes (Oxford Readings in Classical Studies)*, 11–32. Oxford.

Hooley, Daniel M. 1997. *The Knotted Thong: Structures of Mimesis in Persius*. Ann Arbor, MI.

Hubbard, Margaret. 1973. 'The *Odes*'. In Charles Desmond Nuttall Costa, ed. *Horace*, 1–28. London.

Hunter, Richard. 2004. *Plato's Symposium*. Oxford.

Johnson, Timothy S. 2007. *A Symposion of Praise: Horace Returns to Lyric in Odes IV*. Madison, WI.

———2012. *Horace's Iambic Criticism: Casting Blame (Iambikē Poiēsis)*. Leiden.

Johnson, Walter Ralph. 1982. *The Idea of Lyric: Lyric Modes in Ancient and Modern Poetry*. Berkeley, CA.

———1993. *Horace and the Dialectic of Freedom: Readings in* Epistles *1*. Ithaca, NY.

Keane, Catherine. 2006. *Figuring Genre in Roman Satire*. Oxford.

Kennedy, Duncan F. 1993. *The Arts of Love: Five Essays in the Discourse of Roman Love Elegy*. Cambridge.

Kiessling, Adolph, and Richard Heinze. 1999. *Q. Horatius Flaccus: Satiren*. Zurich. Original 1921.

Kilpatrick, Ross. 1986. *The Poetry of Friendship: Horace, Epistles I*. Edmonton.

Knorr, Ortwin. 2006. 'Horace's Ship Ode (*Odes* 1.14) in context: a metaphorical love-triangle'. *Transactions of the American Philological Association* 136: 149–69.

Knox, Peter. 1985. 'Wine, water, and Callimachean polemics'. *Harvard Studies in Classical Philology* 89: 107–19.

Konstan, David. 1994. *Sexual Symmetry: Love in the Ancient Novel and Related Genres*. Princeton, NJ.

Kurke, Leslie. 1991. *The Traffic in Praise: Pindar and the Poetics of Social Economy*. Ithaca, NY.

Labate, Mario. 1984. *L'arte di farsi amare: modelli culturali e progetto didascalico nell'elegia ovidiana*. Pisa.

——— 2009. 'Il sermo oraziano e i generi letterari'. Trans. [as 'Horatian *Sermo* and genres of literature'] Kirk Freudenburg. In Kirk Freudenburg, ed. *Horace: Satires and Epistles (Oxford Readings in Classical Literature)*, 102–21. Oxford.

Laird, Andrew. 2007. 'The *Ars Poetica*'. In Stephen Harrison, ed. *The Cambridge Companion to Horace*, 132–43. Cambridge.

Lamb, W. R. M., ed. and trans. 1925. *Symposium. Plato in Twelve Volumes*, vol. 4, *Lysis, Symposium, Gorgias*, 172–223. London.

——— 1967. *Meno. Plato in Twelve Volumes*, vol. 2, *Laches, Protagoras, Meno, Euthydemus*, 70–100. Cambridge, MA.

Lana, Italo. 1993. 'Le guerre civili et la pace nella poesia di Orazio'. In Scevola Mariotti et al., eds. *Atti del convegno di Venosa: 8–15 Novembre 1992*, 59–74. Venosa.

Lewis, Michael. 2008. *Derrida and Lacan: Another Writing*. Edinburgh.

Lloyd-Jones, Hugh. 1990. *Greek Comedy, Hellenistic Literatures, Greek Religion, and Miscellanea: the Academic Papers of Sir Hugh Lloyd-Jones*. Oxford.

Lombardo, Stanley, and Diane Rayor, trans. 1988. *Callimachus: Hymns, Epigrams, Select Fragments*. Baltimore, MD.

Lorenz, Sven. 2007. 'Catullus and Martial'. In Marilyn Skinner, ed. *A Companion to Catullus*, 418–38. Malden, MA.

Lowrie, Michèle. 1997. *Horace's Narrative Odes*. Oxford.

——— 2009. 'A parade of lyric predecessors: C. 1.12–18'. In Michèle Lowrie, ed. *Horace: Odes and Epodes (Oxford Readings in Classical Studies)*, 337–55. Oxford.

Lyne, R. O. A. M. 1980. *The Latin Love Poets: From Catullus to Horace*. Oxford.

Mankin, David. 1995. *Horace: Epodes*. Cambridge.

——— 2010. 'The *Epodes*: Genre, Themes, and Arrangement'. In Gregson Davis, ed. *A Companion to Horace*, 93–104. Malden, MA.

Mayer, Roland. 1986. 'Horace's Epistles 1 and philosophy'. *American Journal of Philology* 107: 55–73.

——— 1994. *Horace: Epistles: Book I*. Cambridge.

——— 2005. 'Sleeping with the enemy: satire and philosophy'. In Kirk Freudenburg, ed. *Cambridge Companion to Roman Satire*, 146–59. Cambridge.

—— 2012. *Horace: Odes: Book I*. Cambridge.

McCarter, Stephanie. 2015. *Horace Between Freedom and Slavery: The First Book of* Epistles. Madison, WI.

McGlathery, Daniel. 1998. 'Reversals of Platonic love in Petronius's *Satyricon'*. In David H. J. Larmour, Paul Allen Miller and Charles Platter, eds. *Rethinking Sexuality: Foucault and Classical Antiquity*, 204–27. Princeton, NJ.

McNeill, Randall L. B. 2001. *Horace: Image, Identity, and Audience*. Baltimore, MD.

Miller, Paul Allen. 1994. *Lyric Texts and Lyric Consciousness: The Birth of Genre from Archaic Greece to Augustan Rome*. London.

—— 1998. 'The bodily grotesque in Roman satire: images of sterility', *Arethusa* 31: 257–83.

—— 2004. *Subjecting Verses: Latin Love Elegy and the Emergence of the Real*. Princeton, NJ.

—— 2005. *Latin Verse Satire: An Anthology and Reader*. London.

—— 2013a. 'Imitations of immortality: Du Bellay's *Les Regrets*, Petrarch, Horace, and Ovid'. *Intertexts* 17: 23–51.

—— 2013b. Review of Beard, Mary. 2014. *Laughter in Ancient Rome: On Joking, Tickling, and Cracking Up*. *Hermathena* 194, 218–22.

—— 2015. 'Placing the self in the field of truth: irony and self-fashioning in ancient and postmodern rhetorical theory'. *Arethusa* 48: 313–37.

—— 2018. 'Discipline and punish: Horatian satire and the formation of the self'. In Monica Gale and David Scourfield, eds. *Texts and Violence in the Roman World*, 87–109. Cambridge.

Miller, Paul Allen, and Charles Platter. 2010. *Plato's Apology of Socrates: A Commentary*. Norman, OK.

Moles, John. 1985. 'Cynicism in Horace. Epistles I'. *Papers of the Liverpool Latin Seminar* 5: 33–60.

—— 2007. 'Philosophy and ethics'. In Stephen Harrison, ed. *The Cambridge Companion to Horace*, 165–80. Cambridge.

Moritz, L. A. 1976. 'Snow and spring: Horace's Soracte Ode again'. *Greece and Rome* 23: 169–76.

Morrison, Andrew D. 2016. 'Lycambae spretus infido gener/aut acer hostis Bupalo: Horace's *Epodes* and the Greek iambic tradition'. In Philippa Bather and Claire Stocks, eds. *Horace's Epodes: Contexts, Intertexts, & Receptions*, 31–62. Oxford.

Muecke, Frances. 1997. *Horace: Satires II*. Liverpool.

—— 2007. 'The Satires'. In Stephen Harrison, ed. *The Cambridge Companion to Horace*, 105–20. Cambridge.

Nehamas, Alexander. 1998. *The Art of Living: Socratic Reflections from Plato to Foucault*. Berkeley, CA.

Nietzsche, Friedrich. 1997. *Twilight of the Idols: Or, How to Philosophize with the Hammer*. Trans. Richard Polt. Indianapolis, IN.

Nisbet, Robin. 2007. 'Horace: life and chronology'. In Stephen Harrison, ed. *The Cambridge Companion to Horace*, 7–21. Cambridge.

—— 2009. 'The word order of Horace's *Odes*'. In Michèle Lowrie, ed. *Horace: Odes and Epodes (Oxford Readings in Classical Studies)*, 378–400. Oxford.

Nisbet, Robin, and Margaret Hubbard. 1970. *A Commentary on Horace: Odes Book I*. Oxford.

—— 1978. *A Commentary on Horace: Odes Book II*. Oxford.

Nisbet, Robin, and Niall Rudd. 2004. *A Commentary on Horace: Odes Book III*. Oxford.

Oberhelman, Steven and David Armstrong. 1995. 'Satire as poetry and the impossibility of metathesis in Horace's *Satires*'. In Dirk Obink, ed. *Philodemus and Poetry: Poetic Theory and Practice in Lucretius, Philodemus, and Horace*, 233–57. Oxford.

O'Connor, Joseph F. 1990. 'Horace's *Cena Nasidieni* and poetry's fast'. *Classical Journal* 86: 23–34.

Oliensis, Ellen. 1997. 'The erotics of *Amicitia*: readings in Tibullus, Propertius, and Horace'. In Judith P. Hallett and Marilyn B. Skinner, eds. *Roman Sexualities*, 151–71. Princeton, NJ.

—— 1998. *Horace and the Rhetoric of Authority*. Cambridge.

—— 2007. 'Erotics and gender'. In Stephen Harrison, ed. *The Cambridge Companion to Horace*, 221–34. Cambridge.

—— 2009. 'Canidia, Canicula, and the decorum of Horace's *Epodes*'. In Michèle Lowrie, ed. *Horace: Odes and Epodes (Oxford Readings in Classical Studies)*, 160–87. Oxford.

Ormand, Kirk. 2005. 'Impossible Lesbians in Ovid's Metamorphoses'. In Ronnie Ancona and Ellen Greene, eds. *Gendered Dynamics in Latin Love Poetry*, 79–100. Baltimore, MD.

Page, Denys. 1955. *Sappho and Alcaeus: An Introduction to the Study of Ancient Lesbian Poetry*. Oxford.

Plaza, Maria. 2006. *The Function of Humour in Roman Verse Satire: Laughing and Lying*. Oxford.

Porter, David H. 1987. *Horace's Poetic Journey: A Reading of Odes 1–3*. Princeton, NJ.

Préaux, Jean. 1968. *Q. Horatius Flaccus Epistulae: Liber Primus*. Paris.

Putnam, Michael C. J. 1996. *Artifices of Eternity: Horace's Fourth Book of Odes*. Ithaca, NY.

Quinn, Kenneth. 1980. *Horace: The Odes*. London.

Reckford, Kenneth J. 2009a. *Recognizing Persius*. Princeton, NJ.

——— 2009b. 'Studies in Persius'. In Maria Plaza, ed. *Persius and Juvenal (Oxford Readings in Classical Studies)*, 17–56. Oxford.

Richlin, Amy. 1992. *The Garden of Priapus: Sexuality and Aggression in Roman Humor*, rev. ed. Oxford.

Rolfe, John C. 1962. *Horace: Satires and Epistles*, rev. ed. Boston, MA.

Roller, Matthew B. 2001. *Constructing Autocracy: Aristocrats and Emperors in Julio-Claudian Rome*. Princeton, NJ.

Roochnik, David. 2012. 'Humour'. In Gerald A. Press, ed. *The Continuum Companion to Plato*, 108–10. London.

Rorty, Richard. 1989. *Contingency, Irony, and Solidarity*. Cambridge.

Rossi, Luigi. 2009. 'Orazio, un lirico greco senza musica'. Trans. [as 'Horace, a Greek lyrist without music'.] Maya Jessica Alapin et al. In Michèle Lowrie, ed. *Horace: Odes and Epodes (Oxford Readings in Classical Studies)*, 356–77. Oxford.

Rudd, Niall. 1960. 'Patterns in Horatian lyric'. *American Journal of Philology* 81: 373–92.

——— trans. 1979. *Horace: Satires and Epistles; Persius: Satires*. London.

——— 1982. *The Satires of Horace*. Berkeley, CA.

——— ed. 1989. *Horace: Epistles Book II and Epistle to the Pisones ('Ars Poetica')*. Cambridge.

Ruffell, Ian A. 2003. 'Beyond satire: popular invective and the segregation of literature'. *Journal of Roman Studies* 93: 35–65.

Salkever, Stephen G. 1993. 'Socrates' Aspasian oration: the play of politics and philosophy in Plato's *Menexenus*'. *American Political Science Review* 87: 133–43.

Santirocco, Matthew S. 1986. *Unity and Design in Horace's Odes*. Chapel Hill, NC.

Schlegel, Catherine M. 2005. *Satire and the Threat of Speech: Horace's Satires Book 1*. Madison, WI.

Scodel, Ruth. 2010. 'Iambos and parody'. In James J. Clauss and Martine Cuypers, eds. *A Companion to Hellenistic Literature*, 251–66. Malden, MA.

Scolnicov, Samuel. 2012. 'Irony'. In Gerald A. Press, ed. *The Continuum Companion to Plato*, 110–11. London.

Sheets, George A. 2007. 'Elements of style in Catullus'. In Marilyn Skinner, ed. *A Companion to Catullus*, 190–211. Malden, MA.

Shields, M. G. 1958. '*Odes* 1.9: a study in imaginative unity'. *Phoenix* 12: 166–73.

Stampacchia, Giulia. 1982. 'Schiavitù e libertà nelle "Satire" di Orazio'. *Index* 11: 193–219.

Syme, Ronald. 1960. *The Roman Revolution*. Oxford.

Tarrant, Richard. 2007. 'Horace and Roman literary history'. In Stephen Harrison, ed. *The Cambridge Companion to Horace*, 63–76. Cambridge.

Thesleff, Holger. 2012. 'Play'. In Gerald A. Press, ed. *The Continuum Companion to Plato*, 123–5. London.

Thomas, Richard. 2007. 'Horace and Hellenistic poetry'. In Stephen Harrison, ed. *The Cambridge Companion to Horace*, 50–62. Cambridge.

Traina, Alfonso. 2009. 'Horace and Aristippus: the *Epistles* and the art of *Convivere*'. In Kirk Freudenburg, ed. *Horace: Satires and Epistles (Oxford Readings in Classical Studies)*, 287–307. Oxford.

Uzzi, Jeannine Diddle. 2005. *Children in the Visual Arts of Imperial Rome*. Cambridge.

Vecchi, Lorenzo De. 2013. *Orazio: Satire*. Roma.

Veyne, Paul. 2001a. 'En guise d'introduction'. In Paul Veyne. *La société romaine*, i–xlvi. Paris.

——— 2001b. 'La famille et l'amour sous le Haut-Empire romaine'. In Paul Veyne, *La société romaine*, 88–130. Paris.

Walters, Jonathan. 1997. 'Invading the Roman body: manliness and impenetrability in Roman thought'. In Judith P. Hallett and Marilyn B. Skinner, eds. *Roman Sexualities*, 29–43. Princeton, NJ.

Watson, Lindsay C. 2003. *A Commentary on Horace's* Epodes. Oxford.

——— 2007. 'The Epodes: Horace's Archilochus?' In Stephen Harrison, ed. *The Cambridge Companion to Horace*, 93–104. Cambridge.

Welch, Tara. 2008. 'Horace's journey through Arcadia'. *Transactions of the American Philological Association* 138: 47–74.

West, Martin Lichfield. 1989. *Iambi et elegi graeci: ante Alexandrum cantati*, rev. ed. New York.

White, Peter. 1993. *Promised Verse: Poets in the Society of Augustan Rome*. Cambridge, MA.

——— 2007. 'Friendship, patronage, and Horatian socio-poetics'. In Stephen Harrison, ed. *The Cambridge Companion to Horace*, 195–206. Cambridge.

Wickham, Edward C. with the assistance of Heathcote William Garrod. 1901. *Q. Horati Flacci: Opera*, 2nd ed. Oxford.

Wilkinson, L. P. 1946. *Horace and His Lyric Poetry*. Cambridge.

Williams, Gordon. 2009. '*Libertino patre natus*: true or false?' In Kirk Freudenburg, ed. *Horace: Satires and Epistles (Oxford Readings in Classical Studies)*, 138–55. Oxford.

Wirszubski, Chaim. 1950. *Libertas as a Political Idea at Rome During the Late Republic and Early Principate*. Cambridge.

Wray, David. 2001. *Catullus and the Poetics of Roman Manhood*. Cambridge.

INDEX